AMERICAN FOREIGN POLICY
Third Edition

HENRY A. KISSINGER

AMERICAN

FOREIGN POLICY

Third Edition

W · W · NORTON & COMPANY

New York · London

THE ESSAY "CENTRAL ISSUES OF AMERICAN FOREIGN POLICY"
COPYRIGHT © 1968 BY THE BROOKINGS INSTITUTION

ISBN 0 393 05634 1 cloth edition
ISBN 0 393 05641 4 paper edition

4 5 6 7 8 9 0

CONTENTS

CONTENTS

6

PREFACE TO THE THIRD EDITION

The publisher of this volume in early 1969 brought together three essays I had written before I came to Washington as Assistant to the President for National Security Affairs. Toward the end of 1973, after my appointment as Secretary of State, the publisher suggested that it might be useful to readers to add to an expanded edition some of my public statements as a government official. This Third Edition updates the previous edition with a fuller selection of speeches made during my tenure in office.

They cover the range of contemporary topics: relations with allies, adversaries and developing nations; political, military and economic challenges; problems in the Middle East, Latin America, Africa, and Asia; and issues facing the international community and the United Nations. More importantly, they all bear on the fundamental necessity of American foreign policy, that is, to restore our national consensus on our broader purposes in the world.

Henry A. Kissinger
Washington, D.C.
April, 1977

ONE

DOMESTIC STRUCTURE
AND FOREIGN POLICY

I. THE ROLE OF DOMESTIC STRUCTURE

IN THE traditional conception, international relations are conducted by political units treated almost as personalities. The domestic structure is taken as given; foreign policy begins where domestic policy ends.

But this approach is appropriate only to stable periods because then the various components of the international system generally have similar conceptions of the "rules of the game." If the domestic structures are based on commensurable notions of what is just, a consensus about permissible aims and methods of foreign policy develops. If domestic structures are reasonably stable, temptations to use an adventurous foreign policy to achieve domestic cohesion are at a minimum. In these conditions, leaders will generally apply the same criteria and hold similar views about what constitutes a "reasonable" demand. This does not guarantee agreement, but it provides the condition for a meaningful dialogue, that is, it sets the stage for traditional diplomacy.

When the domestic structures are based on fundamentally different conceptions of what is just, the conduct of international affairs grows more complex. Then it becomes difficult even to define the nature of disagreement because what seems most obvious to one side appears most problematic to the other. A policy dilemma arises because the pros and cons of a given course seem evenly balanced. The definition of what constitutes a problem and what criteria are relevant in "solving" it reflects to a considerable extent the domestic notions of what is just, the pressures produced by the decision-making process, and the experience which forms the leaders in their rise to eminence. When domestic structures—and the concept of legitimacy on which they are based—differ widely, statesmen can still meet, but their ability to persuade has been reduced for they no longer speak the same language.

This can occur even when no universal claims are made. Incompatible domestic structures can passively generate a gulf, simply because of the difficulty of achieving a consensus about the nature of "reasonable" aims and methods. But when one or more states claim universal applicability for their particular structure, schisms grow deep indeed. In that event, the domestic structure becomes not only an obstacle to understanding but one of the principal issues in international affairs. Its requirements condition the conception of alternatives; survival seems involved in every dispute. The symbolic aspect of foreign policy begins to overshadow the substantive component. It becomes difficult to consider a dispute "on its merits" because the disagreement seems finally to turn not on a specific issue but on a set of values as expressed in domestic arrangements. The consequences of such a state of affairs were explained by Edmund Burke during the French Revolution:

I never thought we could make peace with the system; because it was not for the sake of an object we pursued in rivalry with each other, but with the system itself that we were at war. As I understood the matter, we were at war not with its conduct but with its existence; convinced that its existence and its hostility were the same.[1]

Of course, the domestic structure is not irrelevant in any historical period. At a minimum, it determines the amount of the total social effort which can be devoted to foreign policy. The wars of the kings who governed by divine right were limited because feudal rulers, bound by customary law, could not levy income taxes or conscript their subjects. The French Revolution, which based its policy on a doctrine of popular will, mobilized resources on a truly national scale for the first time. This was one of the principal reasons for the startling successes of French arms against a hostile Europe which possessed greater over-all power. The ideological regimes of the twentieth century have utilized a still larger share of the national effort. This has enabled them to hold their own against an environment possessing far superior resources.

Aside from the allocation of resources, the domestic structure crucially affects the way the actions of other states are interpreted. To some extent, of course, every society finds itself in an environment not of its own making and has some of the main lines of its foreign policy imposed on it. Indeed, the pressure of the environment can grow so strong that it permits only one interpretation of its significance; Prussia in the eighteenth century and Israel in the contemporary period may have found themselves in this position.

But for the majority of states the margin of decision has been greater. The actual choice has been determined to a considerable degree by their interpretation of the environment and by their leaders' conception of alternatives. Napoleon rejected peace offers beyond the dreams of the kings who had ruled France by "divine right" because he was convinced

1. Edmund Burke, *Works* (London, 1826), Vol. VIII, pp. 214–215.

that *any* settlement which demonstrated the limitations of his power was tantamount to his downfall. That Russia seeks to surround itself with a belt of friendly states in Eastern Europe is a product of geography and history. That it is attempting to do so by imposing a domestic structure based on a particular ideology is a result of conceptions supplied by its domestic structure.

The domestic structure is decisive finally in the elaboration of positive goals. The most difficult, indeed tragic, aspect of foreign policy is how to deal with the problem of conjecture. When the scope for action is greatest, knowledge on which to base such action is small or ambiguous. When knowledge becomes available, the ability to affect events is usually at a minimum. In 1936, no one could know whether Hitler was a misunderstood nationalist or a maniac. By the time certainty was achieved, it had to be paid for with millions of lives.

The conjectural element of foreign policy—the need to gear actions to an assessment that cannot be proved true when it is made—is never more crucial than in a revolutionary period. Then, the old order is obviously disintegrating while the shape of its replacement is highly uncertain. Everything depends, therefore, on some conception of the future. But varying domestic structures can easily produce different assessments of the significance of existing trends and, more importantly, clashing criteria for resolving these differences. This is the dilemma of our time.

Problems are novel; their scale is vast; their nature is often abstract and always psychological. In the past, international relations were confined to a limited geographic area. The various continents pursued their relations essentially in isolation from each other. Until the eighteenth century, other continents impinged on Europe only sporadically and for relatively brief periods. And when Europe extended its sway over much of the world, foreign policy became limited to the Western Powers with the single exception of Japan. The international system of the nineteenth century was to all practical purposes identical with the concert of Europe.

The period after World War II marks the first era of truly global foreign policy. Each major state is capable of producing consequences in every part of the globe by a direct application of its power or because ideas can be transmitted almost instantaneously or because ideological rivalry gives vast symbolic significance even to issues which are minor in geopolitical terms. The mere act of adjusting perspectives to so huge a scale would produce major dislocations. This problem is compounded by the emergence of so many new states. Since 1945, the number of participants in the international system has nearly doubled. In previous periods the addition of even one or two new states tended to lead to decades of instability until a new equilibrium was established and accepted. The emergence of scores of new states has magnified this difficulty many times over.

These upheavals would be challenge enough, but they are overshadowed by the risks posed by modern technology. Peace is maintained through the threat of mutual destruction based on weapons for which there has been no operational experience. Deterrence—the policy of preventing an action by confronting the opponent with risks he is unwilling to run—depends in the first instance on psychological criteria. What the potential aggressor believes is more crucial than what is objectively true. Deterrence occurs above all in the minds of men.

To achieve an international consensus on the significance of these developments would be a major task even if domestic structures were comparable. It becomes especially difficult when domestic structures differ widely and when universal claims are made on behalf of them. A systematic assessment of the impact of domestic structure on the conduct of international affairs would have to treat such factors as historical traditions, social values, and the economic system. But this would far transcend the scope of this essay. For the purposes of this discussion we shall confine ourselves to sketching the impact of two factors only: administrative structure and the formative experience of leadership groups.

II. THE IMPACT OF THE ADMINISTRATIVE STRUCTURE

In the contemporary period, the very nature of the governmental structure introduces an element of rigidity which operates more or less independently of the convictions of statesmen or the ideology which they represent. Issues are too complex and relevant facts too manifold to be dealt with on the basis of personal intuition. An institutionalization of decision-making is an inevitable by-product of the risks of international affairs in the nuclear age. Moreover, almost every modern state is dedicated to some theory of "planning"—the attempt to structure the future by understanding and, if necessary, manipulating the environment. Planning involves a quest for predictability and, above all, for "objectivity." There is a deliberate effort to reduce the relevant elements of a problem to a standard of average performance. The vast bureaucratic mechanisms that emerge develop a momentum and a vested interest of their own. As they grow more complex, their internal standards of operation are not necessarily commensurable with those of other countries or even with other bureaucratic structures in the same country. There is a trend toward autarky. A paradoxical consequence may be that increased control over the domestic environment is purchased at the price of loss of flexibility in international affairs.

The purpose of bureaucracy is to devise a standard operating procedure which can cope effectively with most problems. A bureaucracy is efficient if the matters which it handles routinely are, in fact, the most frequent and if its procedures are relevant to their solution. If those criteria are met, the energies of the top leadership are freed to deal creatively with the unexpected occurrence or with the need for innovation. Bureaucracy becomes an obstacle when what it defines as routine does not address the most significant range of issues or when its prescribed mode of action proves irrelevant to the problem.

When this occurs, the bureaucracy absorbs the energies of top executives in reconciling what is expected with what happens; the analysis of where one is overwhelms the consideration of where one should be going. Serving the machine becomes a more absorbing occupation than defining its purpose. Success consists in moving the administrative machine to the point of decision, leaving relatively little energy for analyzing the merit of this decision. The quest for "objectivity"— while desirable theoretically—involves the danger that means and ends are confused, that an average standard of performance is exalted as the only valid one. Attention tends to be diverted from the act of choice—which is the ultimate test of statesmanship—to the accumulation of facts. Decisions can be avoided until a crisis brooks no further delay, until the events themselves have removed the element of ambiguity. But at that point the scope for constructive action is at a minimum. Certainty is purchased at the cost of creativity.

Something like this seems to be characteristic of modern bureaucratic states whatever their ideology. In societies with a pragmatic tradition, such as the United States, there develops a greater concern with an analysis of where one is than where one is going. What passes for planning is frequently the projection of the familiar into the future. In societies based on ideology, doctrine is institutionalized and exegesis takes the place of innovation. Creativity must make so many concessions to orthodoxy that it may exhaust itself in doctrinal adaptations. In short, the accumulation of knowledge of the bureaucracy and the impersonality of its method of arriving at decisions can be achieved at a high price. Decision-making can grow so complex that the process of producing a bureaucratic consensus may overshadow the purpose of the effort.

While all thoughtful administrators would grant in the abstract that these dangers exist, they find it difficult to act on their knowledge. Lip service is paid to planning; indeed planning staffs proliferate. However, they suffer from two debilities. The "operating" elements may not take the planning effort seriously. Plans become esoteric exercises which are accepted largely because they imply no practical consequence. They are a sop to administrative theory. At the same time, since planning staffs have a high incentive to try to be "useful," there is a bias against novel conceptions which are difficult to adapt to an administrative mold. It is one thing to assign an individual or a group the task of looking ahead; this is a far cry from providing an environment which encourages an understanding for deeper historical, sociological, and economic trends. The need to provide a memorandum may outweigh the imperatives of creative thought. The quest for objectivity creates a temptation to see in the future an updated version of the present. Yet true innovation is bound to run counter to prevailing standards. The dilemma of modern bureaucracy is that while every creative act is lonely, not every lonely act is creative. Formal criteria are little help in solving this problem because the unique cannot be expressed "objectively."

The rigidity in the policies of the technologically advanced societies is in no small part due to the complexity of decision-making. Crucial problems may—and frequently do—go unrecognized for a long time. But once the decision-making apparatus has disgorged a policy, it becomes very difficult to change it. The alternative to the status quo is the prospect of repeating the whole anguishing process of arriving at decisions. This explains to some extent the curious phenomenon that decisions taken with enormous doubt and perhaps with a close division become practically sacrosanct once adopted. The whole administrative machinery swings behind their implementation as if activity could still all doubts.

Moreover, the reputation, indeed the political survival, of most leaders depends on their ability to realize their goals, however these may have been arrived at. Whether these goals are desirable is relatively less crucial. The time span by which administrative success is measured is considerably shorter than that by which historical achievement is determined. In heavily bureaucratized societies all pressures emphasize the first of these accomplishments.

Then, too, the staffs on which modern executives come to depend develop a momentum of their own. What starts out as an aid to decision-makers often turns into a practically autonomous organization whose internal problems structure and sometimes compound the issues which it was originally designed to solve. The decision-maker will always be aware of the morale of his staff. Though he has the authority, he cannot overrule it too frequently without impairing its efficiency; and he may, in any event, lack the knowledge to do so. Placating the staff then becomes a major preoccupation of the executive. A form of administrative democracy results, in which a decision often reflects an attainable consensus rather than substantive conviction (or at least the two imperceptibly merge). The internal requirements of the bureaucracy may come to predominate over the purposes which it was intended to serve. This is probably even more true in highly institutionalized Communist states—such as the U.S.S.R.—than in the United States.

When the administrative machine grows very elaborate, the various levels of the decision-making process are separated by chasms which are obscured from the outside world by the complexity of the apparatus. Research often becomes a means to buy time and to assuage consciences. Studying a problem can turn into an escape from coming to grips with it. In the process, the gap between the technical competence of research staffs and what hard-pressed political leaders are capable of absorbing widens constantly. This heightens the insecurity of the executive and may thus compound either rigidity or arbitrariness or both. In many fields—strategy being a prime example—decision-makers may find it difficult to give as many hours to a problem as the expert has had years to study it. The ultimate decision often depends less on knowledge than on the ability to brief the top administrator —to present the facts in such a way that they can be absorbed rapidly. The effectiveness of briefing, however, puts a premium on theatrical qualities. Not everything that sounds plausible is correct, and many things which are correct may not sound plausible when they are first presented; and a second hearing is rare. The stage aspect of briefing may leave the decision-maker with a gnawing feeling of having been taken —even, and perhaps especially, when he does not know quite how.

Sophistication may thus encourage paralysis or a crude popularization which defeats its own purpose. The excessively theoretical approach of many research staffs overlooks the problem of the strain of decision-making in times of crisis. What is relevant for policy depends not only on academic truth but also on what can be implemented under stress. The technical staffs are frequently operating in a framework of theoretical standards while in fact their usefulness depends on essentially psychological criteria. To be politically meaningful, their proposals must involve answers to the following types of questions: Does the executive understand the proposal? Does he believe in it? Does he accept it as a guide to action or as an excuse for doing nothing? But if these kinds of concerns are given too much weight, the requirements of salesmanship will defeat substance.

The pragmatism of executives thus clashes with the theoretical bent of research or planning staffs. Executives as a rule take cognizance of a problem only when it emerges as an administrative issue. They thus unwittingly encourage bureaucratic contests as the only means of generating decisions. Or the various elements of the bureaucracy make a series of nonaggression pacts with each other and thus reduce the decision-maker to a benevolent constitutional monarch. As the special role of the executive increasingly becomes to choose between proposals generated administratively, decision-makers turn into arbiters rather than leaders. Whether they wait until a problem emerges as an administrative issue or until a crisis has demonstrated the irrelevance of the standard operating procedure, the modern decision-makers often find themselves the prisoners of their advisers.

Faced with an administrative machine which is both elaborate and fragmented, the executive is forced into essentially lateral means of control. Many of his public pronouncements, though ostensibly directed to outsiders, perform a perhaps more important role in laying down guidelines for the bureaucracy. The chief significance of a foreign policy speech by the President may thus be that it settles an internal debate in Washington (a public statement is more useful for this purpose than an administrative memorandum because it is harder to reverse). At the same time, the bureaucracy's awareness of this method of control tempts it to shortcut its debates by using pronouncements by the decision-makers as charters for special purposes. The executive thus finds himself confronted by proposals for public declarations which may be innocuous in themselves—and whose bureaucratic significance may be anything but obvious—but which can be used by some agency or department to launch a study or program which will restrict his freedom of decision later on.

All of this drives the executive in the direction of extra-bureaucratic means of decision. The practice of relying on special emissaries or personal envoys is an example; their status outside the bureaucracy frees them from some of its restraints. International agreements are sometimes possible only by ignoring safeguards against capricious action. It is a paradoxical aspect of modern bureaucracies that their quest for objectivity and calculability often leads to impasses which can be overcome only by essentially arbitrary decisions.

Such a mode of operation would involve a great risk of stagnation even in "normal" times. It becomes especially dangerous in a revolutionary period. For then, the problems which are most obtrusive may be least relevant. The issues which are most significant may not be suitable for administrative formulation and even when formulated may not lend themselves to bureaucratic consensus. When the issue is how to transform the existing framework, routine can become an additional obstacle to both comprehension and action.

This problem, serious enough *within* each society, is magnified in the conduct of international affairs. While the formal machinery of decision-making in developed countries shows many similarities, the criteria which influence decisions vary enormously. With each administrative machine increasingly absorbed in its own internal problems, diplomacy loses its flexibility. Leaders are extremely aware of the problems of placating their own bureaucracy; they cannot depart too far from its prescriptions without raising serious morale problems. Decisions are reached so painfully that the very anguish of decision-making acts as a brake on the give-and-take of traditional diplomacy.

This is true even *within* alliances. Meaningful consultation with other nations becomes very difficult when the internal process of decision-making already has some of the characteristics of compacts between quasi-sovereign entities. There is an increasing reluctance to hazard a hard-won domestic consensus in an international forum.

What is true within alliances—that is, among nations which have at least some common objectives—becomes even more acute in relations between antagonistic states or blocs. The gap created when two large bureaucracies generate goals largely in isolation from each other and on the basis of not necessarily commensurable criteria is magnified considerably by an ideological schism. The degree of ideological fervor is not decisive; the problem would exist even if the original ideological commitment had declined on either or both sides. The criteria for bureaucratic decision-making may continue to be influenced by ideology even after its élan has dissipated. Bureaucratic structures generate their own momentum which may more than counterbalance the loss of earlier fanaticism. In the early stages of a revolutionary movement, ideology is crucial and the accident of personalities can be decisive. The Reign of Terror in France was ended by the elimination of a single man, Robespierre. The Bolshevik revolution could hardly have taken place had Lenin not been on the famous train which crossed Germany into Russia. But once a revolution becomes institutionalized, the administrative structures which it has spawned develop their own vested interests. Ideology may grow less significant in creating commitment; it becomes pervasive in supplying criteria of administrative choice. Ideologies prevail by being taken for granted. Orthodoxy substitutes for conviction and produces its own form of rigidity.

In such circumstances, a meaningful dialogue across ideological dividing lines becomes extraordinarily difficult. The more elaborate the administrative structure, the less relevant an individual's view becomes—indeed one of the purposes of bureaucracy is to liberate decision-making from the accident of personalities. Thus while personal convictions may be modified, it requires a really monumental effort to alter bureaucratic commitments. And if change occurs, the bureaucracy prefers to move at its own pace and not be excessively influenced by statements or pressures of foreigners. For all these reasons, diplomacy tends to become rigid or to turn into an abstract bargaining process based on largely formal criteria such as "splitting the difference." Either course is self-defeating: the former because it negates the very purpose of diplomacy; the latter because it subordinates purpose to technique and because it may encourage intransigence. Indeed, the incentive for intransigence increases if it is known that the difference will generally be split.

Ideological differences are compounded because major parts of the world are only in the first stages of administrative evolution. Where the technologically advanced countries suffer from the inertia of overadministration, the developing areas often lack even the rudiments of effective bureaucracy. Where the advanced countries may drown in "facts," the emerging nations are frequently without the most elementary knowledge needed for forming a meaningful judgment or for implementing it once it has been taken. Where large bureaucracies operate in alternating spurts of rigidity and catastrophic (in relation to the bureaucracy) upheaval, the new states tend to make decisions on the basis of almost random pressures. The excessive institutionalization of one and the inadequate structure of the other inhibit international stability.

III. THE NATURE OF LEADERSHIP

WHATEVER one's view about the degree to which choices in international affairs are "objectively" determined, the decisions are made by individuals who will be above all conscious of the seeming multiplicity of options. Their understanding of the nature of their choice depends on many factors, including their experience during their rise to eminence.

The mediating, conciliatory style of British policy in the nineteenth century reflected, in part, the qualities encouraged during careers in Parliament and the values of a cohesive leadership group connected by ties of family and common education. The hysterical cast of the policy of Imperial Germany was given impetus by a domestic structure in which political parties were deprived of responsibility while ministers were obliged to balance a monarch by divine right against a Parliament composed of representatives without any prospect of ever holding office. Consensus could be achieved most easily through fits of national passion which in turn disquieted all of Germany's neighbors. Germany's foreign policy grew unstable because its domestic structure did little to discourage capricious improvisations; it may even have put a premium on them.

The collapse of the essentially aristocratic conception of foreign policy of the nineteenth century has made the career experiences of leaders even more crucial. An aristocracy—if it lives up to its values—will reject the arbitrariness of absolutist rule; and it will base itself on a notion of quality which discourages the temptations of demagoguery inherent in plebiscitarian democracy. Where position is felt to be a birthright, generosity is possible (though not guaranteed); flexibility is not inhibited by a commitment to perpetual success. Where a leader's estimate of himself is not completely dependent on his standing in an administrative structure, measures can be judged in terms of a conception of the future rather than of an almost compulsive desire to avoid even a temporary setback. When statesmen belonged to a community transcending national boundaries, there tended to be consensus on the criteria of what constituted a reasonable proposal. This did not prevent conflicts, but it did define their nature and encourage dialogue. The bane of aristocratic foreign policy was the risk of frivolousness, of a self-confidence unrelated to knowledge, and of too much emphasis on intuition.

In any event, ours is the age of the expert or the charismatic leader. The expert has his constituency—those who have a vested interest in commonly held opinions; elaborating and defining its consensus at a high level has, after all, made him an expert. Since the expert is often the product of the administrative dilemmas described earlier, he is usually in a poor position to transcend them. The charismatic leader, on the other hand, needs a perpetual revolution to maintain his position. Neither the expert nor the charismatic leader operates in an environment which puts a premium on long-range conceptions or on generosity or on subordinating the leader's ego to purposes which transcend his own career.

Leadership groups are formed by at least three factors: their experiences during their rise to eminence; the structure in which they must operate; the values of their society. Three contemporary types will be discussed here: (a) the bureaucratic-pragmatic type, (b) the ideological type, and (c) the revolutionary-charismatic type.

Bureaucratic-pragmatic leadership. The main example of this type of leadership is the American élite—though the leadership groups of other Western countries increasingly approximate the American pattern. Shaped by a society without fundamental social schisms (at least until the race problem became visible) and the product of an environment in which most recognized problems have proved soluble, its approach to policy is *ad hoc,* pragmatic, and somewhat mechanical.

Because pragmatism is based on the conviction that the context of events produces a solution, there is a tendency to await developments. The belief is prevalent that every problem will yield if attacked with sufficient energy. It is inconceivable, therefore, that delay might result in irretrievable disaster; at worst it is thought to require a redoubled effort later on. Problems are segmented into constituent elements, each of which is dealt with by experts in the special difficulty it involves. There is little emphasis or concern for their interrelationship. Technical issues enjoy more careful attention, and receive more sophisticated treatment, than political ones. Though the importance of intangibles is affirmed in theory, it is difficult to obtain a consensus on which factors are significant and even harder to find a meaningful mode for dealing with them. Things are done because one knows how to do them and not because one ought to do them. The criteria for dealing with trends which are conjectural are less well developed than those for immediate crises. Pragmatism, at least in its generally accepted form, is more concerned with method than with judgment; or rather it seeks to reduce judgment to methodology and value to knowledge.

This is reinforced by the special qualities of the professions —law and business—which furnish the core of the leadership groups in America. Lawyers—at least in the Anglo-Saxon tradition—prefer to deal with actual rather than hypothetical cases; they have little confidence in the possibility of stating a future issue abstractly. But planning by its very nature is hypothetical. Its success depends precisely on the ability to transcend the existing framework. Lawyers may be prepared to undertake this task; but they will do well in it only to the extent that they are able to overcome the special qualities encouraged by their profession. What comes naturally to lawyers in the Anglo-Saxon tradition is the sophisticated analysis of a series of *ad hoc* issues which emerge as problems through adversary proceedings. In so far as lawyers draw on the experience which forms them, they have a bias toward awaiting developments and toward operating within the definition of the problem as formulated by its chief spokesmen.

This has several consequences. It compounds the already powerful tendencies within American society to identify foreign policy with the solution of immediate issues. It produces great refinement of issues as they arise, but it also encourages the administrative dilemmas described earlier. Issues are dealt with only as the pressure of events imposes the need for resolving them. Then, each of the contending factions within the bureaucracy has a maximum incentive to state its case in its most extreme form because the ultimate outcome depends, to a considerable extent, on a bargaining process. The premium placed on advocacy turns decision-making into a series of adjustments among special interests—a process more suited to domestic than to foreign policy. This procedure neglects the long range because the future has no administrative constituency and is, therefore, without representation in the adversary proceedings. Problems tend to be slighted until some agency or department is made responsible for them. When this occurs—usually when a difficulty has already grown acute—the relevant department becomes an all-out spokesman for its particular area of responsibility. The outcome usually depends more on the pressures or the persuasiveness of the contending advocates than on a concept of over-all purpose. While these tendencies exist to some extent in all bureaucracies they are particularly pronounced in the American system of government.

This explains in part the peculiar alternation of rigidity and spasms of flexibility in American diplomacy. On a given issue—be it the Berlin crisis or disarmament or the war in Vietnam—there generally exists a great reluctance to develop a negotiating position or a statement of objectives except in the most general terms. This stems from a desire not to prejudge the process of negotiations and above all to retain flexibility in the face of unforeseeable events. But when an approaching conference or some other pressures make the development of a position imperative and some office or individual is assigned the specific task, a sudden change occurs. Both personal and bureaucratic success are then identified with bringing the particular assignment to a conclusion. Where so much stock is placed in negotiating skill, a failure of a conference may be viewed as a reflection on the ability of the negotiator rather than on the objective difficulty of the subject. Confidence in the bargaining process causes American negotiators to be extremely sensitive to the tactical requirements of the conference table—sometimes at the expense of longer-term considerations. In internal discussions, American negotiators—generally irrespective of their previous commitments—often become advocates for the maximum range of concessions; their legal background tempts them to act as mediators between Washington and the country with which they are negotiating.

The attitudes of the business élite reinforce the convictions of the legal profession. The American business executive rises through a process of selection which rewards the ability to manipulate the known—in itself a conciliatory procedure. The special skill of the executive is thought to consist in coordinating well-defined functions rather than in challenging them. The procedure is relatively effective in the business world, where the executive can often substitute decisiveness, long experience, and a wide range of personal acquaintance for reflectiveness. In international affairs, however—especially in a revolutionary situation—the strong will which is one of our business executives' notable traits may produce essentially arbitrary choices. Or unfamiliarity with the subject matter may have the opposite effect of turning the executive into a spokesman for his technical staffs. In either case, the business executive is even more dependent than the lawyer on the bureaucracy's formulation of the issue. The business élite is even less able or willing than the lawyer to recognize that the formulation of an issue, not the technical remedy, is usually the central problem.

All this gives American policy its particular cast. Problems are dealt with as they arise. Agreement on what constitutes a problem generally depends on an emerging crisis which settles the previously inconclusive disputes about priorities. When a problem is recognized, it is dealt with by a mobilization of all resources to overcome the immediate symptoms. This often involves the risk of slighting longer-term issues which may not yet have assumed crisis proportions and of overwhelming, perhaps even undermining, the structure of the area concerned by a flood of American technical experts proposing remedies on an American scale. Administrative decisions emerge from a compromise of conflicting pressures in which accidents of personality or persuasiveness play a crucial role. The compromise often reflects the maxim that "if two parties disagree the truth is usually somewhere in between." But the pedantic application of such truisms causes the various contenders to exaggerate their positions for bargaining purposes or to construct fictitious extremes to make their position appear moderate. In either case, internal bargaining predominates over substance.

The *ad hoc* tendency of our decision-makers and the reliance on adversary proceeding cause issues to be stated in black-and-white terms. This suppresses a feeling for nuance and makes it difficult to recognize the relationship between seemingly discrete events. Even with the perspective of a decade there is little consensus about the relationship between the actions culminating in the Suez fiasco and the French decision to enter the nuclear field; or about the inconsistency between the neutralization of Laos and the step-up of the military effort in Vietnam.

The same quality also produces a relatively low valuation of historical factors. Nations are treated as similar phenomena, and those states presenting similar immediate problems are treated similarly. Since many of our policy-makers first address themselves to an issue when it emerges as their area of responsibility, their approach to it is often highly anecdotal. Great weight is given to what people say and relatively little to the significance of these affirmations in terms of domestic structure or historical background. Agreement may be taken at face value and seen as reflecting more consensus than actually exists. Opposition tends to produce moral outrage which often assumes the form of personal animosity—the attitude of some American policy-makers toward President de Gaulle is a good example.

The legal background of our policy-makers produces a bias in favor of constitutional solutions. The issue of supra-nationalism or confederalism in Europe has been discussed largely in terms of the right of countries to make independent decisions. Much less weight has been given to the realities which would limit the application of a majority vote against a major country whatever the legal arrangements. (The fight over the application of Article 19 of the United Nations Charter was based on the same attitude.) Similarly, legal terms such as "integration" and "assignment" sometimes become ends in themselves and thus obscure the operational reality to which they refer. In short, the American leadership groups show high competence in dealing with technical issues, and much less virtuosity in mastering a historical process. And the policies of other Western countries exhibit variations of the American pattern. A lesser pragmatism in continental Europe is counterbalanced by a smaller ability to play a world-role.

The ideological type of leadership. As has been discussed above, the impact of ideology can persist long after its initial fervor has been spent. Whatever the ideological commitment of individual leaders, a lifetime spent in the Communist hierarchy must influence their basic categories of thought—especially since Communist ideology continues to perform important functions. It still furnishes the standard of truth and the guarantee of ultimate success. It provides a means for maintaining cohesion among the various Communist parties of the world. It supplies criteria for the settlement of disputes both within the bureaucracy of individual Communist countries and among the various Communist states.

However attenuated, Communist ideology is, in part, responsible for international tensions. This is less because of specific Marxist tactical prescriptions—with respect to which Communists have shown a high degree of flexibility—than because of the basic Marxist-Leninist categories for interpreting reality. Communist leaders never tire of affirming that Marxism-Leninism is the key element of their self-proclaimed superiority over the outside world; as Marxist-Leninists they are convinced that they understand the historical process better than the non-Communist world does.

The essence of Marxism-Leninism—and the reason that normal diplomacy with Communist states is so difficult—is the view that "objective" factors such as the social structure, the economic process, and, above all, the class struggle are more important than the personal convictions of statesmen. Belief in the predominance of objective factors explains the Soviet approach to the problem of security. If personal convictions are "subjective," Soviet security cannot be allowed to rest on the good will of other statesmen, especially those of a different social system. This produces a quest for what may be described as absolute security—the attempt to be so strong as to be independent of the decisions of other countries. But absolute security for one country means absolute insecurity for all others; it can be achieved only by reducing other states to impotence. Thus an essentially defensive foreign policy can grow indistinguishable from traditional aggression.

The belief in the predominance of objective factors explains why, in the past, periods of détente have proved so precarious. When there is a choice between Western good will or a physical gain, the pressures to choose the latter have been overwhelming. The wartime friendship with the West was sacrificed to the possibility of establishing Communist-controlled governments in Eastern Europe. The spirit of Geneva did not survive the temptations offered by the prospect of undermining the Western position in the Middle East. The many overtures of the Kennedy administration were rebuffed until the Cuban missile crisis demonstrated that the balance of forces was not in fact favorable for a test of strength.

The reliance on objective factors has complicated negotiations between the West and the Communist countries. Communist negotiators find it difficult to admit that they could be swayed by the arguments of men who have, by definition, an inferior grasp of the laws of historical development. No matter what is said, they think that they understand their Western counterpart better than he understands himself. Concessions are possible, but they are made to "reality," not to individuals or to a bargaining process. Diplomacy becomes difficult when one of the parties considers the key element to negotiation—the give-and-take of the process of bargaining—as but a superstructure for factors not part of the negotiation itself.

Finally, whatever the decline in ideological fervor, orthodoxy requires the maintenance of a posture of ideological hostility to the non-Communist world even during a period of coexistence. Thus, in a reply to a Chinese challenge, the Communist Party of the U.S.S.R. declared: "We fully support the destruction of capitalism. We not only believe in the inevitable death of capitalism but we are doing everything possible for it to be accomplished through class struggle as quickly as possible." [2]

The wariness toward the outside world is reinforced by the

2. "The Soviet Reply to the Chinese Letter," open letter of the Central Committee of the Communist Party of the Soviet Union as it appeared in *Pravda*, July 14, 1963, pp. 1–4; *The Current Digest of the Soviet Press* Vol. XV, No. 28 (August 7, 1963), p. 23.

personal experiences which Communist leaders have had on the road to eminence. In a system where there is no legitimate succession, a great deal of energy is absorbed in internal maneuvering. Leaders rise to the top by eliminating—sometimes physically, always bureaucratically—all possible opponents. Stalin had all individuals who helped him into power executed. Khrushchev disgraced Kaganovich, whose protegé he had been, and turned on Marshal Zhukov six months after being saved by him from a conspiracy of his other colleagues. Brezhnev and Kosygin owed their careers to Khrushchev; they nevertheless overthrew him and started a campaign of calumny against him within twenty-four hours of his dismissal.

Anyone succeeding in Communist leadership struggles must be single-minded, unemotional, dedicated, and, above all, motivated by an enormous desire for power. Nothing in the personal experience of Soviet leaders would lead them to accept protestations of good will at face value. Suspiciousness is inherent in their domestic position. It is unlikely that their attitude toward the outside world is more benign than toward their own colleagues or that they would expect more consideration from it.

The combination of personal qualities and ideological structure also affects relations *among* Communist states. Since national rivalries are thought to be the result of class conflict, they are expected to disappear wherever Socialism has triumphed. When disagreements occur they are dealt with by analogy to internal Communist disputes: by attempting to ostracize and then to destroy the opponent. The tendency to treat different opinions as manifestations of heresy causes disagreements to harden into bitter schisms. The debate between Communist China and the U.S.S.R. is in many respects more acrimonious than that between the U.S.S.R. and the non-Communist world.

Even though the basic conceptual categories of Communist leadership groups are similar, the impact of the domestic structure of the individual Communist states on international relations varies greatly. It makes a considerable difference whether an ideology has become institutionalized, as in the Soviet Union, or whether it is still impelled by its early revolutionary fervor, as in Communist China. Where ideology has become institutionalized a special form of pragmatism may develop. It may be just as empirical as that of the United States but it will operate in a different realm of "reality." A different philosophical basis leads to the emergence of another set of categories for the settlement of disputes, and these in turn generate another range of problems.

A Communist bureaucratic structure, however pragmatic, will have different priorities from ours; it will give greater weight to doctrinal considerations and conceptual problems. It is more than ritual when speeches of senior Soviet leaders begin with hour-long recitals of Communist ideology. Even if it were ritual, it must affect the definition of what is considered reasonable in internal arguments. Bureaucratization and pragmatism may lead to a loss of élan; they do not guarantee convergence of Western and Soviet thinking.

The more revolutionary manifestations of Communism, such as Communist China, still possess more ideological fervor, but, paradoxically, their structure may permit a wider latitude for new departures. Tactical intransigence and ideological vitality should not be confused with structural rigidity. Because the leadership bases its rule on a prestige which transcends bureaucratic authority, it has not yet given so many hostages to the administrative structure. If the leadership should change—or if its attitudes are modified—policy could probably be altered much more dramatically in Communist China than in the more institutionalized Communist countries.

The charismatic-revolutionary type of leadership. The contemporary international order is heavily influenced by yet another leadership type: the charismatic revolutionary leader. For many of the leaders of the new nations the bureaucratic-pragmatic approach of the West is irrelevant because they are more interested in the future which they wish to construct than in the manipulation of the environment which dominates the thinking of the pragmatists. And ideology is not satisfactory because doctrine supplies rigid categories which overshadow the personal experiences which have provided the impetus for so many of the leaders of the new nations.

The type of individual who leads a struggle for independence has been sustained in the risks and suffering of such a course primarily by a commitment to a vision which enabled him to override conditions which had seemed overwhelmingly hostile. Revolutionaries are rarely motivated primarily by material considerations—though the illusion that they are persists in the West. Material incentives do not cause a man to risk his existence and to launch himself into the uncertainties of a revolutionary struggle. If Castro or Sukarno had been principally interested in economics, their talents would have guaranteed them a brilliant career in the societies they overthrew. What made their sacrifices worthwhile to them was a vision of the future—or a quest for political power. To revolutionaries the significant reality is the world which they are striving to bring about, not the world they are fighting to overcome.

This difference in perspective accounts for the inconclusiveness of much of the dialogue between the West and many of the leaders of the new countries. The West has a tendency to believe that the tensions in the emerging nations are caused by a low level of economic activity. To the apostles of economic development, raising the gross national product seems the key to political stability. They believe that it should receive the highest priority from the political leaders of new countries and supply their chief motivation.

But to the charismatic heads of many of the new nations, economic progress, while not unwelcome, offers too limited a scope for their ambitions. It can be achieved only by slow, painful, highly technical measures which contrast with the heroic exertions of the struggle for independence. Results are long-delayed; credit for them cannot be clearly established. If Castro were to act on the advice of theorists of economic development, the best he could hope for would be that after some decades he would lead a small progressive country— perhaps a Switzerland of the Caribbean. Compared to the prospect of leading a revolution throughout Latin America, this goal would appear trivial, boring, perhaps even unreal to him.

Moreover, to the extent that economic progress is achieved, it may magnify domestic political instability, at least in its early phases. Economic advance disrupts the traditional political structure. It thus places constant pressures on the incumbent leaders to reestablish the legitimacy of their rule. For this purpose a dramatic foreign policy is particularly apt. Many leaders of the new countries seem convinced that an adventurous foreign policy will not harm prospects for economic development and may even foster it. The competition of the superpowers makes it likely that economic assistance will be forthcoming regardless of the actions of the recipient. Indeed the more obtrusive their foreign policy the greater is their prospect of being wooed by the chief contenders.

The tendency toward a reckless policy is magnified by the

uncertain sense of identity of many of the new nations. National boundaries often correspond to the administrative subdivisions established by the former colonial rulers. States thus have few of the attributes of nineteenth-century European nationalism: common language, common culture, or even common history. In many cases, the only common experience is a century or so of imperial rule. As a result, there is a great pressure toward authoritarian rule, and a high incentive to use foreign policy as a means of bringing about domestic cohesion.

Western-style democracy presupposes that society transcends the political realm; in that case opposition challenges a particular method of achieving common aims but not the existence of the state itself. In many of the new countries, by contrast, the state represents the primary, sometimes the sole, manifestation of social cohesion. Opposition can therefore easily appear as treason—apart from the fact that leaders who have spent several decades running the risks of revolutionary struggle or who have achieved power by a coup d'état are not likely to favor a system of government which makes them dispensable. Indeed the attraction of Communism for many of these leaders is not Marxist-Leninist economic theory but the legitimacy for authoritarian rule which it provides.

No matter what the system of government, many of the leaders of the new nations use foreign policy as a means to escape intractable internal difficulties and as a device to achieve domestic cohesion. The international arena provides an opportunity for the dramatic measures which are impossible at home. These are often cast in an anti-Western mold because this is the easiest way to re-create the struggle against imperial rule which is the principal unifying element for many new nations. The incentive is particularly strong because the rivalry of the nuclear powers eliminates many of the risks which previously were associated with an adventurous foreign policy—especially if that foreign policy is directed against the West, which lacks any effective sanctions.

Traditional military pressure is largely precluded by the nuclear stalemate and respect for world opinion. But the West is neither prepared nor able to use the sanction which weighs most heavily on the new countries: the deliberate exploitation of their weak domestic structure. In many areas the ability to foment domestic unrest is a more potent weapon than traditional arms. Many of the leaders of the new countries will be prepared to ignore the classical panoply of power; but they will be very sensitive to the threat of domestic upheaval. States with a high capacity for exploiting domestic instability can use it as a tool of foreign policy. China, though lacking almost all forms of classical long-range military strength, is a growing factor in Africa. Weak states may be more concerned with a country's capacity to organize domestic unrest in their territory than with its capacity for physical destruction.

Conclusion. Contemporary domestic structures thus present an unprecedented challenge to the emergence of a stable international order. The bureaucratic-pragmatic societies concentrate on the manipulation of an empirical reality which they treat as given; the ideological societies are split between an essentially bureaucratic approach (though in a different realm of reality than the bureaucratic-pragmatic structures) and a group using ideology mainly for revolutionary ends. The new nations, in so far as they are active in international affairs, have a high incentive to seek in foreign policy the perpetuation of charismatic leadership.

These differences are a major obstacle to a consensus on what constitutes a "reasonable" proposal. A common diagnosis of the existing situation is hard to achieve, and it is even more difficult to concert measures for a solution. The situation is complicated by the one feature all types of leadership have in common: the premium put on short-term goals and the domestic need to succeed at all times. In the bureaucratic societies policy emerges from a compromise which often produces the least common denominator, and it is implemented by individuals whose reputation is made by administering the status quo. The leadership of the institutionalized ideological state may be even more the prisoner of essentially corporate bodies. Neither leadership can afford radical changes of course for they result in profound repercussions in its administrative structure. And the charismatic leaders of the new nations are like tightrope artists—one false step and they will plunge from their perch.

IV. DOMESTIC STRUCTURE AND FOREIGN POLICY: THE PROSPECTS FOR WORLD ORDER

MANY contemporary divisions are thus traceable to differences in domestic structure. But are there not countervailing factors? What about the spread of technology and its associated rationality, or the adoption on a global scale of many Western political forms? Unfortunately the process of "Westernization" does not inevitably produce a similar concept of reality. For what matters is not the institutions or the technology, but the significance which is attached to them. And this differs according to the evolution of the society concerned.

The term "nation" does not mean the same thing when applied to such various phenomena as India, France, and Nigeria. Similarly, technology is likely to have a different significance for different peoples, depending on how and when it was acquired.

Any society is part of an evolutionary process which proceeds by means of two seemingly contradictory mechanisms. On the one hand, the span of possible adaptations is delimited by the physical environment, the internal structure, and, above all, by previous choices. On the other hand, evolution proceeds not in a straight line but through a series of complicated variations which appear anything but obvious to the chief actors. In retrospect a choice may seem to have been nearly random or else to have represented the only available alternative. In either case, the choice is not an isolated act but an accumulation of previous decisions reflecting history or tradition and values as well as the immediate pressures of the need for survival. And each decision delimits the range of possible future adaptations.

Young societies are in a position to make radical changes of course which are highly impractical at a later stage. As a society becomes more elaborate and as its tradition is firmly established, its choices with respect to its internal organization grow more restricted. If a highly articulated social unit attempts basic shifts, it runs the risk of doing violence to its internal organization, to its history and values as embodied in its structure. When it accepts institutions or values developed elsewhere it must adapt them to what its structure can absorb. The institutions of any political unit must therefore be viewed in historical context for that alone can give an indication of their future. Societies—even when their institutions are similar—may be like ships passing in the night which find themselves but temporarily in the same place.

Is there then no hope for cooperation and stability? Is our international system doomed to incomprehension and its members to mounting frustration?

It must be admitted that if the domestic structures were considered in isolation, the prognosis would not be too hopeful. But domestic structures do not exist in a vacuum. They must respond to the requirements of the environment. And here all states find themselves face to face with the necessity of avoiding a nuclear holocaust. While this condition does not restrain all nations equally, it nevertheless defines a common task which technology will impose on even more countries as a direct responsibility.

Then, too, a certain similarity in the forms of administration may bring about common criteria of rationality, as Professor Jaguaribe has pointed out.[3] Science and technology will spread. Improved communications may lead to the emergence of a common culture. The fissures between domestic structures and the different stages of evolution are important, but they may be outweighed by the increasing interdependence of humanity.

It would be tempting to end on this note and to base the hope for peace on the self-evidence of the need for it. But this would be too pat. The deepest problem of the contemporary international order may be that most of the debates which form the headlines of the day are peripheral to the basic division described in this essay. The cleavage is not over particular political arrangements—except as symptoms—but between two styles of policy and two philosophical perspectives.

The two styles can be defined as the political as against the revolutionary approach to order or, reduced to personalities, as the distinction between the statesman and the prophet.

The statesman manipulates reality; his first goal is survival; he feels responsible not only for the best but also for the worst conceivable outcome. His view of human nature is wary; he is conscious of many great hopes which have failed, of many good intentions that could not be realized, of selfishness and ambition and violence. He is, therefore, inclined to erect hedges against the possibility that even the most brilliant idea might prove abortive and that the most eloquent formulation might hide ulterior motives. He will try to avoid certain experiments, not because he would object to the results

3. "World Order, Rationality, and Socioeconomic Development," *Daedalus*, Vol. XCV (Spring 1966), pp. 607–626.

if they succeeded, but because he would feel himself responsible for the consequences if they failed. He is suspicious of those who personalize foreign policy, for history teaches him the fragility of structures dependent on individuals. To the statesman, gradualism is the essence of stability; he represents an era of average performance, of gradual change and slow construction.

By contrast, the prophet is less concerned with manipulating than with creating reality. What is possible interests him less than what is "right." He offers his vision as the test and his good faith as a guarantee. He believes in total solutions; he is less absorbed in methodology than in purpose. He believes in the perfectibility of man. His approach is timeless and not dependent on circumstances. He objects to gradualism as an unnecessary concession to circumstance. He will risk everything because his vision is the primary significant reality to him. Paradoxically, his more optimistic view of human nature makes him more intolerant than the statesman. If truth is both knowable and attainable, only immorality or stupidity can keep man from realizing it. The prophet represents an era of exaltation, of great upheavals, of vast accomplishments, but also of enormous disasters.

The encounter between the political and the prophetic approach to policy is always somewhat inconclusive and frustrating. The test of the statesman is the permanence of the international structure under stress. The test of the prophet is inherent in his vision. The statesman will seek to reduce the prophet's intuition to precise measures; he judges ideas on their utility and not on their "truth." To the prophet this approach is almost sacrilegious because it represents the triumph of expediency over universal principles. To the statesman negotiation is the mechanism of stability because it presupposes that maintenance of the existing order is more

important than any dispute within it. To the prophet negotiations can have only symbolic value—as a means of convert-
ing or demoralizing the opponent; truth, by definition,
cannot be compromised.

Both approaches have prevailed at different periods in
history. The political approach dominated European foreign
policy between the end of the religious wars and the French
Revolution and then again between the Congress of Vienna
and the outbreak of World War I. The prophetic mode was
in the ascendant during the great upheavals of the religious
struggles and the period of the French Revolution, and in
the contemporary uprisings in major parts of the world.

Both modes have produced considerable accomplishments,
though the prophetic style is likely to involve the greater
dislocations and more suffering. Each has its nemesis. The
nemesis of the statesman is that equilibrium, though it may
be the condition of stability, does not supply its own motivation; that of the prophet is the impossibility of sustaining a
mood of exaltation without the risk of submerging man in the
vastness of a vision and reducing him to a mere figure to be
manipulated.

As for the difference in philosophical perspective, it may
reflect the divergence of the two lines of thought which since
the Renaissance have distinguished the West from the part of
the world now called underdeveloped (with Russia occupying an intermediary position). The West is deeply committed
to the notion that the real world is external to the observer,
that knowledge consists of recording and classifying data
—the more accurately the better. Cultures which escaped the
early impact of Newtonian thinking have retained the essentially pre-Newtonian view that the real world is almost
completely *internal* to the observer.

Although this attitude was a liability for centuries—because it prevented the development of the technology and consumer goods which the West enjoyed—it offers great flexibility with respect to the contemporary revolutionary turmoil. It enables the societies which do not share our cultural mode to alter reality by influencing the perspective of the observer—a process which we are largely unprepared to handle or even to perceive. And this can be accomplished under contemporary conditions without sacrificing technological progress. Technology comes as a gift; acquiring it in its advanced form does not presuppose the philosophical commitment that discovering it imposed on the West. Empirical reality has a much different significance for many of the new countries than for the West because in a certain sense they never went through the process of discovering it (with Russia again occupying an intermediary position). At the same time, the difference in philosophical perspective may cause us to seem cold, supercilious, lacking in compassion. The instability of the contemporary world order may thus have at its core a philosophical schism which makes the issues producing most political debates seem largely tangential.

Such differences in style and philosophical perspective are not unprecedented. What is novel is the global scale on which they occur and the risks which the failure to overcome them would entail. Historically, cleavages of lesser magnitude have been worked out dialectically, with one style of policy or one philosophical approach dominant in one era only to give way later to another conception of reality. And the transition was rarely free of violence. The challenge of our time is whether we can deal consciously and creatively with what in previous centuries was adjusted through a series of more or less violent and frequently catastrophic upheavals. We must construct an international order *before* a crisis imposes it as a necessity.

This is a question not of blueprints, but of attitudes. In

fact the overconcern with technical blueprints is itself a symp-
ton of our difficulties. Before the problem of order can be
"dealt" with—even philosophically—we must be certain that
the right questions are being asked.

We can point to some hopeful signs. The most sensitive
thinkers of the West have recognized that excessive empiri-
cism may lead to stagnation. In many of the new countries—
and in some Communist ones as well—the second or third
generation of leaders is in the process of freeing itself from
the fervor and dogmatism of the early revolutionary period
and of relating their actions to an environment which they
helped to create. But these are as yet only the first tentative
signs of progress on a course whose significance is not always
understood. Indeed it is characteristic of an age of turmoil
that it produces so many immediate issues that little time is
left to penetrate their deeper meaning. The most serious
problem therefore becomes the need to acquire a sufficiently
wide perspective so that the present does not overwhelm the
future.

TWO

CENTRAL ISSUES OF AMERICAN FOREIGN POLICY

The twentieth century has known little repose. Since the turn of the century, international crises have been increasing in both frequency and severity. The contemporary unrest, although less apocalyptic than the two world wars which spawned it, is even more profoundly revolutionary in nature.

The essence of a revolution is that it appears to contemporaries as a series of more or less unrelated upheavals. The temptation is great to treat each issue as an immediate and isolated problem which once surmounted will permit the fundamental stability of the international order to reassert itself. But the crises which form the headlines of the day are symptoms of deep-seated structural problems. The international system which produced stability for a century collapsed under the impact of two world wars. The age of the superpowers, which temporarily replaced it, is nearing its end. The current international environment is in turmoil because its essential elements are all in flux simultaneously. This essay will concentrate on structural and conceptual problems rather than specific policy issues.

I. THE STRUCTURAL PROBLEM

FOR THE first time, foreign policy has become global. In the past, the various continents conducted their foreign policy essentially in isolation. Throughout much of history, the foreign policy of Europe was scarcely affected by events in Asia. When, in the late eighteenth and nineteenth centuries, the European powers were extending their influence throughout the world, the effective decisions continued to be made in only a few great European capitals. Today, statesmen face the unprecedented problem of formulating policy for well over a hundred countries. Every nation, no matter how insignificant, participates in international affairs. Ideas are transmitted almost instantaneously. What used to be considered domestic events can now have world-wide consequences.

The revolutionary character of our age can be summed up in three general statements: (a) the number of participants in the international order has increased and their nature has altered; (b) their technical ability to affect each other has vastly grown; (c) the scope of their purposes has expanded.

Whenever the participants in the international system change, a period of profound dislocation is inevitable. They can change because new states enter the political system, or because there is a change in values as to what constitutes legitimate rule, or, finally, because of the reduction in influence of some traditional units. In our period, all of these factors have combined. Since the end of the Second World War, several score of new states have come into being. In the nineteenth century the emergence of even a few new nations produced decades of adjustment, and after the First World War, the successor states of the Austro-Hungarian Empire were never assimilated. Our age has yet to find a structure which matches the responsibilities of the new nations to their aspirations.

As the number of participants has increased, technology has multiplied the resources available for the conduct of foreign policy. A scientific revolution has, for all practical purposes, removed technical limits from the exercise of power in foreign policy. It has magnified insecurities because it has made survival seem to depend on the accidents of a technological breakthrough.

This trend has been compounded by the nature of contemporary domestic structures. As long as the states' ability to mobilize resources was limited, the severity of their conflicts had definite bounds. In the eighteenth century, custom restricted the demands rulers by "divine right" could make upon their subjects; a philosophy of minimum government performed the same role through much of the nineteenth century. Our period has seen the culmination of a process started by the French Revolution: the basing of governmental legitimacy on popular support. Even totalitarian regimes are aberrations of a democratic legitimacy; they depend on popular consensus even when they manufacture it through propaganda and pressure. In such a situation, the consensus is decisive; limitations of tradition are essentially irrelevant. It is an ironic result of the democratization of politics that it has enabled states to marshal ever more resources for their competition.

Ideological conflict compounds these instabilities. In the great periods of cabinet diplomacy, diplomats spoke the same language, not only in the sense that French was the lingua franca, but more importantly because they tended to understand intangibles in the same manner. A similar outlook about aims and methods eases the tasks of diplomacy—it may even be a precondition for it. In the absence of such a consensus, diplomats can still meet, but they lose the ability to persuade. More time is spent on defining contending positions than in resolving them. What seems most reasonable to one side will appear most problematical to the other.

When there is ideological conflict, political loyalties no longer coincide with political boundaries. Conflicts among states merge with divisions within nations; the dividing line between domestic and foreign policy begins to disappear. At least some states feel threatened not only by the foreign policy of other countries but also, and perhaps especially, by domestic transformations. A liberalized Communist regime in Prague—which had in no way challenged Soviet preeminence in foreign policy—caused the Kremlin to believe that its vital interests were threatened and to respond by occupying the country without even the pretext of legality.

The tensions produced by ideological conflict are exacerbated by the reduction in influence of the states that were considered great powers before the First World War. The world has become militarily bipolar. Only two powers—the United States and the Union of Soviet Socialist Republics—possess the full panoply of military might. Over the next decade, no other country or group of countries will be capable of challenging their physical preeminence. Indeed, the gap in military strength between the two giant nuclear countries and the rest of the world is likely to increase rather than diminish over that period.

Military bipolarity is a source of rigidity in foreign policy. The guardians of the equilibrium of the nineteenth century were prepared to respond to change with counteradjustment; the policy-makers of the superpowers in the second half of the twentieth century have much less confidence in the ability of the equilibrium to right itself after disturbance. Whatever "balance" there is between the superpowers is regarded as both precarious and inflexible. A bipolar world loses the perspective for nuance; a gain for one side appears as an absolute loss for the other. Every issue seems to involve a question of survival. The smaller countries are torn between a desire for protection and a wish to escape big-power dominance. Each of the superpowers is beset by the desire to maintain its preeminence among its allies, to increase its influence among the uncommitted, and to enhance its security vis-à-vis its opponent. The fact that some of these objectives may well prove incompatible adds to the strain on the international system.

But the age of the superpowers is now drawing to an end. Military bipolarity has not only failed to prevent, it has actually encouraged political multipolarity. Weaker allies have good reason to believe that their defense is in the overwhelming interest of their senior partner. Hence, they see no need to purchase its support by acquiescence in its policies. The new nations feel protected by the rivalry of the superpowers, and their nationalism leads to ever bolder assertions of self-will. Traditional uses of power have become less feasible, and new forms of pressure have emerged as a result of transnational loyalties and weak domestic structures.

This political multipolarity does not necessarily guarantee

stability. Rigidity is diminished, but so is manageability. Nationalism may succeed in curbing the preeminence of the superpowers; it remains to be seen whether it can supply an integrating concept more successfully in this century than in the last. Few countries have the interest and only the superpowers have the resources to become informed about global issues. As a result, diplomacy is often geared to domestic politics and more concerned with striking a pose than contributing to international order. Equilibrium is difficult to achieve among states widely divergent in values, goals, expectations, and previous experience.

The greatest need of the contemporary international system is an agreed concept of order. In its absence, the awesome available power is unrestrained by any consensus as to legitimacy; ideology and nationalism, in their different ways, deepen international schisms. Many of the elements of stability which characterized the international system in the nineteenth century cannot be re-created in the modern age. The stable technology, the multiplicity of major powers, the limited domestic claims, and the frontiers which permitted adjustments are gone forever. A new concept of international order is essential; without it stability will prove elusive.

This problem is particularly serious for the United States. Whatever our intentions or policies, the fact that the United States disposes of the greatest single aggregate of material power in the world is inescapable. A new international order is inconceivable without a significant American contribution. But the nature of this contribution has altered. For the two decades after 1945, our international activities were based on the assumption that technology plus managerial skills gave us the ability to reshape the international system and to bring about domestic transformations in "emerging countries." This direct "operational" concept of international order has proved too simple. Political multipolarity makes it impossible to impose an American design. Our deepest challenge will be to evoke the creativity of a pluralistic world, to base order on political multipolarity even though overwhelming military strength will remain with the two superpowers.

II. THE LIMITS OF BIPOLARITY: THE NATURE OF POWER IN THE MODERN PERIOD

THROUGHOUT history, military power was considered the final recourse. Statesmen treated the acquisition of additional power as an obvious and paramount objective. As recently as twenty-five years ago, it would have been inconceivable that a country could possess *too much* strength for effective political use; every increment of power was—at least theoretically—politically effective. The minimum aim was to assure the impermeability of the territory. Until the Second World War, a state's strength could be measured by its ability to protect its population from attack.

The nuclear age has destroyed this traditional measure. Increasing strength no longer necessarily confers the ability to protect the population. No foreseeable force level—not even full-scale ballistic missile defenses—can prevent levels of damage eclipsing those of the two world wars. In these conditions, the major problem is to discipline power so that it bears a rational relationship to the objectives likely to be in dispute. The paradox of contemporary military strength is that a gargantuan increase in power has eroded its relationship to policy. The major nuclear powers are capable of devastating each other. But they have great difficulty translating this capability into policy except to prevent direct challenges to their own survival—and this condition is interpreted with increasing strictness. The capacity to destroy is difficult to translate into a plausible threat even against countries with no capacity for retaliation. The margin of superiority of the superpowers over the other states is widening; yet other nations have an unprecedented scope for autonomous action. In relations with many domestically weak countries, a radio transmitter can be a more effective form of pressure than a squadron of B-52s. In other words, power no longer translates automatically into influence. This does not mean that impotence increases influence, only that power does not automatically confer it.

This state of affairs has profound consequences for traditional notions of balance of power. In the past, stability has always presupposed the existence of an equilibrium of power which prevented one state from imposing its will on the others.

The traditional criteria for the balance of power were territorial. A state could gain overwhelming superiority only by conquest; hence, as long as territorial expansion was foreclosed, or severely limited, the equilibrium was likely to be preserved. In the contemporary period, this is no longer true. Some conquests add little to effective military strength; major increases in power are possible entirely through developments within the territory of a sovereign state. China gained more in real military power through the acquisition of nuclear weapons than if it had conquered all of Southeast Asia. If the Soviet Union had occupied Western Europe but had remained without nuclear weapons, it would be less powerful than it is now with its existing nuclear arsenal within its present borders. In other words, the really fundamental changes in the balance of power have all occurred *within* the territorial limits of sovereign states. Clearly, there is an urgent need to analyze just what is understood by power—as well as by balance of power—in the nuclear age.

This would be difficult enough were technology stable. It becomes enormously complicated when a scientific revolution produces an upheaval in weapons technology at five-year intervals. Slogans like "superiority," "parity," "assured destruction," compete unencumbered by clear definitions of their operational military significance, much less a consensus on their political implications. The gap between experts and decision-makers is widening.

In short, as power has grown more awesome, it has also turned abstract, intangible, elusive. Deterrence has become the dominant military policy. But deterrence depends above all on psychological criteria. It seeks to keep an opponent from a given course by posing unacceptable risks. For purposes of deterrence, the opponent's calculations are decisive. A bluff taken seriously is more useful than a serious threat interpreted as a bluff. For political purposes, the meaningful measurement of military strength is the assessment of it by the other side. Psychological criteria vie in importance with strategic doctrine.

The abstract nature of modern power affects domestic disputes profoundly. Deterrence is tested negatively by things which do *not* happen. But it is never possible to demonstrate *why* something has not occurred. Is it because we are pursuing the best possible policy or only a marginally effective one? Bitter debate even among those who believe in the necessity of defense policy is inevitable and bound to be inconclusive. Moreover, the longer peace is maintained—or the more successful deterrence is—the more it furnishes arguments for those who are opposed to the very premises of defense policy. Perhaps there was no need for preparedness in the first place because the opponent never meant to attack. In the modern state, national security is likely to be a highly divisive domestic issue.

The enormity of modern power has destroyed its cumulative impact to a considerable extent. Throughout history the use of force set a precedent; it demonstrated a capacity to use power for national ends. In the twentieth century any use of force sets up inhibitions against resorting to it again. Whatever the outcome of the war in Vietnam, it is clear that it has greatly diminished American willingness to become involved in this form of warfare elsewhere. Its utility as a precedent has therefore been importantly undermined.

The difficulty of forming a conception of power is paralleled by the problem of how to use it diplomatically. In the past, measures to increase readiness signaled the mounting seriousness with which an issue was viewed.[1] But such measures have become less obvious and more dangerous when weapons are always at a high state of readiness—solid-fuel missiles require less than ten minutes to be fired—and are hidden either under the ground or under the oceans. With respect to nuclear weapons, signaling increased readiness has to take place in a narrow range between the danger of failure and the risk of a preemptive strike.

Even when only conventional weapons are involved, the question of what constitutes a politically meaningful threat is increasingly complicated. After the capture of the *Pueblo,* the United States called up thirteen thousand reservists and moved an aircraft carrier into the waters off the shores of Korea. Did the fact that we had to call up reserves when challenged by a fifth-rate military power convey that we

1. Sometimes these measures got out of control; the mobilization schedules were one of the principal reasons for the outbreak of the First World War.

meant to act or that we were overextended? Did the move of the aircraft carrier indicate a decision to retaliate or was it intended primarily to strike a pose?

The problem is illustrated dramatically by the war in Vietnam. A massive breakdown of communication occurred not only within the policy-making machinery in the United States but also between the United States and Hanoi. Over the past five years, the U.S. government has found it difficult, if not impossible, to define what it understood by victory. President Johnson extended an open-ended offer for unconditional negotiations. Yet our troops were deployed as if this offer had not been made. The deployment was based on purely military considerations; it did not take into account the possibility that our troops might have to support a negotiation—the timing of which we had, in effect, left to the opponent. Strategy divorced from foreign policy proved sterile.

These perplexities have spurred new interest in arms-control negotiations, especially those dealing with strategic missiles. These negotiations can be important for the peace and security of the world. But to be effective, they require an intellectual resolution of the issues which have bedeviled the formulation of military policy. Unless we are able to give an operational meaning to terms such as "superiority" or "stability," negotiations will lack criteria by which to judge progress.

Thus, whatever the course—a continuation of the arms race or arms control—a new look at American national security policy is essential. Over ten years have passed since the last comprehensive, bipartisan, high-level reevaluation of all aspects of national security: the Gaither Committee. A new administration should move quickly to bring about such a review. It should deal with some of the following problems: (a) a definition of the national interest and national security over the next decade; (b) the nature of military power in that period; (c) the relationship of military power to political influence; (d) implications and feasibility (both military and political) of various postures—superiority, parity, and so on; (e) the implications (both political and military) of new developments such as MIRV (multiple individually targeted reentry vehicles) and ballistic missile defenses; (f) the prospects for arms control, including specific measures to moderate the arms race.

III. POLITICAL MULTIPOLARITY: THE CHANGED NATURE OF ALLIANCES

No AREA of policy illustrates more dramatically the tensions between political multipolarity and military bipolarity than the field of alliance policy. For a decade and a half after the Second World War, the United States identified security with alliances. A global network of relationships grew up based on the proposition that deterrence of aggression required the largest possible grouping of powers.

This system of alliances was always in difficulty outside the Atlantic area because it tried to apply principles drawn from the multipolar world of the eighteenth and nineteenth centuries when several major powers of roughly equal strength existed. Then, indeed, it was impossible for one country to achieve dominance if several others combined to prevent it. But this was not the case in the era of the superpowers of the forties and fifties. Outside Europe, our allies added to our strength only marginally; they were in no position to reinforce each other's capabilities.

Alliances, to be effective, must meet four conditions: (1) a common objective—usually defense against a common danger; (2) a degree of joint policy at least sufficient to define the *casus belli;* (3) some technical means of cooperation in case common action is decided upon; (4) a penalty for noncooperation—that is, the possibility of being refused assistance must exist—otherwise protection will be taken for granted and the mutuality of obligation will break down.

In the system of alliances developed by the United States after the Second World War, these conditions have never been met outside the North Atlantic Treaty Organization (NATO). In the Southeast Asia Treaty Organization (SEATO) and the Central Treaty Organization (CENTO), to which we belong in all but name, there has been no consensus as to the danger. Pakistan's motive for obtaining U.S. arms was not security against a Communist attack but protection against India. The Arab members of CENTO armed not against the U.S.S.R. but against Israel. Lacking a conception of common interests, the members of these alliances have never been able to develop common policies with respect to issues of war and peace. Had they been able to do so, such policies might well have been stillborn anyway, because the technical means of cooperation have been lacking. Most allies have neither the resources nor the will to render mutual support. A state which finds it difficult to maintain order or coherence of policy at home does not increase its strength by combining with states suffering similar disabilities.

In these circumstances, SEATO and CENTO have grown moribund as instruments of collective action. Because the United States has often seemed more eager to engage in the defense of its SEATO and CENTO allies than they themselves, they have become convinced that noncooperation will have no cost. In fact, they have been able to give the impression that it would be worse for us than for them if they fell to Communism. SEATO and CENTO have become, in effect, unilateral American guarantees. At best, they provide a legal basis for bilateral U.S. aid.

The case is different with NATO. Here we are united with countries of similar traditions and domestic structures. At the start, there was a common conception of the threat. The technical means for cooperation existed. Mechanisms for developing common policies came into being—especially in the military field. Thus in its first decade and a half, NATO was a dynamic and creative institution.

Today, however, NATO is in disarray as well. Actions by the United States—above all, frequent unilateral changes of policy—are partially responsible. But the most important cause is the transformation of the international environment, specifically the decline in the preeminence of the superpowers and the emergence of political multipolarity. Where the alliances outside of Europe have never been vital because they failed to take into account the military bipolarity of the fifties, NATO is in difficulties because it has yet to adjust to the political multipolarity of the late sixties.

When NATO was founded in 1949, Europeans had a dual fear: the danger of an imminent Soviet attack and the prospect of eventual U.S. withdrawal. In the late 1960s, however, the fear of Soviet invasion has declined. Even the attack on Czechoslovakia is likely to restore anxiety about Soviet military aggression only temporarily. At the same time, two decades of American military presence in Europe coupled with American predominance in NATO planning have sharply reduced the fear that America might wash its hands of European concerns.

When NATO was formed, moreover, the principal threat to world peace seemed to lie in a Soviet attack on Europe. In recent years, the view has grown that equally grave risks are likely to arise in trouble spots outside Europe. To most Europeans, these do not appear as immediate threats to their independence or security. The irony here is striking. In the fifties, Europeans were asking for American assistance in Asia and the Middle East with the argument that they were defending the greater interests of freedom. The United States replied that these very interests required American aloofness. Today, the roles are precisely reversed. It is Europe that evades our entreaties to play a global role; that is to say, Europeans do not consider their interests at stake in America's extra-European involvement.

These are symptoms of deeper, structural problems, however. One problem, paradoxically, is the growth of European economic strength and political self-confidence. At the end of the Second World War, Europe was dependent on the United States for economic assistance, political stability, and military protection. As long as Europe needed the shelter of a superpower, American predominance was inevitable. In relations with the United States, European statesmen acted as lobbyists rather than as diplomats. Their influence depended less on the weight of their countries than on the impact of their personalities. A form of consultation evolved whereby Europeans sought to influence American actions by giving us a reputation to uphold or—to put it more crudely—by oscillating between flattery and almost plaintive appeals for reassurance. The United States, secure in its predominance, in turn concentrated on soothing occasional European outbreaks of insecurity rather than on analyzing their causes.

Tutelage is a comfortable relationship for the senior partner, but it is demoralizing in the long run. It breeds illusions of omniscience on one side and attitudes of impotent irresponsibility on the other. In any event, the United States could not expect to perpetuate the accident of Europe's postwar exhaustion into a permanent pattern of international relations. Europe's economic recovery inevitably led to a return to more traditional political pressures.

These changes in Europe were bound to lead to a difficult transitional period. They could have resulted in a new partnership between the United States and an economically resurgent and politically united Europe, as had been envisaged by many of the early advocates of Atlantic unity. However, the European situation has not resolved itself in that way. Thoughtful Europeans know that Europe must unite in some form if it is to play a major role in the long run. They are aware, too, that Europe does not make even approximately the defense effort of which it is capable. But European unity is stymied, and domestic politics has almost everywhere dominated security policy. The result is a massive frustration which expresses itself in special testiness toward the United States.

These strains have been complicated by the growth of Soviet nuclear power. The changed nature of power in the modern period has affected NATO profoundly. As the risks of nuclear war have become enormous, the credibility of traditional pledges of support has inevitably been reduced. In the past, a country would carry out a commitment because, it could plausibly be argued, the consequences of not doing so were worse than those of coming to the ally's assistance. This is no longer self-evident. In each of the last three annual statements by the Secretary of Defense on the U.S. defense posture, the estimate of *dead* in a general nuclear war ranged from 40 to 120 million. This figure will, if anything, increase. It will become more and more difficult to demonstrate that *anything* is worse than the elimination of over half of a society in a matter of days. The more NATO relies on strategic nuclear war as a counter to all forms of attack, the less credible its pledges will be.

The consciousness of nuclear threat by the two superpowers

has undermined allied relationships in yet another way. For understandable reasons, the superpowers have sought to make the nuclear environment more predictable—witness the nuclear test ban treaty and the nonproliferation treaty. But the blind spot in our policy has been the failure to understand that, in the absence of full consultation, our allies see in these talks the possible forerunner of a more comprehensive arrangement affecting their vital interests negotiated without them. Strategic arms talks thus emphasize the need of political understanding in acute form. The pattern of negotiating an agreement first and then giving our allies an opportunity— even a full one—to comment is intolerable in the long run. It puts the onus of failure on them, and it prevents them from doing more than quibble about a framework with which they may disagree. Strains have been reinforced by the uncertain American response to the Soviet invasion of Czechoslovakia— especially the reluctance to give up the prospect of a summit meeting. Atlantic relations, for all their seemingly normalcy, thus face a profound crisis.

This state of affairs has been especially difficult for those Americans who deserve most credit for forging existing Atlantic relations. Two decades of hegemony have produced the illusion that present Atlantic arrangements are "natural," that wise policy consists of making the existing framework more tolerable. "Leadership" and "partnership" are invoked, but the content given to these words is usually that which will support the existing pattern. European unity is advocated to enable Europeans to share burdens on a world-wide scale.

Such a view fails to take into account the realities of political multipolarity. The aim of returning to the "great days of the Marshall Plan" is impossible. Nothing would sunder Atlantic relationships so surely as the attempt to reassert the notions of leadership appropriate to the early days of NATO.

In the bipolar world of the forties and fifties, order could be equated with military security; integrated command arrangements sufficed as the principal bond of unity. In the sixties, security, while still important, has not been enough. Every crisis from Berlin to Czechoslovakia has seen the call for "strengthening NATO" confined to military dispositions. Within months a malaise has become obvious again because the overriding need for a common political conception has not been recognized. The challenge of the seventies will be to forge unity with political measures.

It is not "natural" that the major decisions about the defense of an area so potentially powerful as Western Europe should be made three thousand miles away. It is not "normal" that Atlantic policies should be geared to American conceptions. In the forties and fifties, practicing unity—through formal resolutions and periodic reassurances—was profoundly important as a symbol of the end of our isolationism. In the decade ahead, we cannot aim at unity as an end in itself; it must emerge from common conceptions and new structures.

"Burden-sharing" will not supply that impetus. Countries do not assume burdens because it is fair, only because it is necessary. While there are strong arguments for Atlantic partnership and European unity, enabling Europe to play a global role is not one of them. A nation assumes responsibilities not only because it has resources but because it has a certain view of its own destiny. Through the greater part of its history—until the Second World War—the United States possessed the resources but not the philosophy for a global role. Today, the poorest Western European country—Portugal —has the widest commitments outside Europe because its historic image of itself has become bound up with its overseas possessions. This condition is unlikely to be met by any other European country—with the possible exception of Great

Britain—no matter what its increase in power. Partially as the result of decolonization, Europeans are unlikely to conduct a significant global policy whatever their resources or their degree of unity. Cooperation between the United States and Europe must concentrate on issues within the Atlantic area rather than global partnership.

Even within the Atlantic area, a more equitable distribution of responsibilities has two prerequisites: there must be some consensus in the analysis of the international situation, at least as it affects Europe; there must be a conviction that the United States cannot or will not carry all the burdens alone. Neither condition is met today. The traditional notion of American leadership tends to stifle European incentives for autonomy. Improved consultation—the remedy usually proposed—can only alleviate, not remove, the difficulty.

The problem of consultation is complex, of course. No doubt unilateral American action has compounded the uneasiness produced by American predominance and European weakness. The shift in emphasis of American policy, from the NATO multilateral force to the nonproliferation treaty, and frequent unilateral changes in strategic doctrine, have all tended to produce disquiet and to undermine the domestic position of ministers who had staked their futures on supporting the American viewpoint.

It is far from self-evident, however, that more extensive consultation within the existing framework can be more than a palliative. One problem concerns technical competence. In any large bureaucracy—and an international consultative process has many similarities to domestic administrative procedures—the weight given to advice bears some relation to the competence it reflects. If one partner possesses all the technical competence, the process of consultation is likely to remain barren. The minimum requirement for effective consultation is that each ally have enough knowledge to give meaningful advice.

But there are even more important limits to the process of consultation. The losing party in a domestic dispute has three choices: (a) it can accept the setback with the expectation of winning another battle later on—this is the usual bureaucratic attitude and it is based on the assurance of another hearing; (b) if advice is consistently ignored, it can resign and go into opposition; (c) as the opposition party, it can have the purpose either of inducing the existing government to change its course or of replacing it. If all these avenues are closed, violence or mounting frustration are the consequences.

Only the first option is open to sovereign states bound together by an alliance, since they obviously cannot resign or go into opposition without wrecking the alliance. They cannot affect the process by which their partners' decision-makers are chosen despite the fact that this may be crucial for their fate. Indeed, as long as the need to maintain the alliance overrides all other concerns, disagreement is likely to be stifled. Advice without responsibility and disagreement without an outlet can turn consultation into a frustrating exercise which compounds rather than alleviates discord.

Consultation is especially difficult when it lacks an integrating over-all framework. The consultation about the non-proliferation treaty concerned specific provisions but not the underlying general philosophy which was of the deepest concern to many of our allies, especially Italy and the Federal Republic of Germany. During periods of détente, each ally makes its own approach to Eastern Europe or the U.S.S.R. without attempting to further a coherent Western enterprise. During periods of crisis, there is pressure for American reassurance but not for a clearly defined common philosophy. In these circumstances, consultation runs the risk of being irrelevant. The issues it "solves" are peripheral; the central issues are inadequately articulated. It deals haphazardly in answers to undefined questions.

Such a relationship is not healthy in the long run. Even with the best will, the present structure encourages American unilateralism and European irresponsibility. This is a serious problem for the United States. If the United States remains the trustee of every non-Communist area, it will exhaust its psychological resources. No country can act wisely simultaneously in every part of the globe at every moment of time. A more pluralistic world—especially in relationships with friends—is profoundly in our long-term interest. Political multipolarity, while difficult to get used to, is the precondition for a new period of creativity. Painful as it may be to admit, we could benefit from a counterweight that would discipline our occasional impetuosity and, by supplying historical perspective, modify our penchant for abstract and "final" solutions.

All of this suggests that there is no alternative to European unity either for the United States or for Europe. In its absence, the malaise can only be alleviated, not ended. Ultimately, this is a problem primarily for the Europeans. In the recent past, the United States has often defeated its purposes by committing itself to one particular form of European unity —that of federalism. It has also complicated British membership in the Common Market by making it a direct objective of American policy.

In the next decade the architectonic approach to Atlantic policy will no longer be possible. The American contribution must be more philosophical; it will have to consist more of understanding and quiet, behind-the-scenes encouragement than of the propagation of formal institutional structures. Involved here is the American conception of how nations cooperate. A tradition of legalism and habits of predominance have produced a tendency to multiply formal arrangements.

But growing European autonomy forces us to learn that nations cooperate less because they have a legal obligation to do so than because they have common purposes. Command arrangements cannot substitute for common interests. Coordinated strategy will be empty unless it reflects shared political concepts. The chance of disagreements on peripheral issues may be the price for unity on issues that really matter. The memory of European impotence and American tutelage should not delude us into believing that we understand Europe's problems better than it does itself. Third-force dangers are not avoided by legal formulas, and, more important, they have been overdrawn. It is hard to visualize a "deal" between the Soviet Union and Europe which would jeopardize our interests without jeopardizing European interests first. In any event, a sense of responsibility in Europe will be a much better counter to Soviet efforts to undermine unity than American tutelage.

In short, our relations with Europeans are better founded on developing a community of interests than on the elaboration of formal legal obligations. No precise blueprint for such an arrangement is possible because different fields of activity have different needs. In the military sphere, for example, modern technology will impose a greater degree of integration than is necessary in other areas. Whatever their formal autonomy, it is almost inconceivable that our allies would prefer to go to war without the support of the United States, given the relatively small nuclear forces in prospect for them. Close coordination between Europe and the United States in the military sphere is dictated by self-interest, and Europe has more to gain from it than the United States.

For this very reason, it is in our interest that Europeans

should assume much greater responsibility for developing doctrine and force levels in NATO, perhaps by vitalizing such institutions as the West European Union (WEU), perhaps by alternative arrangements. The Supreme Allied Commander should in time be a European.

Military arrangements are not enough, however. Under current conditions, no statesman will risk a cataclysm simply to fulfill a legal obligation. He will do so only if a degree of *political* cooperation has been established which links the fate of each partner with the survival of all the others. This requires an entirely new order of political creativity.

Coordination is especially necessary in East-West relations. The conventional view is that NATO can be as useful an instrument for détente as for defense. This is doubtful—at least in NATO's present form. A military alliance, one of the chief cohesive links of which is its integrated command arrangement, is not the best instrument for flexible diplomacy. Turning NATO into an instrument of détente might reduce its security contribution without achieving a relaxation of tensions. A diplomatic confrontation of NATO and the Warsaw Pact would have all the rigidities of the bipolar military world. It would raise fears in Western Europe of an American-Soviet condominium, and it would tend to legitimize the Soviet hegemonical position in Eastern Europe. Above all, it would fail to take advantage of the flexibility afforded by greater Western European unity and autonomy. As Europe gains structure, its attraction for Eastern Europe is bound to increase. The major initiatives to improve relations between Western and Eastern Europe should originate in Europe with the United States in a reserve position.

Such an approach can work only if there is a real consensus as to objectives. Philosophical agreement can make possible flexibility of method. This will require a form of consultation much more substantial than that which now exists and a far more effective and coherent European contribution.

To be sure, events in Czechoslovakia demonstrate the limits of Eastern European autonomy that the Soviet Union is now prepared to tolerate. But the Soviet Union may not be willing indefinitely to use the Red Army primarily against allies as it has done three times in a decade and a half. In any event, no Western policy can guarantee a more favorable evolution in Central Europe; all it can do is to take advantage of an opportunity if it arises.

Policy outside Europe is likely to be divergent. Given the changed European perspective, an effort to bring about global burden-sharing might only produce stagnation. The allies would be able to agree primarily on doing nothing. Any crisis occurring anywhere would turn automatically and organically world-wide. American acceptance of European autonomy implies also European acceptance of a degree of American autonomy with respect to areas in which, for understandable reasons, European concern has lessened.

There may be opportunities for cooperation in hitherto purely national efforts—for example, our space program. European participation in it could help to remedy the "technological gap."

Finally, under present circumstances, an especially meaningful community of interests can be developed in the social sphere. All modern states face problems of bureaucratization, pollution, environmental control, urban growth. These problems know no national considerations. If the nations of the Atlantic work together on these issues—through either private or governmental channels or both—a new generation habituated to cooperative efforts could develop similar to that spawned in different circumstances by the Marshall Plan.

It is high time that the nations bordering the Atlantic deal

—formally, systematically, and at the highest level—with questions such as these: (a) What are the relative roles of Europe and the United States in East-West contacts? (b) Is a division of functions conceivable in which Western Europe plays the principal role in relation to Eastern Europe while the United States concentrates on relationships with the U.S.S.R.? (c) What forms of political consultation does this require? (d) In what areas of the world is common action possible? Where are divergent courses indicated? How are differences to be handled?

Thus, we face the root questions of a multipolar world. How much unity should we want? How much diversity can we stand? These questions never have a final answer within a pluralistic society. Adjusting the balance between integration and autonomy will be the key challenge of emerging Atlantic relations.

IV. BIPOLARITY AND MULTIPOLARITY: THE CONCEPTUAL PROBLEM

IN THE YEARS ahead, the most profound challenge to American policy will be philosophical: to develop some concept of order in a world which is bipolar militarily but multipolar politically. But a philosophical deepening will not come easily to those brought up in the American tradition of foreign policy.

Our political society was one of the few which was *consciously* created at a point in time. At least until the emergence of the race problem, we were blessed by the absence of conflicts between classes and over ultimate ends. These factors produced the characteristic aspects of American foreign policy: a certain manipulativeness and pragmatism, a conviction that the normal pattern of international relations was harmonious, a reluctance to think in structural terms, a belief in final answers—all qualities which reflect a sense of self-sufficiency not far removed from a sense of omnipotence. Yet the contemporary dilemma is that there are no total solutions; we live in a world gripped by revolutions in technology, values, and institutions. We are immersed in an unending process, not in a quest for a final destination. The deepest problems of equilibrium are not physical but psychological or moral. The shape of the future will depend ultimately on convictions which far transcend the physical balance of power.

The New Nations and Political Legitimacy. This challenge is especially crucial with respect to the new nations. Future historians are likely to class the confusion and torment in the emerging countries with the great movements of religious awakening. Continents which had been dormant for centuries suddenly develop political consciousness. Regions which for scores of years had considered foreign rule as natural struggle for independence. Yet it is a curious nationalism which defines itself not as in Europe by common language or culture but often primarily by the common experience of foreign rule. Boundaries—especially in Africa—have tended to follow the administrative convenience of the colonial powers rather than linguistic or tribal lines. The new nations have faced problems both of identity and of political authority. They often lack social cohesiveness entirely, or they are split into competing groups, each with a highly developed sense of identity.

It is no accident that between the Berlin crisis and the invasion of Czechoslovakia, the principal threats to peace came from the emerging areas. Domestic weakness encourages foreign intervention. The temptation to deflect domestic dissatisfactions into foreign adventures is ever present. Leaders feel little sense of responsibility to an over-all international equilibrium; they are much more conscious of their local grievances. The rivalry of the superpowers offers many opportunities for blackmail.

Yet their relations with other countries are not the most significant aspect of the turmoil of the new countries. It is in the new countries that questions of the purpose of political life and the meaning of political legitimacy—key issues also in the modern state—pose themselves in their most acute form. The new nations weigh little in the physical balance of power. But the forces unleashed in the emergence of so many new states may well affect the moral balance of the world—the convictions which form the structure for the world of to-morrow. This adds a new dimension to the problem of multi-polarity.

Almost all of the new countries suffer from a revolutionary malaise: revolutions succeed through the coming together of all resentments. But the elimination of existing structures compounds the difficulty of establishing political consensus. A successful revolution leaves as its legacy a profound disloca-tion. In the new countries, contrary to all revolutionary expectations, the task of construction emerges as less glamor-ous and more complex than the struggle for freedom; the exaltation of the quest for independence cannot be perpetu-ated. Sooner or later, positive goals must replace resentment of the former colonial power as a motive force. In the absence of autonomous social forces, this unifying role tends to be per-formed by the state.

But the assumption of this role by the state does not pro-duce stability. When social cohesiveness is slight, the struggle for control of authority is correspondingly more bitter. When government is the principal, sometimes the sole, expression of national identity, opposition comes to be considered treason. The profound social or religious schisms of many of the new nations turn the control of political authority quite literally into a matter of life and death. Where political obligation follows racial, religious, or tribal lines, self-restraint breaks down. Domestic conflicts assume the character of civil war. Such traditional authority as exists is personal or feudal. The problem is to make it "legitimate"—to develop a notion of political obligation which depends on legal norms rather than on coercive power or personal loyalty.

This process took centuries in Europe. It must be accomplished in decades in the new nations, where preconditions of success are less favorable than at comparable periods in Europe. The new countries are subject to outside pressures; there is a premium on foreign adventures to bring about domestic cohesiveness. Their lack of domestic structure compounds the already great international instabilities.

The American role in the new nations' efforts to build legitimate authority is in need of serious reexamination. The dominant American view about political structure has been that it will follow more or less automatically upon economic progress and that it will take the form of constitutional democracy.

Both assumptions are subject to serious questions. In every advanced country, political stability preceded rather than emerged from the process of industrialization. Where the rudiments of popular institutions did not exist at the beginning of the Industrial Revolution, they did not receive their impetus from it. To be sure, representative institutions were broadened and elaborated as the countries prospered, but their significant features antedated economic development and are not attributable to it. In fact, the system of government which brought about industrialization—whether popular or authoritarian—has tended to be confirmed rather than radically changed by this achievement.

Nor is democracy a natural evolution of nationalism. In the last century, democracy was accepted by a ruling class whose estimate of itself was founded outside the political process. It was buttressed by a middle class, holding a political philosophy in which the state was considered to be a referee of the ultimately important social forces rather than the principal focus of national consciousness. Professional revolutionaries were rarely involved; their bias is seldom democratic.

The pluralism of the West had many causes which cannot be duplicated elsewhere. These included a church organization outside the control of the state and therefore symbolizing the limitation of government power; the Greco-Roman philosophical tradition of justice based on human dignity, reinforced later by the Christian ethic; an emerging bourgeoisie; a stalemate in religious wars imposing tolerance as a practical necessity and a multiplicity of states. Industrialization was by no means the most significant of these factors. Had any of the others been missing, the Western political evolution could have been quite different.

This is why Communism has never succeeded in the industrialized Western countries for which its theory was devised; its greatest successes have been in developing societies. This is no accident. Industrialization—in its early phases—multiplies dislocations. It smashes the traditional framework. It requires a system of values which makes the sacrifices involved in capital formation tolerable and which furnishes some integrating principles to contain psychological frustrations.

Communism is able to supply legitimacy for the sacrifices inseparably connected with capital formation in an age when the maxims of laissez faire are no longer acceptable. And Leninism has the attraction of providing a rationale for holding on to power. Many of the leaders of the new countries are revolutionaries who sustained themselves through the struggle for independence by visions of the transformations to be brought about after victory. They are not predisposed even to admit the possibility of giving up power in their hour of triumph. Since they usually began their struggle for independence while in a small minority and sustained it against heavy odds, they are not likely to be repelled by the notion that it is possible to "force men to be free."

The ironic feature of the current situation is that Marxism, professing a materialistic philosophy, is accepted only where it does not exist: in some new countries and among protest movements of the advanced democratic countries. Its appeal is its idealistic component and not its economic theory. It offers a doctrine of substantive change and an explanation of final purposes. Its philosophy has totally failed to inspire the younger generation in Communist countries, where its bureaucratic reality is obvious.

On the other hand, the United States, professing an idealistic philosophy, often fails to gain acceptance for democratic values because of its heavy reliance on economic factors. It has answers to technical dislocations but has not been able to contribute much to building a political and moral consensus. It offers a procedure for change but little content for it.

The problem of political legitimacy is the key to political stability in regions containing two-thirds of the world's population. A stable domestic system in the new countries will not automatically produce international order, but international order is impossible without it. An American agenda must include some conception of what we understand by political legitimacy. In an age of instantaneous communication, we cannot pretend that what happens to over two-thirds of humanity is of no concern or interest to the United States. This does not mean that our goal should be to transfer American institutions to the new nations—even less that we should impose them. Nor should we define the problem as how to prevent the spread of Communism. Our goal should be to build a moral consensus which can make a pluralistic world creative rather than destructive.

Irrelevance to one of the great revolutions of our time will mean that we will ultimately be engulfed by it—if not physically, then psychologically. Already some of the protest movements have made heroes of leaders in repressive new countries. The absurdity of founding a claim for freedom on protagonists of the totalitarian state—such as Guevara or Ho or Mao—underlines the impact of the travail of the new countries on older societies which share none of their technical but some of their spiritual problems, especially the problem of the nature of authority in the modern world. To a young generation in rebellion against bureaucracy and bored with material comfort, these societies offer at least the challenge of unlimited opportunity (and occasionally unlimited manipulativeness) in the quest for justice.

A world which is bipolar militarily and multipolar politically thus confronts an additional problem. Side by side with the physical balance of power, there exists a psychological balance based on intangibles of value and belief. The presuppositions of the physical equilibrium have changed drastically; those of the psychological balance remain to be discovered.

The Problem of Soviet Intentions. Nothing has been more difficult for Americans to assimilate in the nuclear age than the fact that even enmity is complex. In the Soviet Union, we confront an opponent whose public pronouncements are insistently hostile. Yet the nuclear age imposes a degree of co-operation and an absolute limit to conflicts.

The military relationship with the Soviet Union is difficult enough; the political one confronts us with a profound conceptual problem. A society which regards peace as the normal condition tends to ascribe tension not to structural causes but to wicked or shortsighted individuals. Peace is thought to result either from the automatic operation of economic forces or from the emergence of a more benign leadership abroad.

The debate about Soviet trends between "hard-liners" and "soft-liners" illustrates this problem. Both sides tend to agree that the purpose of American policy is to encourage a more benign evolution of Soviet society—the original purpose of containment was, after all, to bring about the *domestic* transformation of the U.S.S.R. They are at one that a settlement presupposes a change in the Soviet system. Both groups imply that the nature of a possible settlement is perfectly obvious. But the apostles of containment have never specified the American negotiating program to be undertaken from the position of strength their policy was designed to achieve. The advocates of relaxation of tensions have been no more precise; they have been more concerned with atmosphere than with the substance of talks.

In fact, the difference between the "hawks" and "doves" has usually concerned timing: the hawks have maintained that a Soviet change of heart, while inevitable, was still in the future, whereas the doves have argued that it has already taken place. Many of the hawks tend to consider all negotiations as fruitless. Many of the doves argue—or did before Czechoslovakia—that the biggest step toward peace has already been accomplished by a Soviet change of heart about the cold war; negotiations need only remove some essentially technical obstacles.

The difference affects—and sometimes poisons—the entire American debate about foreign policy. Left-wing critics of American foreign policy seem incapable of attacking U.S. actions without elevating our opponent (whether it happens to be Mao or Castro or Ho) to a pedestal. If they discern some stupidity or self-interest on our side, they assume that the other side must be virtuous. They then criticize the United States for opposing the other side. The right follows the same logic in reverse: they presuppose *our* good intentions and conclude that the other side must be perverse in opposing us.

Both the left and the right judge largely in terms of intentions. In the process, whatever the issue—whether Berlin or Vietnam—more attention is paid to whether to get to the conference room than what to do once we arrive there. The dispute over Communist intentions has diverted attention from elaborating our own purposes. In some quarters, the test of dedication to peace has been whether one interprets Soviet intentions in the most favorable manner.

It should be obvious, however, that the Soviet domestic situation is complex and its relationship to foreign policy far from obvious. It is true that the risks of general nuclear war should be as unacceptable to Moscow as to Washington; but this truism does not automatically produce détente. It also seems to lessen the risks involved in local intervention. No doubt the current generation of Communist leaders lacks the ideological dynamism of their predecessors who made the revolution; at the same time, they have at their disposal a military machine of unprecedented strength, and they must deal with a bureaucracy of formidable vested interests. Unquestionably, Soviet consumers press their leaders to satisfy their demands; but it is equally true that an expanding modern economy is able to supply *both* guns and butter. Some Soviet leaders may have become more pragmatic; but in an elaborated Communist state, the results of pragmatism are complex. Once power is seized and industrialization is largely accomplished, the Communist Party faces a difficult situation. It is not needed to conduct the government, and it has no real function in running the economy (though it tries to do both). In order to justify its continued existence and command, it may develop a vested interest in vigilance against outside danger and thus in perpetuating a fairly high level of tension.

It is beyond the scope of this essay to go into detail on the issue of internal Communist evolution. But it may be appropriate to inquire why, in the past, every period of détente has proved stillborn. There have been at least five periods of peaceful coexistence since the Bolshevik seizure of power, one in each decade of the Soviet state. Each was hailed in the West as ushering in a new era of reconciliation and as signifying the long-awaited final change in Soviet purposes. Each ended abruptly with a new period of intransigence, which was generally ascribed to a victory of Soviet hard-liners rather than to the dynamics of the system. There were undoubtedly many reasons for this. But the tendency of many in the West to be content with changes of Soviet tone and to confuse atmosphere with substance surely did not help matters. It has enabled the Communist leaders to postpone the choice which they must make sooner or later: whether to use détente as a device to lull the West or whether to move toward a resolution of the outstanding differences. As long as this choice is postponed, the possibility exists that latent crises may run away with the principal protagonists, as happened in the Middle East and perhaps even in Czechoslovakia.

The eagerness of many in the West to emphasize the liberalizing implications of Soviet economic trends and to make favorable interpretation of Soviet intentions a test of good faith may have the paradoxical consequence of strengthening the Soviet hard-liners. Soviet troops had hardly arrived in Prague when some Western leaders began to insist that the invasion would not affect the quest for détente while others continued to indicate a nostalgia for high-level meetings. Such an attitude hardly serves the cause of peace. The risk is great that if there is no penalty for intransigence there is no incentive for conciliation. The Kremlin may use negotiations —including arms control—as a safety valve to dissipate Western suspicions rather than as a serious endeavor to resolve concrete disputes or to remove the scourge of nuclear war.

If we focus our policy discussions on Soviet purposes, we confuse the debate in two ways: Soviet trends are too ambiguous to offer a reliable guide—it is possible that not even Soviet leaders fully understand the dynamics of their system; it deflects us from articulating the purposes we should pursue, whatever Soviet intentions. Peace will not, in any event, result from one grand settlement but from a long diplomatic process, and this process requires some clarity as to our destination. Confusing foreign policy with psychotherapy deprives us of criteria by which to judge the political foundations of international order.

The obsession with Soviet intentions causes the West to be smug during periods of détente and panicky during crises. A benign Soviet tone is equated with the achievement of peace; Soviet hostility is considered to be the signal for a new period of tension and usually evokes purely military countermeasures. The West is thus never ready for a Soviet change of course; it has been equally unprepared for détente and intransigence.

These lines are being written while outrage at the Soviet invasion of Czechoslovakia is still strong. There is a tendency to focus on military implications or to speak of strengthening unity in the abstract. But if history is a guide, there will be a new Soviet peace offensive sooner or later. Thus, reflecting about the nature of détente seems most important while its achievement appears most problematical. If we are not to be doomed to repeat the past, it may be well to learn some of its lessons: we should not again confuse a change of tone with a change of heart. We should not pose false inconsistencies between allied unity and détente; indeed, a true relaxation of tensions presupposes Western unity. We should concentrate negotiations on the concrete issues that threaten peace, such as intervention in the third world. Moderating the arms race must also be high on the agenda. None of this is possible without a concrete idea of what we understand by peace and a creative world order.

V. AN INQUIRY INTO THE AMERICAN NATIONAL INTEREST

WHEREVER we turn, then, the central task of American foreign policy is to analyze anew the current international environment and to develop some concepts which will enable us to contribute to the emergence of a stable order.

First, we must recognize the existence of profound structural problems that are to a considerable extent independent of the intentions of the principal protagonists and that cannot be solved merely by good will. The vacuum in Central Europe and the decline of the Western European countries would have disturbed the world equilibrium regardless of the domestic structure of the Soviet Union. A strong China has historically tended to establish suzerainty over its neighbors; in fact, one special problem of dealing with China—Communism apart—is that it has had no experience in conducting foreign policy with equals. China has been either dominant or subjected.

To understand the structural issue, it is necessary to undertake an inquiry, from which we have historically shied away, into the essence of our national interest and into the premises of our foreign policy. It is part of American folklore that, while other nations have interests, we have responsibilities; while other nations are concerned with equilibrium, we are concerned with the legal requirements of peace. We have a tendency to offer our altruism as a guarantee of our reliability: "We have no quarrel with the Communists," Secretary of State Rusk said on one occasion; "all our quarrels are on behalf of other people."

Such an attitude makes it difficult to develop a conception of our role in the world. It inhibits other nations from gearing their policy to ours in a confident way—a "disinterested" policy is likely to be considered "unreliable." A mature conception of our interest in the world would obviously have to take into account the widespread interest in stability and peaceful change. It would deal with two fundamental questions: What is it in our interest to prevent? What should we seek to accomplish?

The answer to the first question is complicated by an often-repeated proposition that we must resist aggression anywhere it occurs since peace is indivisible. A corollary is the argument that we do not oppose the fact of particular changes but the method by which they are brought about. We find it hard to articulate a truly vital interest which we would defend however "legal" the challenge. This leads to an undifferentiated globalism and confusion about our purposes. The abstract concept of aggression causes us to multiply our commitments. But the denial that our interests are involved diminishes our staying power when we try to carry out these commitments.

Part of the reason for our difficulties is our reluctance to think in terms of power and equilibrium. In 1949, for example, a State Department memorandum justified NATO as follows: "[The treaty] obligates the parties to defend the purposes and principles of the United Nations, the freedom, common heritage and civilization of the parties and their free institutions based upon the principles of democracy, individual liberty and the role of law. It obligates them to act in defense of peace and security. It is directed against no one; it is directed solely against aggression. It seeks not to influence any shifting balance of power but to strengthen a balance of principle."

But principle, however lofty, must at some point be related to practice; historically, stability has always coincided with an equilibrium that made physical domination difficult. Interest is not necessarily amoral; moral consequences can spring from interested acts. Britain did not contribute any the less to international order for having a clear-cut concept of its interest which required it to prevent the domination of the Continent by a single power (no matter in what way it was threatened) and the control of the seas by anybody (even if the immediate intentions were not hostile). A new American administration confronts the challenge of relating our commitments to our interests and our obligations to our purposes.

The task of defining positive goals is more difficult but even more important. The first two decades after the end of the Second World War posed problems well suited to the American approach to international relations. Wherever we turned, massive dislocations required attention. Our pragmatic, *ad hoc* tendency was an advantage in a world clamoring for technical remedies. Our legal bent contributed to the development of many instruments of stability.

In the late sixties, the situation is more complex. The United States is no longer in a position to operate programs globally; it has to encourage them. It can no longer impose its preferred solution; it must seek to evoke it. In the forties and fifties, we offered remedies; in the late sixties and in the seventies our role will have to be to contribute to a structure that will foster the initiative of others. We are a superpower physically, but our designs can be meaningful only if they generate willing cooperation. We can continue to contribute to defense and positive programs, but we must seek to encourage and not stifle a sense of local responsibility. Our contribution should not be the sole or principal effort, but it should make the difference between success and failure.

This task requires a different kind of creativity and another form of patience than we have displayed in the past. Enthusiasm, belief in progress, and the invincible conviction that American remedies can work everywhere must give way to an understanding of historical trends, an ordering of our preferences, and above all an understanding of the difference our preferences can in fact make.

The dilemma is that there can be no stability without equilibrium but, equally, equilibrium is not a purpose with which we can respond to the travail of our world. A sense of mission is clearly a legacy of American history; to most Americans, America has always stood for something other than its own grandeur. But a clearer understanding of America's interests and of the requirements of equilibrium can give perspective to our idealism and lead to humane and moderate objectives, especially in relation to political and social change. Thus our conception of world order must have deeper purposes than stability but greater restraints on our behavior than would result if it were approached only in a fit of enthusiasm.

Whether such a leap of the imagination is possible in the modern bureaucratic state remains to be seen. New administrations come to power convinced of the need for goals and for comprehensive concepts. Sooner, rather than later, they find themselves subjected to the pressures of the immediate and the particular. Part of the reason is the pragmatic, issue-oriented bias of our decision-makers. But the fundamental reason may be the pervasiveness of modern bureaucracy.

What started out as an aid to decision-making has developed a momentum of its own. Increasingly, the policy-maker is more conscious of the pressures and the morale of his staff than of the purpose this staff is supposed to serve. The policy-maker becomes a referee among quasi-autonomous bureaucratic bodies. Success consists of moving the administrative machinery to the point of decision, leaving relatively little energy for analyzing the decision's merit. The modern bureaucratic state widens the range of technical choices while limiting the capacity to make them.

An even more serious problem is posed by the change of ethic of precisely the most idealistic element of American youth. The idealism of the fifties during the Kennedy era expressed itself in self-confident, often zealous, institution building. Today, however, many in the younger generation consider the management of power irrelevant, perhaps even immoral. While the idea of service retains a potent influence, it does so largely with respect to problems which are clearly *not* connected with the strategic aspects of American foreign policy; the Peace Corps is a good example. The new ethic of freedom is not "civic"; it is indifferent or even hostile to systems and notions of order. Management is equated with manipulation. Structural designs are perceived as systems of "domination"—not of order. The generation which has come of age after the fifties has had Vietnam as its introduction to world politics. It has no memory of occasions when American-supported structural innovations were successful or of the motivations which prompted these enterprises.

Partly as a result of the generation gap, the American mood oscillates dangerously between being ashamed of power and expecting too much of it. The former attitude deprecates the use or possession of force; the latter is overly receptive to the possibilities of absolute action and overly indifferent to the likely consequences. The danger of a rejection of power is that it may result in a nihilistic perfectionism which disdains the gradual and seeks to destroy what does not conform to its notion of utopia. The danger of an overconcern with force is that policy-makers may respond to clamor by a series of spasmodic gestures and stylistic maneuvers and then recoil before their implications.

These essentially psychological problems cannot be overemphasized. It is the essence of a satisfied, advanced society that it puts a premium on operating within familiar procedures and concepts. It draws its motivation from the present, and it defines excellence by the ability to manipulate an established framework. But for the major part of humanity, the present becomes endurable only through a vision of the future. To most Americans—including most American leaders —the significant reality is what they see around them. But for most of the world—including many of the leaders of the new nations—the significant reality is what they wish to bring about. If we remain nothing but the managers of our physical patrimony, we will grow increasingly irrelevant. And since there can be no stability without us, the prospects of world order will decline.

We require a new burst of creativity, however, not so much for the sake of other countries as for our own people, especially the youth. The contemporary unrest is no doubt exploited by some whose purposes are all too clear. But that it is there to exploit is proof of a profound dissatisfaction with the merely managerial and consumer-oriented qualities of the modern state and with a world which seems to generate crises by inertia. The modern bureaucratic state, for all its panoply of strength, often finds itself shaken to its foundations by seemingly trivial causes. Its brittleness and the world-wide revolution of youth—especially in advanced countries and among the relatively affluent—suggest a spiritual void, an al-most metaphysical boredom with a political environment that increasingly emphasizes bureaucratic challenges and is dedi-cated to no deeper purpose than material comfort.

Our unrest has no easy remedy. Nor is the solution to be found primarily in the realm of foreign policy. Yet a deeper nontechnical challenge would surely help us regain a sense of direction. The best and most prideful expressions of American purposes in the world have been those in which we acted in concert with others. Our influence in these situations has de-pended on achieving a reputation as a member of such a concert. To act consistently abroad we must be able to gen-erate coalitions of shared purposes. Regional groupings supported by the United States will have to take over major responsibility for their immediate areas, with the United States being concerned more with the over-all framework of order than with the management of every regional enterprise.

In the best of circumstances, the next administration will be beset by crises. In almost every area of the world, we have been living off capital—warding off the immediate, rarely dealing with underlying problems. These difficulties are likely to multiply when it becomes apparent that one of the legacies of the war in Vietnam will be a strong American reluctance to risk overseas involvements.

A new administration has the right to ask for compassion and understanding from the American people. But it must found its claim not on pat technical answers to difficult issues; it must above all ask the right questions. It must recognize that, in the field of foreign policy, we will never be able to contribute to building a stable and creative world order unless we first form some conception of it.

THREE

THE YEAR OF EUROPE

*Address to the Associated Press
Annual Luncheon, New York, April 23, 1973*

This year has been called the Year of Europe, but not because Europe was less important in 1972 or in 1969. The Alliance between the United States and Europe has been the cornerstone of all postwar foreign policy. It provided the political framework for American engagements in Europe and marked the definitive end of U.S. isolationism. It ensured the sense of security that allowed Europe to recover from the devastation of the war. It reconciled former enemies. It was the stimulus for an unprecedented endeavor in European unity and the principal means to forge the common policies that safeguarded Western security in an era of prolonged tension and confrontation. Our values, our goals and our basic interests are most closely identified with those of Europe.

I. A NEW ERA

1973 is the Year of Europe because the era that was shaped by decisions of a generation ago is ending. The success of those policies has produced new realities that require new approaches:

The revival of Western Europe is an established fact, as is the historic success of its movement toward economic unification.

The East-West strategic military balance has shifted from American preponderance to near equality, bringing with it the necessity for a new understanding of the requirements of our common security.

Other areas of the world have grown in importance. Japan has emerged as a major power center. In many fields, "Atlantic" solutions, to be viable, must include Japan.

We are in a period of relaxation of tensions. But as the rigid divisions of the past two decades diminish, new assertions of national identity and national rivalry emerge.

Problems have arisen, unforeseen a generation ago, which require new types of cooperative action. Ensuring the supply of energy for industrialized nations is an example.

These factors have produced a dramatic transformation of the psychological climate in the West—a change which is the most profound current challenge to Western statesmanship. In Europe a new generation—to whom war and its dislocations are not personal experiences—takes stability for granted. But it is less committed to the unity that made peace possible and to the effort required to maintain it. In the United States, decades of global burdens have fostered, and the frustrations of the war in Southeast Asia have accentuated, a reluctance to sustain global involvements on the basis of preponderant American responsibility.

Inevitably this period of transition will have its strains. There have been complaints in America that Europe ignores its wider responsibilities in pursuing economic self-interest too one-sidely, and that Europe is not carrying its fair share of the burden of the common defense. There have been complaints in Europe that America is out to divide Europe economically, or to desert Europe militarily, or to bypass Europe diplomatically. Europeans appeal to the United States to accept their independence and their occasionally severe criticism of us in the name of Atlantic unity, while at the same time they ask for a veto on our independent policies— also in the name of Atlantic unity.

Our challenge is whether a unity forged by a common perception of danger can draw new purpose from shared positive aspirations. If we permit the Atlantic partnership to atrophy, or to erode through neglect, carelessness, or mistrust, we risk what has been achieved, and we shall miss our historic opportunity for even greater achievement.

In the forties and fifties the task was economic reconstruction and security against the danger of attack. The West responded with courage and imagination. Today the need is to make the Atlantic relationship as dynamic a force in building a new structure of peace, less geared to crisis and more conscious of opportunities, drawing its inspirations from its goals rather than its fears. The Atlantic nations must join in a fresh act of creation, equal to that undertaken by the postwar generation of leaders of Europe and America.

This is why President Nixon is embarking on a personal and direct approach to the leaders of Western Europe. In his discussions with the heads of government of Britain, Italy, the Federal Republic of Germany, and France, the Secretary General of NATO and other European leaders, it is the President's purpose to lay the basis for a new era of creativity in the West.

His approach will be to deal with Atlantic problems comprehensively. The political, military and economic issues in Atlantic relations are linked by reality, not by our choice nor for the tactical purpose of trading one off against the other. The solutions will not be worthy of the opportunity if left to technicians. They must be addressed at the highest level.

In 1972 the President transformed relations with our adversaries to lighten the burdens of fear and suspicion. In 1973 we can gain the same sense of historical achievement by reinvigorating shared ideals and common purposes with our friends.

The United States proposes to its Atlantic partners that, by the time the President travels to Europe toward the end of the year, we will have worked out a new Atlantic charter setting the goals for the future—a blueprint that builds on the past without becoming its prisoner, deals with the problems our success has created, and creates for the Atlantic nations a new relationship in whose progress Japan can share. We ask our friends in Europe, Canada, and ultimately Japan to join us in this effort. This is what we mean by the Year of Europe.

II. PROBLEMS IN ATLANTIC RELATIONSHIPS

THE PROBLEMS in Atlantic relationships are real. They have arisen in part because during the fifties and sixties the Atlantic community organized itself in different ways in the many different dimensions of its common enterprise.

In economic relations, the European community has increasingly stressed its regional personality; the United States, at the same time, must act as part of, and be responsible for, a wider international trade and monetary system. We must reconcile these two perspectives.

In our collective defense, we are still organized on the principle of unity and integration, but in radically different strategic conditions. The full implications of this change have yet to be faced.

Diplomacy is the subject of frequent consultations, but is

essentially being conducted by traditional nation states. The United States has global interests and responsibilities. Our European allies have regional interests. These are not necessarily in conflict, but in the new era neither are they automatically identical.

In short, we deal with each other regionally and even competitively in economic matters, on an integrated basis in defense, and as nation states in diplomacy. When the various collective institutions were rudimentary, the potential inconsistency in their modes of operation was not a problem. But after a generation of evolution and with the new weight and strength of our allies, the various parts of the construction are not always in harmony and sometimes obstruct each other.

If we want to foster unity, we can no longer ignore these problems. The Atlantic nations must find a solution for the management of their diversity, to serve the common objectives which underlie their unity. We can no longer afford to pursue national or regional self-interest without a unifying framework. We cannot hold together if each country or region asserts its autonomy whenever it is to its benefit and invokes unity to curtail the independence of others.

We must strike a new balance between self-interest and the common interest. We must identify interests and positive values beyond security in order to engage once again the commitment of peoples and parliaments. We need a shared view of the world we seek to build.

III. AGENDA FOR THE FUTURE

Economics. No element of American postwar policy has been more consistent than our support of European unity. We encouraged it at every turn. We knew that a united Europe would be a more independent partner. But we assumed, perhaps too uncritically, that our common interests would be assured by our long history of cooperation. We expected that political unity would follow economic integration, and that a unified Europe working cooperatively with us in an Atlantic partnership would ease many of our international burdens.

It is clear that many of these expectations are not being fulfilled.

We and Europe have benefited from European economic integration. Increased trade within Europe has stimulated the growth of European economies and the expansion of trade in both directions across the Atlantic. But we cannot ignore the fact that Europe's economic success and its transformation from a recipient of our aid to a strong competitor has produced a certain amount of friction. There has been turbulence and a sense of rivalry in international monetary relations.

In trade, the natural economic weight of a market of 250 million people has pressed other states to seek special arrangements to protect their access to it. The prospect of a closed trading system embracing the European Community and a growing number of other nations in Europe, the Mediterranean, and Africa appears to be at the expense of the United

States and other nations which are excluded. In agriculture, where the United States has a comparative advantage, we are particularly concerned that Community protective policies may restrict access for our products.

This divergence comes at a time when we are experiencing a chronic and growing deficit in our balance of payments and protectionist pressures of our own. Europeans in turn question our investment policies and doubt our continued commitment to their economic unity.

The gradual accumulation of sometimes petty, sometimes major economic disputes must be ended and be replaced by a determined commitment on both sides of the Atlantic to find cooperative solutions.

The United States will continue to support the unification of Europe. We have no intention of destroying what we worked so hard to help build. For us European unity is what it has always been—not an end in itself but a means to the strengthening of the West. We shall continue to support European unity as a component of a larger Atlantic partnership.

This year we begin comprehensive trade negotiations with Europe as well as with Japan. We shall also continue to press the effort to reform the monetary system so that it promotes stability rather than constant disruptions. A new equilibrium must be achieved in trade and monetary relations. We see these negotiations as an historic opportunity for positive achievement. They must engage the top political leaders, for they require above all a commitment of political will. If they are left solely to the experts the inevitable competitiveness of economic interests will dominate the debate. The influence of pressure groups and special interests will become pervasive. There will be no overriding sense of direction. There will be no framework for the generous solutions or mutual concessions essential to preserve a vital Atlantic partnership.

It is the responsibility of national leaders to ensure that economic negotiations serve larger political purposes. They must recognize that economic rivalry, if carried on without restraint, will in the end damage other relationships.

The United States intends to adopt a broad political approach that does justice to our overriding political interest in an open and balanced trading order with both Europe and Japan. This is the spirit of the President's trade bill and of his speech to the International Monetary Fund last year. It will guide our strategy in the trade and monetary talks. We see these negotiations not as a test of strength, but as a test of joint statesmanship.

Defense. Atlantic unity has always come most naturally in the field of defense. For many years the military threats to Europe were unambiguous, the requirements to meet them were generally agreed on both sides of the Atlantic, and America's responsibility was preeminent and obvious. Today we remain united on the objective of collective defense, but we face the new challenge of maintaining it under radically changed strategic conditions and with the new opportunity of enhancing our security through negotiated reductions of forces.

The West no longer holds the nuclear predominance that permitted it in the fifties and sixties to rely almost solely on a strategy of massive nuclear retaliation. Because under conditions of nuclear parity such a strategy invites mutual suicide, the Alliance must have other choices. The collective ability to resist attack in Western Europe by means of flexible responses has become central to a rational strategy and crucial to the maintenance of peace. For this reason, the United States has maintained substantial conventional forces in Europe and our NATO allies have embarked on a significant effort to modernize and improve their own military establishments.

While the Atlantic Alliance is committed to a strategy of flexible response in principle, the requirements of flexibility are complex and expensive. Flexibility by its nature requires sensitivity to new conditions and continual consultation among the allies to respond to changing circumstances. And we must give substance to the defense posture that our strategy defines. Flexible response cannot be simply a slogan wrapped around the defense structure that emerges from lowest common denominator compromises driven by domestic considerations. It must be seen by ourselves and by potential adversaries as a credible, substantial and rational posture of defense.

A great deal remains to be accomplished to give reality to the goal of flexible response:

• There are deficiencies in important areas of our conventional defense.

• There are still unresolved issues in our doctrine—for example, on the crucial question of the role of tactical nuclear weapons.

• There are anomalies in NATO deployments as well as in its logistics structure.

To maintain the military balance that has ensured stability in Europe for 25 years, the Alliance has no choice but to address these needs and to reach an agreement on our defense requirements. This task is all the more difficult because the lessening of tensions has given new impetus to arguments that it is safe to begin reducing forces unilaterally. And unbridled economic competition can sap the impulse for common defense. All governments of the Western Alliance face a major challenge in educating their peoples to the realities of security in the 1970s.

The President has asked me to state that America remains committed to doing its fair share in Atlantic defense. He is adamantly opposed to unilateral withdrawals of U.S. forces from Europe. But we owe to our peoples a rational defense posture, at the safest minimum size and cost, with burdens equitably shared. This is what the President believes must result from the dialogue with our allies in 1973.

When this is achieved the necessary American forces will be maintained in Europe, not simply as a hostage to trigger our nuclear weapons, but as an essential contribution to an agreed and intelligible structure of Western defense. This too will enable us to engage our adversaries intelligently in negotiations for mutual balanced reductions.

In the next few weeks, the United States will present to NATO the product of our own preparations for the negotiations on mutual balanced force reductions which will begin this year. We hope that it will be a contribution to a broader dialogue on security. Our approach is designed not from the point of view of special American, but of general Alliance interests. Our position will reflect the President's view that these negotiations are not a subterfuge to withdraw U.S. forces regardless of consequences. No formula for reductions is defensible—whatever its domestic appeal or political rationale —if it undermines security.

Our objective in the dialogue on defense is a new consensus on security addressed to new conditions and to the hopeful new possibilities of effective arms limitations.

Diplomacy. We have entered a truly remarkable period of East-West diplomacy. The last two years have produced an agreement on Berlin, a treaty between West Germany and the U.S.S.R., a SALT agreement, the beginning of negotiations on a European security conference and on mutual balanced force reductions, and a series of significant practical bilateral agreements between Western and Eastern countries, including a dramatic change in bilateral relations between the U.S. and U.S.S.R. These were not isolated actions, but steps on a course charted in 1969 and carried forward as a collective effort. Our approach to détente stressed that negotiations had to be concrete, not atmospheric, and that concessions should be reciprocal. We expect to carry forward the policy of relaxation of tensions on this basis.

Yet this very success has created its own problems. There is an increasing uneasiness—all the more insidious for rarely being made explicit—that superpower diplomacy might sacrifice the interests of traditional allies and other friends. Where our allies' interests have been affected by our bilateral negotiations, as in the talks on the limitations of strategic arms, we have been scrupulous in consulting them; where our allies are directly involved, as in the negotiations on Mutual Balanced Force Reductions, our approach is to proceed jointly on the basis of agreed positions. Yet some of our friends in Europe have seemed unwilling to accord America the same trust in our motives that they received from us or to grant us the same tactical flexibility that they employed in pursuit of their own policies. The United States is now often taken to task for flexibility where we used to be criticized for rigidity.

All of this underlines the necessity to articulate a clear set of common objectives together with our allies. Once that is accomplished, it will be quite feasible, indeed desirable, for the several allies to pursue these goals with considerable tactical flexibility. If we agree on common objectives, it will become a technical question whether a particular measure is pursued in a particular forum or whether to proceed bilaterally or multilaterally. Then those allies who seek reassurance of America's commitment will find it not in verbal reaffirmations of loyalty, but in an agreed framework of purpose.

We do not need to agree on all policies. In many areas of the world our approaches will differ, especially outside of Europe. But we do require an understanding of what should be done jointly and of the limits we should impose on the scope of our autonomy.

We have no intention of buying an illusory tranquility at the expense of our friends. The United States will never knowingly sacrifice the interests of others. But the perception of common interests is not automatic; it requires constant redefinition. The relaxation of tensions to which we are committed makes allied cohesion indispensable, yet more difficult. We must ensure that the momentum of détente is maintained by common objectives rather than by drift, escapism or complacency.

America's Contribution. The agenda I have outlined here is not an American prescription but an appeal for a joint effort of creativity. The historic opportunity for this generation is to build a new structure of international relations for the decades ahead. A revitalized Atlantic partnership is indispensable for it.

The United States is prepared to make its contribution:

We will continue to support European unity. Based on the principles of partnership, we will make concessions to its further growth. We will expect to be met in a spirit of reciprocity.

We will not disengage from our solemn commitments to our allies. We will maintain our forces and not withdraw from Europe unilaterally. In turn, we expect from each ally a fair share of the common effort for the common defense.

We shall continue to pursue the relaxation of tensions with our adversaries on the basis of concrete negotiations in the common interest. We welcome the participation of our friends in a constructive East-West dialogue.

We will never consciously injure the interests of our friends in Europe or in Asia. We expect in return that their policies will take seriously our interests and our responsibilities.

We are prepared to work cooperatively on new common problems we face. Energy, for example, raises the challenging issues of assurance of supply, impact of oil revenues on international currency stability, the nature of common political and strategic interests, and long-range relations of oil-consuming to oil-producing countries. This could be an area of competition; it should be an area of collaboration.

Just as Europe's autonomy is not an end in itself, so the Atlantic Community cannot be an exclusive club. Japan must be a principal partner in our common enterprise.

We hope that our friends in Europe will meet us in this spirit. We have before us the example of the great accomplishments of the past decades—and the opportunity to match and dwarf them. This is the task ahead. This is how, in the 1970s, the Atlantic nations can truly serve our peoples and the cause of peace.

FOUR

THE NATURE OF THE
NATIONAL DIALOGUE

Address to the Pacem in Terris *III*
Conference, Washington, October 8, 1973

THIS IS an important anniversary. A year ago today—on October 8, 1972—came the breakthrough in the Paris negotiations which led soon afterward to the end of American military involvement in Vietnam. It is strangely difficult now to recapture the emotion of that moment of hope and uncertainty when suddenly years of suffering and division were giving way to new possibilities for reconciliation.

We meet, too, at a time when renewed conflict in the Middle East reminds us that international stability is always precarious and never to be taken for granted. *Pacem in terris* remains regrettably elusive. However well we contain this crisis as we have contained others, we must still ask ourselves what we seek beyond the management of conflict.

The need for a dialogue about national purposes has never been more urgent and no assembly is better suited for such a discussion than these gathered here tonight.

Dramatic changes in recent years have transformed America's position and role in the world:

• For most of the postwar period, America enjoyed predominance in physical resources and political power. Now,

like most other nations in history, we find that our most difficult task is how to apply limited means to the accomplishment
of carefully defined ends. We can no longer overwhelm our
problems; we must master them with imagination, understanding, and patience.

• For a generation our preoccupation was to prevent the
Cold War from degenerating into a hot war. Today, when the
danger of global conflict has diminished, we face the more
profound problem of defining what we mean by peace and
determining the ultimate purpose of improved international
relations.

• For two decades the solidarity of our alliances seemed as
constant as the threats to our security. Now our allies have
regained strength and self-confidence, and relations with adversaries have improved. All this has given rise to uncertainties over the sharing of burdens with friends and the impact
of reduced tensions on the cohesion of alliances.

• Thus even as we have mastered the art of containing crises,
our concern with the nature of a more permanent international
order has grown. Questions once obscured by more insistent
needs now demand our attention: What is true national interest? To what end stability? What is the relationship of peace
to justice?

It is characteristic of periods of upheaval that to those who
live through them they appear as a series of haphazard events.
Symptoms obscure basic issues and historical trends. The
urgent tends to dominate the important. Too often goals are
presented as abstract utopias, safe havens from pressing events.

But a debate to be fruitful must define what can reasonably
be asked of foreign policy and at what pace progress can be
achieved. Otherwise it turns into competing catalogues of the
desirable rather than informed comparisons of the possible.
Dialogue degenerates into tactical skirmishing.

The current public discussion reflects some interesting and significant shifts in perspective:

• A foreign policy once considered excessively moralistic is now looked upon by some as excessively pragmatic.

• The government was criticized in 1969 for holding back East-West trade with certain countries until there was progress in their foreign policies. Now we are criticized for not holding back East-West trade until there are changes in those same countries' domestic policies.

• The administration's foreign policy, once decried as too Cold War oriented, is now attacked as too insensitive to the profound moral antagonism between Communism and freedom. One consequence of this intellectual shift is a gap between conception and performance on some major issues of policy:

• The desirability of peace and détente is affirmed, but both the inducements to progress and the penalties to confrontation are restricted by legislation.

• Expressions of concern for human values in other countries are coupled with failure to support the very programs designed to help developing areas improve their economic and social conditions.

• The declared objective of maintaining a responsible American international role clashes with nationalistic pressures in trade and monetary negotiations and with calls for unilateral withdrawal from alliance obligations.

It is clear that we face genuine moral dilemmas and important policy choices. But it is also clear that we need to define the framework of our dialogue more perceptively and understandingly.

I. THE COMPETING ELEMENTS
OF FOREIGN POLICY

FOREIGN POLICY must begin with the understanding that it
involves relationships between sovereign countries. Sovereignty
has been defined as a will uncontrolled by others; that is what
gives foreign policy its contingent and ever incomplete
character. For disagreements among sovereign states can be
settled only by negotiation or by power, by compromise or by
imposition. Which of these methods prevails depends on the
values, the strengths, and the domestic systems of the countries
involved. A nation's values define what is just; its strength
determines what is possible; its domestic structure decides what
policies can in fact be implemented and sustained.

Thus foreign policy involves two partially conflicting endeavors: defining the interests, purposes, and values of a society
and relating them to the interests, purposes, and values of
others.

The policy-maker, therefore, must strike a balance between
what is desirable and what is possible. Progress will always
be measured in partial steps and in the relative satisfaction
of alternative goals. Tension is unavoidable between values,
which are invariably cast in maximum terms, and efforts to
promote them, which of necessity involve compromise. Foreign
policy is explained domestically in terms of justice. But what
is defined as justice at home becomes the subject of negotiation abroad. It is thus no accident that many nations, includ-

ing our own, view the international arena as a forum in which virtue is thwarted by the clever practice of foreigners.

In a community of sovereign states, the quest for peace involves a paradox: The attempt to impose absolute justice by one side will be seen as absolute injustice by all others; the quest for total security for some turns into total insecurity for the remainder. Stability depends on the relative satisfaction and therefore also the relative dissatisfaction of the various states. The pursuit of peace must therefore begin with a pragmatic concept of coexistence—especially in a period of ideological conflict.

We must, of course, avoid becoming obsessed with stability. An excessively pragmatic policy will be empty of vision and humanity. It will lack not only direction, but also roots and heart. General de Gaulle wrote in his memoirs that "France cannot be France without greatness." By the same token, America cannot be true to itself without moral purpose. This country has always had a sense of mission. Americans have always held the view that America stood for something above and beyond its material achievements. A purely pragmatic policy provides no criteria for other nations to assess our performance and no standards to which the American people can rally.

But when policy becomes excessively moralistic, it may turn quixotic or dangerous. A presumed monopoly on truth obstructs negotiation and accommodation. Good results may be given up in the quest for ever-elusive ideal solutions. Policy may fall prey to ineffectual posturing or adventuristic crusades.

The prerequisite for a fruitful national debate is that the policy-makers and critics appreciate each other's perspectives and respect each other's purposes. The policy-maker must understand that the critic is obliged to stress imperfections in order to challenge assumptions and to goad actions. But equally the critic should acknowledge the complexity and inherent ambiguity of the policy-maker's choices. The policy-maker must be concerned with the best that can be achieved, not just the best that can be imagined. He has to act in a fog of incomplete knowledge without the information that will be available later to the analyst. He knows—or should know—that he is responsible for the consequences of disaster as well as for the benefits of success. He may have to qualify some goals not because they would be undesirable if reached, but because the risks of failure outweigh potential gains. He must often settle for the gradual, much as he might prefer the immediate. He must compromise with others, and this means to some extent compromising with himself.

The outsider demonstrates his morality by the precision of his perceptions and the loftiness of his ideals. The policy-maker expresses his morality by implementing a sequence of imperfections and partial solutions in pursuit of *his* ideals.

There must be understanding, as well, of the crucial importance of timing. Opportunities cannot be hoarded; once past, they are usually irretrievable. New relationships in a fluid transitional period—such as today—are delicate and vulnerable; they must be nurtured if they are to thrive. We cannot pull up young shoots periodically to see whether the roots are still there or whether there is some marginally better location for them.

We are now at such a time of tenuous beginnings. Western Europe and Japan have joined us in an effort to reinvigorate our relationships. The Soviet Union has begun to practice foreign policy—at least partially—as a relationship between states rather than as international civil war. The People's Republic of China has emerged from two decades of isolation. The developing countries are impatient for economic and social change. A new dimension of unprecedented challenges

—in food, oceans, energy, environment—demands global co-operation.

We are at one of those rare moments where through a combination of fortuitous circumstances and design man seems in a position to shape his future. What we need is the confidence to discuss issues without bitter strife, the wisdom to define together the nature of our world, as well as the vision to chart together a more just future.

II. DÉTENTE WITH THE SOVIET UNION

NOTHING demonstrates this need more urgently than our relationship with the Soviet Union.

This administration has never had any illusions about the Soviet system. We have always insisted that progress in technical fields, such as trade, had to follow—and reflect—progress toward more stable international relations. We have maintained a strong military balance and a flexible defense posture as a buttress to stability. We have insisted that disarmament had to be mutual. We have judged movement in our relations with the Soviet Union, not by atmospherics, but by how well concrete problems are resolved and by whether there is responsible international conduct.

Coexistence to us continues to have a very precise meaning:

We will oppose the attempt by any country to achieve a position of predominance either globally or regionally.

• We will resist any attempt to exploit a policy of détente to weaken our alliances.

• We will react if relaxation of tensions is used as a cover to exacerbate conflicts in international trouble spots.

The Soviet Union cannot disregard these principles in any area of the world without imperiling its entire relationship with the United States.

On this basis we have succeeded in transforming U.S.-Soviet relations in many important ways. Our two countries have concluded an historic accord to limit strategic arms. We have substantially reduced the risk of direct U.S.-Soviet confrontation in crisis areas. The problem of Berlin has been resolved by negotiation. We and our allies have engaged the Soviet Union in negotiations on major issues of European security, including a reduction of military forces in Central Europe. We have reached a series of bilateral agreements on cooperation—health, environment, space, science and technology, as well as trade. These accords are designed to create a vested interest in cooperation and restraint.

Until recently the goals of détente were not an issue. The necessity of shifting from confrontation toward negotiation seemed so overwhelming that goals beyond the settlement of international disputes were never raised. But now progress has been made—and already taken for granted. We are engaged in an intense debate on whether we should make changes in Soviet society a precondition for further progress —or indeed for following through on commitments already made. The cutting edge of this problem is the congressional effort to condition most-favored-nation trade status for other countries on changes in their domestic systems.

This is a genuine moral dilemma. There are genuine moral concerns—on both sides of the argument. So let us not address this as a debate between those who are morally sensitive and those who are not, between those who care for justice and those who are oblivious to humane values. The attitude of the American people and government has been made emphatically clear on countless occasions, in ways that have produced effective results. The exit tax on emigration is not being collected and we have received assurances that it will not be reapplied; hardship cases submitted to the Soviet government are being given specific attention; the rate of Jewish emigration has been in the terms of thousands where it was once a trickle. We will continue our vigorous efforts on these matters.

But the real debate goes far beyond this: Should we now tie demands which were never raised during negotiations to agreements that have already been concluded? Should we require as a formal condition internal changes that we heretofore sought to foster in an evolutionary manner?

Let us remember what the MFN question specifically involves. The very term "most favored nation" is misleading in its implication of preferential treatment. What we are talking about is whether to allow *normal* economic relations to develop—of the kind we now have with over one hundred other countries and which the Soviet Union enjoyed until 1951. The issue is whether to abolish discriminatory trade restrictions that were imposed at the height of the Cold War. Indeed, at that time the Soviet government discouraged commerce because it feared the domestic impact of normal trading relations with the West on its society.

The demand that Moscow modify its domestic policy is a precondition for MFN or détente was never made while we were negotiating; now it is inserted after both sides have carefully shaped an overall mosaic. Thus it raises questions about our entire bilateral relationship.

Finally the issue affects not only our relationship with the Soviet Union, but also with many other countries whose internal structures we find incompatible with our own. Conditions imposed on one country could inhibit expanding relations with others, such as the People's Republic of China.

We shall never condone the suppression of fundamental liberties. We shall urge humane principles and use our influence to promote justice. But the issue comes down to the limits of such efforts. How hard can we press without provoking the Soviet leadership into returning to practices in its foreign policy that increase international tensions? Are we ready to face the crises and increased defense budgets that a return to Cold War conditions would spawn? And will this encourage full emigration or enhance the well-being or nourish the hope for liberty of the peoples of Eastern Europe and the Soviet Union? Is it détente that has prompted repression—or is it détente that has generated the ferment and the demand for openness which we are now witnessing?

For half a century we have objected to Communist efforts to alter the domestic structures of other countries. For a generation of Cold War we sought to ease the risks produced by competing ideologies. Are we now to come full circle and *insist* on domestic compatibility as a condition of progress?

These questions have no easy answers. The government may underestimate the margin of concessions available to us. But a fair debate must admit that they *are* genuine questions, the answers to which could affect the fate of all of us.

Our policy with respect to détente is clear: We shall resist aggressive foreign policies. Détente cannot survive irresponsibility in any area, including the Middle East. As for the internal policies of closed systems, the United States will never forget that the antagonism between freedom and its enemies is part of the reality of the modern age. We are not neutral in that struggle. As long as we remain powerful we will use our influence to promote freedom, as we always have. But in the nuclear age we are obliged to recognize that the issue of war and peace also involves human lives and that the attainment of peace is a profound moral concern.

III. THE WORLD AS IT IS AND THE WORLD WE SEEK

ADDRESSING THE United Nations General Assembly two weeks ago, I described our goal as a world where power blocs and balances are no longer relevant; where justice, not stability, can be our overriding preoccupation; where countries consider cooperation in the world interest to be in their national interest.

But we cannot move toward the world of the future without first maintaining peace in the world as it is. These very days we are vividly reminded that this requires vigilance and a continuing commitment.

So our journey must start from where we are now. This is a time of lessened tension, of greater equilibrium, of diffused power. But if the world is better than our earlier fears, it still falls far short of our hopes. To deal with the present does not mean that we are content with it.

The most striking feature of the contemporary period—the feature that gives complexity as well as hope—is the radical transformation in the nature of power. Throughout history power has generally been homogeneous. Military, economic, and political potential were closely related. To be powerful a nation had to be strong in all categories. Today the vocabulary of strength is more complex. Military muscle does not guarantee political influence. Economic giants can be militarily weak, and military strength may not be able to obscure economic weakness. Countries·can exert political influence even when they have neither military nor economic strength.

It is wrong to speak of only one balance of power, for there are several which have to be related to each other. In the military sphere, there are two superpowers. In economic terms, there are at least five major groupings. Politically, many more centers of influence have emerged; some eighty new nations have come into being since the end of World War II and regional groups are assuming ever increasing importance.

Above all, whatever the measure of power, its political utility has changed. Throughout history increases in military power—however slight—could be turned into specific political advantage. With the overwhelming arsenals of the nuclear age, however, the pursuit of marginal advantage is both pointless and potentially suicidal. Once sufficiency is reached, additional increments of power do not translate into usable political strength; and attempts to achieve tactical gains can lead to cataclysm.

This environment both puts a premium on stability and makes it difficult to maintain. Today's striving for equilibrium should not be compared to the balance of power of previous periods. The very notion of "operating" a classical balance of power disintegrates when the change required to upset the balance is so large that it cannot be achieved by limited means.

More specifically, there is no parallel with the nineteenth century. Then, the principal countries shared essentially similar concepts of legitimacy and accepted the basic structure of the existing international order. Small adjustments in strength were significant. The "balance" operated in a relatively confined geographic area. None of these factors obtain today.

Nor when we talk of equilibrium do we mean a simplistic mechanical model devoid of purpose. The constantly shifting alliances that maintained equilibrium in previous centuries are neither appropriate nor possible in our time. In an age of ideological schism the distinction between friends and adversaries is an objective reality. We share ideals as well as interests with our friends, and we know that the strength of our friendships is crucial to the lowering of tensions with our opponents.

When we refer to five or six or seven major centers of power, the point being made is not that others are excluded but that a few short years ago everyone agreed that there were only two. The diminishing tensions and the emergence of new centers of power has meant greater freedom of action and greater importance for all other nations. In this setting, our immediate aim has been to build a stable network of relationships that offers hope of sparing mankind the scourges of war. An interdependent world community cannot tolerate either big power confrontations or recurrent regional crises.

But peace must be more than the absence of conflict. We perceive stability as the bridge to the realization of human aspirations, not an end in itself. We have learned much about containing crises, but we have not removed their roots. We have begun to accommodate our differences, but we have not affirmed our commonality. We may have improved the mastery of equilibrium, but we have not yet attained justice.

In the encyclical *Pacem in Terris,* Pope John sketched a greater vision. He foresaw "that no political community is able to pursue its own interests and develop itself in isolation," for "there is a growing awareness of all human beings that they are members of a world community."

The opportunities of mankind now transcend nationalism, and can only be dealt with by nations acting in concert:

- For the first time in generations mankind is in a position to shape a new and peaceful international order. But do we have the imagination and determination to carry forward this still fragile task of creation?
- For the first time in history we may have the technical knowledge to satisfy man's basic needs. The imperatives of the modern world respect no national borders and must inevitably open all societies to the world around them. But do we have the political will to join together to accomplish this great end?

If this vision is to be realized, America's active involvement is inescapable. History will judge us by our deeds, not by our good intentions.

But it cannot be the work of any one country. And it cannot be the undertaking of any one administration or one branch of government or one party. To build truly is to chart a course that will be carried on by future leaders because it has the enduring support of the American people.

So let us search for a fresh consensus. Let us restore a spirit of understanding between the legislative and the executive, between the government and the press, between the people and their public servants. Let us learn once again to debate our methods and not our motives, to focus on our destiny and not on our divisions. Let us all contribute our different views and perspectives but let us, once again, see ourselves as engaged in a common enterprise. If we are to shape a world community we must first restore community at home.

With Americans working together, America can work with others toward man's eternal goal of *pacem in terris*—peace abroad, peace at home, and peace within ourselves.

FIVE

THE QUEST FOR PEACE IN
THE MIDDLE EAST

*Address to the Peace Conference on the
Middle East, Geneva, December 21, 1973*

WE ARE convened here at a moment of historic opportunity for the cause of peace in the Middle East, and for the cause of peace in the world. For the first time in a generation the peoples of the Middle East are sitting together to turn their talents to the challenge of a lasting peace.

All of us must have the wisdom to grasp this moment—to break the shackles of the past, and to create at last a new hope for the future.

Two months ago, what we now refer to as the fourth Arab-Israeli war was coming to an end. Today, there is the respite of an imperfect cease fire, but the shadow of war still hangs over the Middle East. Either we begin today the process of correcting the conditions which produced that conflict, or we doom untold tens of thousands to travail, sorrow, and further inconclusive bloodshed.

When the history of our era is written, it will speak not of a series of Arab-Israeli wars, but of one war broken by periods of uneasy armistices and temporary cease fires. That war has already lasted twenty-five years. Whether future histories will call this the era of the twenty-five-year Arab-Israeli war, or the thirty-year war, or the fifty-year war, rests in large measure in our hands. And above all, it rests in the hands of the Israeli and Arab governments, not only those whose distinguished representatives are seated around this table, but also those who are absent and who we all hope will join us soon.

We are challenged by emotions so deeply felt—by causes so passionately believed and pursued—that the tragic march from cataclysm to cataclysm, each more costly and indecisive than the last, sometimes seems preordained. Yet our presence here today—in itself a momentous accomplishment—is a symbol of rejection of this fatalistic view. Respect for the forces of history does not mean blind submission to those forces.

There is an Arab saying, *Illi Fat Mat,* which means that the past is dead. Let us resolve here today that we will overcome the legacy of hatred and suffering. Let us overcome old myths with new hope. Let us make the Middle East worthy of the messages of hope and reconciliation that have been carried forward from its stark soil by three great religions.

Today there is hope for the future, for the conflict is no longer looked upon entirely in terms of irreconcilable absolutes. The passionate ideologies of the past have, in part at least, been replaced by a recognition that all the peoples concerned have earned, by their sacrifice, a long period of peace.

From two recent trips through the Middle East I have the impression that people on both sides have had enough of bloodshed. No further proof of heroism is necessary; no military point remains to be made. The Middle East—so often the source of mankind's inspiration—is challenged to another act of hope and reconciliation—significant not only for its own peoples but for all mankind.

What does each side seek? Both answer with a single word: peace. But peace has of course a concrete meaning for each. One side seeks the recovery of sovereignty and the redress of grievances suffered by a displaced people. The other seeks security and recognition of its legitimacy as a nation. The common goal of peace must be broad enough to embrace all these aspirations.

For the United States, our objective is such a peace.

We cannot promise success, but we can promise dedication. We cannot guarantee a smooth journey toward our goal, but we can assure you of an unswerving quest for justice.

The United States will make a determined and unflagging effort.

President Nixon has sent me here because for five years he has endeavored to build a new structure of international peace in which ties with old friends are strengthened, and new and constructive relationships replace distrust and confrontation with adversaries.

But world peace remains tenuous and incomplete so long as the Middle East is in perpetual crisis. Its turmoil is a threat to the hopes of all of us in this room.

It is time to end this turmoil.

The question is not whether there must be peace. The question is, How do we achieve it? What can we do here to launch new beginnings?

First, this Conference must speak with a clear and unequivocal voice: the cease fire called for by the Security Council must be scrupulously adhered to by all concerned. Prior to last October the United States did all it could to prevent a new outbreak of fighting. But we failed because frustration could no longer be contained.

After the fighting began we, in concert with the Soviet Union, helped bring an end to the hostilities by sponsoring a number of resolutions in the Security Council. The six-point agreement of 11 November 1973 consolidated the cease fire. It helped create the minimal conditions necessary for carrying forward our efforts here. All these resolutions and agreements must be strictly implemented.

But regardless of these steps, we recognize that the cease fire remains fragile and tentative. The United States is concerned over the evidence of increased military preparedness. A renewal of hostilities would be both foolhardy and dangerous. We urge all concerned to refrain from the use of force, and to give our efforts here the chance they deserve.

Second, we must understand what can realistically be accomplished at any given moment.

The separation of military forces is certainly the most immediate problem. Disengagement of military forces would help to reduce the danger of a new military outbreak; it would begin the process of building confidence between the two sides.

Based on intensive consultations with the leaders of the Middle East, including many in this room today, I believe that the first work of this Conference should be to achieve early agreement on the separation of military forces, and I believe too that such an agreement is possible.

Serious discussions have already taken place between the military representatives of Egypt and Israel at Kilometer 101. It is important to build promptly on the progress achieved there. And on the Jordanian and Syrian fronts a comparable base for the lessening of tensions and the negotiation of further steps toward peace must be found. Progress toward peace should include *all* parties concerned.

Third, the disengagement of forces is an essential first step— a consolidation of the cease fire and a bridge to the "peaceful and accepted settlement" called for in Security Council

Resolution 242. Our final objective is the implementation in all of the parts of this resolution. This goal has the full support of the United States.

Peace must bring a new relationship among the nations of the Middle East—a relationship that will not only put an end to the state of war which has persisted for the last quarter of a century, but will also permit the peoples of the Middle East to live together in harmony and safety. It must replace the reality of mistrust with a new reality of promise and hope. It must include concrete measures that make war less likely.

A peace agreement must include these elements among others: withdrawals, recognized frontiers, security arrangements such as demilitarized zones, guarantees, a settlement of the legitimate interests of the Palestinians, and a recognition that Jerusalem contains places considered holy by three great religions.

Peace will require that we relate the imperative of withdrawals to the necessities of security, the requirement of guarantees to the sovereignty of the parties, the hopes of the displaced to the realities now existing.

Fourth, we believe there must be realistic negotiations between the parties. Resolution 338 provides just such a process. It is on the parties that the primary responsibility rests. The United States intends to help facilitate these talks in every feasible way, to encourage moderation and the spirit of accommodation. We are prepared to make concrete suggestions to either side if this will help promote practical progress. But we must always remember that while a Middle East settlement is in the interest of us all, it is the people of the area that must live with the results. It must, in the final analysis, be acceptable to them.

Peace, in short, cannot last unless it rests on the consent of the parties concerned. The wisest of realists are those who understand the power of a moral consensus. There is a measure of safety in power to prevent aggression, but there is greater security still in arrangements considered so just that no one wishes to overthrow them.

As we open this Conference we take a momentous step. We are challenging a history of missed opportunities, of mutual fear and bottomless distrust. Our backdrop is a war that has brought anguish and pain, a war that has been costly to both sides, that has brought neither victory nor defeat, that reflected the failure of all our past efforts at peaceful solutions.

Mr. Secretary-General, fellow delegates, President Nixon has sent me here with the purpose of affirming America's commitment to a just and lasting peace.

We do not embark on this task with false expectations. We do not pretend that there are easy answers. A problem that has defied solution for a generation does not yield to simple remedies.

In all efforts for peace the overriding problem is to relate the sense of individual justice to the common good. The great tragedies of history occur not when right confronts wrong, but when two rights face each other.

The problems of the Middle East today have such a character. There is justice on all sides, but there is a greater justice still in finding a truth which merges all aspirations in the realization of a common humanity. It was a Jewish sage who, speaking for all mankind, expressed this problem well: "If I am not for myself, who is for me, but if I am for myself alone, who am I?"

Fellow delegates, in the months ahead we will examine many problems. We will discuss many expedients. We will know success—and I dare say we shall experience deadlock and perhaps occasionally despair.

But let us always keep in mind our final goal:

We can exhaust ourselves in maneuvers or we can remember that this is the first real chance for peace the Middle East has had in three decades.

We can concentrate on our resentments or we can be motivated by the consciousness that this opportunity, once past, will not return.

We can emphasize the very real causes of distrust, or we can remember that if we succeed our children will thank us for what they have been spared.

We can make propaganda or we can try to make progress.

The American attitude is clear. We know we are starting on a journey whose outcome is uncertain and whose progress will be painful. We are conscious that we need wisdom and patience and good will. But we know, too, that the agony of three decades must be overcome and that somehow we have to muster the insight and courage to put an end to the conflict between peoples who have so often ennobled mankind.

So we in the American delegation are here to spare no effort in the quest of a lasting peace in the Middle East, a task which is as worthy as it may be agonizing. If I may quote the words of a poet: "Pain that cannot forget / falls drop by drop / upon the heart / until in our despair / there comes wisdom / through the awful / grace of God."

SIX

THE PROCESS OF DÉTENTE

*Statement Delivered to the Senate Foreign
Relations Committee, September 19, 1974*

I. THE CHALLENGE

SINCE THE dawn of the nuclear age the world's fears of holocaust and its hopes for peace have turned on the relationship between the United States and the Soviet Union.

Throughout history men have sought peace but suffered war; all too often deliberate decisions or miscalculations have brought violence and destruction to a world yearning for tranquility. Tragic as the consequences of violence may have been in the past, the issue of peace and war takes on unprecedented urgency when, for the first time in history, two nations have the capacity to destroy mankind. In the nuclear age, as President Eisenhower pointed out two decades ago, "there is no longer any alternative to peace."

The destructiveness of modern weapons defines the necessity of the task; deep differences in philosophy and interests between the United States and the Soviet Union point up its difficulty. These differences do not spring from misunderstanding, or personalities, or transitory factors:

· They are rooted in history, and in the way the two countries have developed.

· They are nourished by conflicting values and opposing ideologies.

· They are expressed in diverging national interests that produce political and military competition.

· They are influenced by allies and friends whose association we value and whose interests we will not sacrifice.

Paradox confuses our perception of the problem of peaceful coexistence: if peace is pursued to the exclusion of any other goal, other values will be compromised and perhaps lost; but if unconstrained rivalry leads to nuclear conflict, these values, along with everything else, will be destroyed in the resulting holocaust. However competitive they may be at some levels of their relationship, both major nuclear powers must base their policies on the premise that neither can expect to impose its will on the other without running an intolerable risk. The challenge of our time is to reconcile the reality of competition with the imperative of coexistence.

There can be no peaceful international order without a constructive relationship between the United States and the Soviet Union. There will be no international stability unless both the Soviet Union and the United States conduct themselves with restraint and unless they use their enormous power for the benefit of mankind.

Thus we must be clear at the outset on what the term "détente" entails. It is the search for a more constructive relationship with the Soviet Union reflecting the realities I have outlined. It is a continuing process, not a final condition that has been or can be realized at any one specific point in time. And it has been pursued by successive American leaders, though the means have varied, as have world conditions.

Some fundamental principles guide this policy:

The United States cannot base its policy solely on Moscow's good intentions. But neither can we insist that all forward movement must await a convergence of American and Soviet purposes. We seek, regardless of Soviet intentions, to serve peace through a systematic resistance to pressure and conciliatory responses to moderate behavior.

We must oppose aggressive actions and irresponsible behavior. But we must not seek confrontations lightly.

We must maintain a strong national defense while recognizing that in the nuclear age the relationship between military strength and politically usable power is the most complex in all history.

Where the age-old antagonism between freedom and tyranny is concerned, we are not neutral. But other imperatives impose limits on our ability to produce internal changes in foreign countries. Consciousness of our limits is recognition of the necessity of peace—not moral callousness. The preservation of human life and human society are moral values, too.

We must be mature enough to recognize that to be stable a relationship must provide advantages to both sides, and that the most constructive international relationships are those in which both parties perceive an element of gain. Moscow will benefit from certain measures just as we will from others. The balance cannot be struck on each issue every day, but only over the whole range of relations and over a period of time.

II. THE COURSE OF
SOVIET-AMERICAN RELATIONS

In the first two decades of the postwar period, U.S.-Soviet relations were characterized by many fits and starts. Some encouraging developments followed the Cuban missile crisis of 1962, for example. But at the end of the decade the invasion of Czechoslovakia brought progress to a halt and threw a deepening shadow over East-West relations.

During those difficult days some were tempted to conclude that antagonism was the central feature of the relationship and that U.S. policy—even while the Vietnam agony raised questions about the readiness of the American people to sustain a policy of confrontation—had to be geared to this grim reality. Others recommended a basic change of policy: there was a barrage of demands to hold an immediate summit to establish a better atmosphere to launch the Strategic Arms Limitation Talks [SALT], and to end the decades-old trade discrimination against the Soviet Union which was widely criticized as anachronistic, futile, and counterproductive.

These two approaches reflected the extremes of the debate that had dominated most of the postwar period; they also revealed deep-seated differences between the American and the Soviet reactions to the process of international relations.

For many Americans, tensions and enmity in international relations are anomalies, the cause of which is attributed either to deliberate malice or misunderstanding. Malice is to be combated by force, or at least isolation; misunderstanding is to be removed by the strenuous exercise of good will. Communist states, on the other hand, regard tensions as inevitable byproducts of a struggle between opposing social systems.

Most Americans perceive relations between states as either friendly or hostile, both defined in nearly absolute terms. Soviet foreign policy, by comparison, is conducted in a gray area heavily influenced by the Soviet conception of the balance of forces. Thus, Soviet diplomacy is never free of tactical pressures or adjustments, and it is never determined in isolation from the prevailing military balance. For Moscow, East-West contacts and negotiations are in part designed to promote Soviet influence abroad—especially in Western Europe—and to gain formal acceptance of those elements of the status quo most agreeable to Moscow.

The issue, however, is not whether peace and stability serve Soviet purposes, but whether they serve our own. Indeed, to the extent that our attention focuses largely on Soviet intentions we create a latent vulnerability. If détente can be justified only by a basic change in Soviet motivation, the temptation becomes overwhelming to base U.S.-Soviet relations not on realistic appraisal but on tenuous hopes: a change in Soviet tone is taken as a sign of a basic change of philosophy. Atmosphere is confused with substance. Policy oscillates between poles of suspicion and euphoria.

Neither extreme is realistic, and both are dangerous. The hopeful view ignores the fact that we and the Soviets are bound to compete for the foreseeable future. The pessimistic view ignores that we have some parallel interests and that we are compelled to coexist. Détente encourages an environment in which competitors can regulate and restrain their differences and ultimately move from competition to cooperation.

A. AMERICAN GOALS

America's aspiration for the kind of political environment we now call détente is not new.

The effort to achieve a more constructive relationship with the Soviet Union is not made in the name of any one administration, or one party, or for any one period of time. It expresses the continuing desire of the vast majority of the American people for an easing of international tensions, and their expectation that any responsible government will strive for peace. No aspect of our policies, domestic or foreign, enjoys more consistent bipartisan support. No aspect is more in the interest of mankind.

In the postwar period repeated efforts were made to improve our relationship with Moscow. The spirits of Geneva, Camp David, and Glassboro were evanescent moments in a quarter-century otherwise marked by tensions and by sporadic confrontation. What is new in the current period of relaxation of tensions is its duration, the scope of the relationship which has evolved, and the continuity and intensity of consultation which it has produced.

A number of factors have produced this change in the international environment. By the end of the sixties and the beginning of the seventies the time was propitious—no matter what administration was in office in the United States—for a major attempt to improve U.S.-Soviet relations. Contradictory tendencies contested for preeminence in Soviet policy; events could have tipped the scales either toward increased aggressiveness or toward conciliation:

· The fragmentation in the Communist world in the 1960s challenged the leading position of the U.S.S.R. and its claim to be the arbiter of orthodoxy. The U.S.S.R. could have reacted by adopting a more aggressive attitude toward the capitalist world in order to assert its militant vigilance; instead the changing situation and U.S. policy seem to have encouraged Soviet leaders to cooperate in at least a temporary lessening of tension with the West.

· The prospect of achieving a military position of near-parity with the U.S. in strategic forces could have tempted Moscow to use its expanding military capability to strive more determinedly for expansion; in fact it tempered the militancy of some of its actions and sought to stabilize at least some aspects of the military competition through negotiations.

· The very real economic problems of the U.S.S.R. and Eastern Europe could have reinforced autarkic policies and the tendency to create a closed system; in actuality the Soviet Union and its allies have come closer to acknowledging the reality of an interdependent world economy.

· Finally, when faced with the hopes of its own people for greater well-being, the Soviet Government could have continued to stimulate the suspicions of the Cold War to further isolate Soviet society; in fact, it chose—however inadequately and slowly—to seek to calm its public opinion by joining in a relaxation of tensions.

For the United States the choice was clear: to provide as many incentives as possible for those actions by the Soviet Union most conducive to peace and individual well-being and to overcome the swings between illusionary optimism and harsh antagonism that had characterized most of the postwar period. We could capitalize on the tentative beginnings made in the sixties by taking advantage of the compelling new conditions of the 1970s.

We sought to explore every avenue toward an honorable and just accommodation while remaining determined not to settle for mere atmospherics. We relied on a balance of mutual interests rather than Soviet intentions. When challenged—such as in the Middle East, the Caribbean, or Berlin—we always responded firmly. And when Soviet policy moved toward conciliation we sought to turn what may have started as a tactical maneuver into a durable pattern of conduct.

Our approach proceeds from the conviction that in moving forward across a wide spectrum of negotiations, progress in one area adds momentum to progress in other areas. If we succeed, then no agreement stands alone as an isolated accomplishment vulnerable to the next crisis. We did not invent the interrelationship between issues expressed in the so-called linkage concept; it was a reality because of the range of problems and areas in which the interests of the United States and the Soviet Union impinge on each other. We have looked for progress in a series of agreements settling specific political issues and we have sought to relate these to a new standard of international conduct appropriate to the dangers of the nuclear age. By acquiring a stake in this network of relationships with the West, the Soviet Union may become more conscious of what it would lose by a return to confrontation. Indeed it is our hope that it will develop a self-interest in fostering the entire process of relaxation of tensions.

B. THE GLOBAL NECESSITIES

In the late 1940s this nation engaged in a great debate about the role it would play in the postwar world. We forged a bipartisan consensus on which our policies were built for more than two decades. By the end of the 1960s the international environment which molded that consensus had been transformed. What in the fifties had seemed a solid bloc of adversaries had fragmented into competing centers of power and doctrine; old allies had gained new strength and self-assurance; scores of new nations had emerged and formed blocs of their own; and all nations were being swept up in a technology that was compressing the planet and deepening our mutual dependence.

Then, as now, it was clear that the international structure formed in the immediate postwar period was in fundamental flux, and that a new international system was emerging. America's historic opportunity was to help shape a new set of international relationships—more pluralistic, less dominated by military power, less susceptible to confrontation, more open to genuine cooperation among the free and diverse elements of the globe. This new, more positive international environment is possible only if all the major powers—and especially the world's strongest nuclear powers—anchor their policies in the principles of moderation and restraint. They no longer have the power to dominate; they do have the capacity to thwart. They cannot build the new international structure alone; they can make its realization impossible by their rivalry.

Détente is all the more important because of what the creation of a new set of international relations demands of us with respect to other countries and areas. President Ford has assigned the highest priority to maintaining the vitality of our partnerships in Europe, Asia, and Latin America. Our security ties with our allies are essential, but we also believe that recognition of the interdependence of the contemporary world requires cooperation in many other fields. Cooperation becomes more difficult if the United States is perceived by allied public opinion as an obstacle to peace and if public debate is polarized on the issue of whether friendship with the United States is inconsistent with East-West reconciliation.

One important area for invigorated cooperative action is economic policy. The international economic system has been severely tested. The Middle East war demonstrated dramatically the integral relationship between economics and politics. Clearly, whatever the state of our relations with the U.S.S.R., the international economic agenda must be addressed. But the task would be infinitely more complex if we proceeded in a Cold War environment.

International economic problems cut across political dividing lines. All nations, regardless of ideology, face the problems of energy and economic growth, feeding burgeoning populations, regulating the use of the oceans, and preserving the environment.

At a minimum, easing international tensions allows the West to devote more intellectual and material resources to these problems. As security concerns recede, humane concerns come again to the fore. International organizations take on greater significance and responsibility, less obstructed by Cold War antagonisms. The climate of lessened tensions even opens prospects for broader collaboration between East and West. It is significant that some of these global issues—such as energy, cooperation in science and health, and the protection of the environment—have already reached the U.S.-Soviet agenda.

In the present period mankind may be menaced as much by international economic and political chaos as by the danger of war. Avoiding either hazard demands a cooperative world structure for which improved East-West relations are essential.

III. THE EVOLUTION OF DÉTENTE —THE BALANCE OF RISKS AND INCENTIVES

THE COURSE of détente has not been smooth or even. As late as 1969 Soviet-American relations were ambiguous and uncertain. To be sure, negotiations on Berlin and SALT had begun. But the tendency toward confrontation appeared dominant.

We were challenged by Soviet conduct in the Middle East ceasefire of August 1970, during the Syrian invasion of Jordan in September 1970, on the question of a possible Soviet submarine base in Cuba, in actions around Berlin, and during the Indo-Pakistani war. Soviet policy seemed directed toward fashioning a détente in bilateral relations with our Western European allies, while challenging the U.S.

We demonstrated then, and stand ready to do so again, that America will not yield to pressure or the threat of force. We made clear then, as we do today, that détente cannot be pursued selectively in one area or toward one group of countries only. For us détente is indivisible.

Finally, a breakthrough was made in 1971 on several fronts —in the Berlin settlement, in the SALT talks, in other arms control negotiations—that generated the process of détente. It consists of these elements: an elaboration of principles; political discussions to solve outstanding issues and to reach cooperative agreements; economic relations; and arms control negotiations, particularly those concerning strategic arms.

A. THE ELABORATION OF PRINCIPLES

Cooperative relations, in our view, must be more than a series of isolated agreements. They must reflect an acceptance of mutual obligations and of the need for accommodation and restraint.

To set forth principles of behavior in formal documents is hardly to guarantee their observance. But they are reference points against which to judge actions and set goals.

The first of the series of documents is the Statement of Principles signed in Moscow in 1972. It affirms: (1) the necessity of avoiding confrontation; (2) the imperative of mutual restraint; (3) the rejection of attempts to exploit tensions to gain unilateral advantages; (4) the renunciation of claims of special influence in the world; and (5) the willingness, on this new basis, to coexist peacefully and build a firm long-term relationship.

An Agreement for the Prevention of Nuclear War based on

these principles was signed in 1973. It affirms that the objective of the policies of the U.S. and the U.S.S.R. is to remove the danger of nuclear conflict and the use of nuclear weapons. But it emphasizes that this objective presupposes the renunciation of *any* war or threat of war not only by the two nuclear super-powers against each other, but also against allies or third countries. In other words, the principle of restraint is not confined to relations between the U.S. and the U.S.S.R.; it is explicitly extended to include *all* countries.

These statements of principles are not an American concession; indeed we have been affirming them unilaterally for two decades. Nor are they a legal contract; rather they are an aspiration and a yardstick by which we assess Soviet behavior. We have never intended to "rely" on Soviet compliance with every principle; we do seek to elaborate standards of conduct which the Soviet Union would violate only to its cost. And if, over the long term, the more durable relationship takes hold, the basic principles will give it definition, structure, and hope.

B.   POLITICAL DIALOGUE AND COOPERATIVE AGREEMENTS

One of the features of the current phase of U.S.-Soviet relations is the unprecedented consultation between leaders, either face-to-face or through diplomatic channels.

Although consultation has reached a level of candor and frequency without precedent, we know that consultation does not guarantee that policies are compatible. It does provide a mechanism for the resolution of differences before they escalate to the point of public confrontation and commit the prestige of both sides.

The channel between the leaders of the two nations has

proved its worth in many crises; it reduces the risk that either side might feel driven to act or to react on the basis of incomplete or confusing information. The channel of communication has continued without interruption under President Ford.

But crisis management is not an end in itself. The more fundamental goal is the elaboration of a political relationship which in time will make crises less likely to arise.

It was difficult in the past to speak of a U.S.-Soviet bilateral relationship in any normal sense of the phrase. Trade was negligible. Contacts between various institutions and between the peoples of the two countries were at best sporadic. There were no cooperative efforts in science and technology. Cultural exchange was modest. As a result there was no tangible inducement toward cooperation and no penalty for aggressive behavior. Today, by joining our efforts even in such seemingly apolitical fields as medical research or environmental protection, we and the Soviets can benefit not only our two peoples but all mankind; in addition we generate incentives for restraint.

Since 1972 we have concluded agreements on a common effort against cancer, on research to protect the environment, on studying the use of the ocean's resources, on the use of atomic energy for peaceful purposes, on studying methods for conserving energy, on examining construction techniques for regions subject to earthquakes, and on devising new transportation methods. Other bilateral areas for cooperation include an agreement on preventing incidents at sea, an agreement to exchange information and research methods in agriculture, and the training of astronauts for the Soviet-U.S. rendezvous and docking mission planned for 1975.

Each project must be judged by the concrete benefits it brings. But in their sum—in their exchange of information and people as well as in their establishment of joint mechanisms—they also constitute a commitment in both countries to work together across a broad spectrum.

C. THE ECONOMIC COMPONENT

During the period of the Cold War economic contact between ourselves and the U.S.S.R. was virtually nonexistent. Even then many argued that improved economic relations might mitigate international tensions; in fact there were several congressional resolutions to that effect. But recurrent crises prevented any sustained progress.

The period of confrontation should have left little doubt, however, that economic boycott would not transform the Soviet system or impose upon it a conciliatory foreign policy. The U.S.S.R. was quite prepared to maintain heavy military outlays and to concentrate on capital growth by using the resources of the Communist world alone. Moreover, it proved impossible to mount an airtight boycott in practice, since over time, most if not all the other major industrial countries became involved in trade with the East.

The question then became how trade and economic contact —in which the Soviet Union is obviously interested—could serve the purposes of peace. On the one hand, economic relations cannot be separated from the political context. Clearly, we cannot be asked to reward hostile conduct with economic benefits even if in the process we deny ourselves some commercially profitable opportunities. On the other hand, when political relations begin to normalize, it is difficult to explain why economic relations should not be normalized as well.

We have approached the question of economic relations with deliberation and circumspection and as an act of policy not primarily of commercial opportunity. As political relations have improved on a broad basis, economic issues have been dealt with on a comparably broad front. A series of interlocking economic agreements with the U.S.S.R. has been negotiated, side by side with the political progress already noted. The twenty-five-year-old lend-lease debt was settled; the reciprocal extension of Most Favored Nation treatment was negotiated, together with safeguards against the possible disruption of our markets and a series of practical arrangements to facilitate the conduct of business in the U.S.S.R. by American firms; our government credit facilities were made available for trade with the U.S.S.R.; and a maritime agreement regulating the carriage of goods has been signed.

These were all primarily regulatory agreements conferring no immediate benefits on the Soviet Union but serving as blueprints for an expanded economic relationship if the political improvement continued.

This approach commanded widespread domestic approval. It was considered a natural outgrowth of political progress. At no time were issues regarding Soviet domestic political practices raised. Indeed, not until *after* the 1972 agreements was the Soviet domestic order invoked as a reason for arresting or reversing the progress so painstakingly achieved.

The sudden *ex post facto* form of linkage raises serious questions:

· For the Soviet Union, it casts doubt on our reliability as a negotiating partner.

· The significance of trade, originally envisaged as only one ingredient of a complex and evolving relationship, is inflated out of all proportion.

· The hoped-for results of policy become transformed into preconditions for any policy at all.

We recognize the depth and validity of the moral concerns expressed by those who oppose—or put conditions on—expanded trade with the U.S.S.R. But a sense of proportion must be maintained about the leverage our economic relations give us with the U.S.S.R.:

· Denial of economic relations cannot by itself achieve what it failed to do when it was part of a determined policy of political and military confrontation.

· The economic bargaining ability of Most Favored Nation [MFN] status is marginal. MFN grants no special privilege to the U.S.S.R.; in fact it is a misnomer since we have such agreements with over one hundred countries. To enact it would be to remove a discriminatory hold-over of the days of the Cold War. To continue to deny it is more a political than an economic act.

· Trade benefits are not a one-way street; the laws of mutual advantage operate, or there will be no trade.

· The technology that flows to the U.S.S.R. as a result of expanded U.S.-Soviet trade may have a few indirect uses for military production. But with our continuing restrictions on strategic exports, we can maintain adequate controls—and we intend to do so. Moreover, the same technology has been available to the U.S.S.R. and will be increasingly so from other non-Communist sources. Boycott denies us a means of influence and possible commercial gain; it does not deprive the U.S.S.R. of technology.

· The actual and potential flow of credits from the U.S. represents a tiny fraction of the capital available to the U.S.S.R. domestically and elsewhere, including Western Europe and Japan. But it does allow us to exercise some influence through our ability to control the scope of trade relationships.

· Over time, trade and investment may lessen the autarkic tendencies of the Soviet system, invite gradual association of the Soviet economy with the world economy, and foster a degree of interdependence that adds an element of stability to the political equation.

D. THE STRATEGIC RELATIONSHIP

We cannot expect to relax international tensions or achieve a more stable international system should the two strongest nuclear powers conduct an unrestrained strategic arms race. Thus, perhaps the single most important component of our policy toward the Soviet Union is the effort to limit strategic weapons competition.

The competition in which we now find ourselves is historically unique:

· Each side has the capacity to destroy civilization as we know it.

· Failure to maintain equivalence could jeopardize not only our freedom but our very survival.

· The lead time for technological innovation is so long, yet the pace of change so relentless, that the arms race and strategic policy itself are in danger of being driven by technological necessity.

· When nuclear arsenals reach levels involving thousands of launchers and over ten thousand warheads, and when the characteristics of the weapons of the two sides are so incommensurable, it becomes difficult to determine what combination of numbers of strategic weapons and performance capabilities would give one side a militarily and politically useful superiority. At a minimum, clear changes in the strategic balance can be achieved only by efforts so enormous and by increments so large that the very attempt would be highly destabilizing.

· The prospect of a decisive military advantage, even if

theoretically possible, is politically intolerable; neither side will passively permit a massive shift in the nuclear balance. Therefore, the probable outcome of each succeeding round of competition is the restoration of a strategic equilibrium, but at increasingly higher levels of forces.

· The arms race is driven by political as well as military factors. While a decisive advantage is hard to calculate, the *appearance* of inferiority—whatever its actual significance—can have serious political consequences. With weapons that are unlikely to be used and for which there is no operational experience, the psychological impact can be crucial. Thus each side has a high incentive to achieve not only the reality but the appearance of reality. In a very real sense each side shapes the military establishment of the other.

If we are driven to it, the United States will sustain an arms race. Indeed, it is likely that the United States would emerge from such a competition with an edge over the Soviet Union in most significant categories of strategic arms. But the political or military benefit which would flow from such a situation would remain elusive. Indeed, after such an evolution it might well be that *both* sides would be worse off than before the race began. The enormous destructiveness of weapons and the uncertainties regarding their effects combine to make the massive use of such weapons increasingly incredible.

The Soviet Union must realize that the overall relationship with the United States will be less stable if strategic balance is sought through unrestrained competitive programs. Sustaining the buildup requires exhortations by both sides that in time may prove incompatible with restrained international conduct. The very fact of a strategic arms race has a high potential for feeding attitudes of hostility and suspicion on both sides, transforming the fears of those who demand more weapons into self-fulfilling prophecies.

The American people can be asked to bear the cost and political instability of a race which is doomed to stalemate only if it is clear that every effort has been made to prevent it. That is why every President since Eisenhower has pursued negotiations for the limitation of strategic arms while maintaining the military programs essential to strategic balance.

There are more subtle strategic reasons for our interest in SALT. Our supreme strategic purpose is the prevention of nuclear conflict, through the maintenance of sufficient political and strategic power. Estimates of what constitutes "sufficiency" have been contentious. Our judgments have changed with our experience in deploying these weapons and as the Soviets expanded their own nuclear forces. When in the late 1960s it became apparent that the Soviet Union, for practical purposes, had achieved a kind of rough parity with the United States, we adopted the current strategic doctrine.

We determined that stability required strategic forces invulnerable to attack, thus removing the incentive on either side to strike first. Reality reinforced doctrine. As technology advanced, it became apparent that neither side *could* realistically expect to develop a credible disarming capability against the other except through efforts so gigantic as to represent a major threat to political stability.

One result of our doctrine was basing our strategic planning on the assumption that in the unlikely event of nuclear attack, the President should have a wide range of options available in deciding at what level and against what targets to respond. We designed our strategic forces with a substantial measure of flexibility, so that the United States' response need not include an attack on the aggressor's cities—thus inviting the destruction of our own—but could instead hit other targets. Translating this capability into a coherent system of planning became a novel, and as yet uncompleted, task of great complexity; but progress has been made. In our view such flexibility enhances the certainty of retaliation and thereby makes an attack less likely. Above all, it preserves the capability for human decision even in the ultimate crisis.

Another, at first seemingly paradoxical, result was a growing commitment to negotiated agreements on strategic arms. SALT became one means by which we and the Soviet Union could enhance stability by setting mutual constraints on our respective forces and by gradually reaching an understanding of the doctrinal considerations that underlie the deployment of nuclear weapons. Through SALT the two sides can reduce the suspicions and fears which fuel strategic competition. SALT, in the American conception, is a means to achieve strategic stability by methods other than the arms race.

Our specific objectives have been:

1. to break the momentum of ever-increasing levels of armaments;
2. to control certain qualitative aspects—particularly MIRVs [multiple independently targetable reentry vehicles];
3. to moderate the pace of new deployments; and
4. ultimately, to achieve reductions in force levels.

The SALT agreements already signed represent a major contribution to strategic stability and a significant first step toward a longer term and possibly broader agreement.

When the first agreements in 1972 were signed, the future strategic picture was not bright:

· The Soviet Union was engaged in a dynamic program that had closed the numerical gap in ballistic missiles; they were deploying three types of ICBMs [intercontinental ballistic missiles] at a rate of over two hundred annually, and launching on the average eight submarines a year with sixteen ballistic missiles each.

· The United States had ended its numerical buildup in the

late 1960s at a level of 1,054 ICBMs and 656 SLBMs [submarine-launched ballistic missiles]. We were emphasizing technological improvements, particularly in MIRVs, for the Poseidon and Minuteman missiles. Our replacement systems were intended for the late 1970s and early 1980s.

· By most reasonable measurements of strategic power, we held an important advantage, which still continues. But it was also clear that if existing trends were maintained the Soviet Union would first exceed our numerical levels by a considerable margin and then develop the same technologies we had already mastered.

The five-year Interim Agreement which limited anti-ballistic missile defenses and froze the level of ballistic missile forces on both sides represented the essential first step toward a less volatile strategic environment.

· By limiting anti-ballistic missiles [ABMs] to very low levels of deployment, the United States and the Soviet Union removed a potential source of instability; for one side to build an extensive defense for its cities would inevitably be interpreted by the other as a step toward a first-strike capability. Before seeking a disarming capability a potential aggressor would want to protect his population centers from incoming nuclear weapons.

· Some have alleged that the Interim Agreement, which expires in October 1977, penalizes the United States by permitting the Soviet Union to deploy more strategic missile launchers, both land-based and sea-based, than the United States. Such a view is misleading. When the agreement was signed in May 1972, the Soviet Union *already* possessed more land-based ICBMs than the United States and, given the pace of its submarine construction program, over the next few years it could have built virtually twice as many nuclear ballistic missile submarines.

The Interim Agreement confined a dynamic Soviet ICBM program to the then-existing level; it put a ceiling on the heaviest Soviet ICBMs, the weapons that most concern us; and it set an upper limit on the Soviet SLBM program. No American program was abandoned or curtailed. We remained free to deploy multiple warheads. No restraints were placed on bombers—a weapons system in which we have a large advantage. Indeed, the U.S. lead in missile warheads is likely to be somewhat greater at the end of this agreement than at the time of its signature.

The SALT I agreements were the first deliberate attempt by the nuclear superpowers to bring about strategic stability through negotiation. This very process is conducive to further restraint. For example, in the first round of SALT negotiations in 1970–72 both sides bitterly contested the number of ABM sites permitted by the agreement; two years later both sides gave up the right to build more than one site. In sum, we believed when we signed these agreements—and we believe now—that they had reduced the danger of nuclear war, that both sides had acquired some greater interest in restraint, and that the basis had been created for the present effort to reach a broader agreement.

The goal of the current negotiations is an agreement for a ten-year period. We had aimed at extending the Interim Agreement with adjustments in the numbers and new provisions aimed at dealing with the problem of MIRVs. We found, however, that our negotiation for a two- or three-year extension was constantly threatened with irrelevance by the ongoing programs of both sides that were due to be deployed at the end of or just after the period. This distorted the negotiation, and indeed devalued its significance. We shifted to the ten-year approach because the period is long enough to cover all current and planned forces but not so long as to invite hedges that would defeat the purpose of an arms control agreement. In fact it invites a slowing down of planned deployments; further, a period of this length will allow us to set realistic ceilings that represent more than a temporary plateau from which to launch a new cycle in the arms race. Further reductions thus become a realistic objective.

With respect to ceilings on strategic forces, we have defined our goal as essential equivalence in strategic capabilities. What constitutes equivalence involves subjective judgment. Because U.S. and Soviet forces *are* different from each other—in number and size of weapons, in technological refinement, in performance characteristics—they are difficult to compare.

Yet in the negotiations we shall, for example, have to compare heavy bombers in which the United States is ahead with heavy missiles which the U.S.S.R. has emphasized. We shall have to decide whether to insist on equivalence in every category or whether to permit trade-offs in which an advantage in one category compensates for a disadvantage in another. The equation does not remain static. We shall have to relate present advantages to potential developments, existing disparities to future trends. This is a difficult process, but we are confident that it can be solved.

Numerical balance is no longer enough. To achieve stability, it will be necessary to consider as well the impact of technological change in such areas as missile throw weight, multiple reentry vehicles and missile accuracy. The difficulty is that we are dealing not only with disparate levels of forces but with disparate capabilities—MIRV technology being a conspicuous example. The rate of increase of warheads is surging far ahead of the increase in delivery vehicles. This is why the United States considers MIRV limitation an essential component of the next phase of the SALT negotiations. If we fail, the rate of technology will outstrip our capacity to design effective limitations; constantly proliferating warheads of increasing accuracy will overwhelm fixed launchers. An arms race will be virtually inevitable.

The third area for negotiations is the pace of deployments of new or more modern systems. Neither side will remain in its present position without change for another decade. The Soviets are already embarked on testing an initial deployment of a third generation of ICBMs and on a third modification of submarine-launched missiles—though the rate of deployment so far has been far short of the maximum pace of the late sixties.

For our part we are planning to introduce the Trident system, and to replace the B-52 force with the B-1; we also have the capability of improving our Minuteman ICBM system, adding to the number as well as capability of MIRV missiles, and, if we choose, of deploying mobile systems, land based or airborne. Thus, our task is to see whether the two sides can agree to slow the pace of deployment so that modernization is less likely to threaten the overall balance or trigger an excessive reaction.

Finally, a ten-year program gives us a chance to negotiate reductions. Reductions have occasionally been proposed as an alternative to ceilings; they are often seen as more desirable, or, at least, easier to negotiate. In fact, it is a far more complicated problem. Reductions in launchers, for example, if not accompanied by restrictions on the number of warheads, will only magnify vulnerability. The fewer the aim points, the simpler it would be to calculate an attack. At the same time reductions will have to proceed from some base line and must therefore be preceded by agreed ceilings—if only of an interim nature. But a ten-year program should permit the negotiations of stable ceilings resulting from the start of a process of reductions.

Détente is admittedly far from a modern equivalent to the kind of stable peace that characterized most of the nineteenth century. But it is a long step away from the bitter and aggressive spirit that has characterized so much of the postwar period. When linked to such broad and unprecedented projects as SALT, détente takes on added meaning and opens prospects of a more stable peace. SALT agreements should be seen as steps in a process leading to progressively greater stability. It is in that light that SALT and related projects will be judged by history.

IV. AN ASSESSMENT OF DÉTENTE

WHERE HAS the process of détente taken us so far? What are the principles that must continue to guide our course?

Major progress has been made:

· Berlin's potential as Europe's perennial flash point has been substantially reduced through the Quadripartite Agreement of 1971. The U.S. considers strict adherence to the agreement a major test of détente.

· We and our allies are launched on negotiations with the Warsaw Pact and other countries in the European Conference on Security and Cooperation—a conference designed to foster East-West dialogue and cooperation.

· At the same time NATO and the Warsaw Pact are negotiating the reduction of their forces in Central Europe.

· The honorable termination of America's direct military involvement in Indochina and the substantial lowering of regional conflict were made possible by many factors. But this achievement would have been much more difficut—if not impossible—in an era of Soviet and Chinese hostility toward the United States.

· America's principal alliances have proved their durability in a new era. Many feared that détente would undermine them. Instead, détente has helped to place our alliance ties on a more enduring basis by removing the fear that friendship with the United States involved the risk of unnecessary confrontation with the U.S.S.R.

· Many incipient crises with the Soviet Union have been contained or settled without ever reaching the point of public disagreement. The world has been freer of East-West tensions and conflict than in the fifties and sixties.

· A series of bilateral cooperative relations have turned the U.S.-Soviet relationship in a far more positive direction.

· We have achieved unprecedented agreements in arms limitation and measures to avoid accidental war.

· New possibilities for positive U.S.-Soviet cooperation have emerged on issues in which the globe is interdependent— science and technology, environment, energy.

These accomplishments do not guarantee peace. But they have served to lessen the rigidities of the past and offer hope for a better era. Despite fluctuations a trend has been established; the character of international politics has been markedly changed.

It is too early to judge conclusively whether this change should be ascribed to tactical considerations. But in a sense, that is immaterial. For whether the change is temporary and tactical, or lasting and basic, our task is essentially the same: to transform that change into a permanent condition devoted to the purpose of a secure peace and mankind's aspiration for a better life. A tactical change sufficiently prolonged becomes a lasting transformation.

But the whole process can be jeopardized if it is taken for granted. As the Cold War recedes in memory, détente can come to seem so natural that it appears safe to levy progressively greater demands on it. The temptation to combine détente with increasing pressure on the Soviet Union will grow. Such an attitude would be disastrous. We would not accept it from Moscow; Moscow will not accept it from us. We will finally wind up again with the Cold War and fail to achieve either peace or any humane goal.

To be sure, the process of détente raises serious issues for many people. Let me deal with these in terms of the principles which underlie our policfy.

First, if détente is to endure, both sides must benefit.

There is no question that the Soviet Union obtains benefits from détente. On what other grounds would the tough-minded members of the Politiburo sustain it? But the essential point surely must be that détente serves American and world interests as well. If these coincide with some Soviet interests, this will only strengthen the durability of the process.

On the global scale, in terms of the conventional measures of power, influence, and position, our interests have not suffered —they have generally prospered. In many areas of the world the influence and the respect we enjoy are greater than was the case for many years. It is also true that Soviet influence and presence are felt in many parts of the world. But this is a reality that would exist without détente. The record shows that détente does not deny us the opportunity to react to it and to offset it.

Our bilateral relations with the U.S.S.R. are beginning to proliferate across a broad range of activities in our societies. Many of the projects now underway are in their infancy; we have many safeguards against unequal benefits—in our laws, in the agreements themselves, and in plain common sense. Of course, there are instances where the Soviet Union has obtained some particular advantage. But we seek in each agreement or project to provide for benefits that are mutual. We attempt to make sure that there are trade-offs among the various programs that are implemented. Americans surely are the last who need fear hard bargaining or lack confidence in competition.

Second, building a new relationship with the Soviet Union does not entail any devaluation of traditional Alliance relations.

Our approach to relations with the U.S.S.R. has always been, and will continue to be, rooted in the belief that the cohesion of our alliances, and particularly the Atlantic Alliance, is a precondition to establishing a more constructive relationship with the U.S.S.R.

Crucial, indeed unique, as may be our concern with Soviet power, we do not delude ourselves that we should deal with it alone. When we speak of Europe and Japan as representing centers of power and influence, we describe not merely an observable fact but an indispensable element in the equilibrium needed to keep the world at peace. The cooperation and partnership between us transcend formal agreements; they reflect values and traditions not soon, if ever, to be shared with our adversaries.

Inevitably, a greater sense of drama accompanies our dealings with the Soviet Union because the central issues of war and peace cannot be other than dramatic. It was precisely a recognition of this fact and our concern that alliance relations not be taken for granted that led to the American initiative in April of 1973 to put new emphasis on our traditional associations. We sought political acts of will which would transcend the technical issues at hand, symbolize our enduring goals, and thus enhance our fundamental bonds. Much has been accomplished. The complications attendant to adapting U.S.-European relations should not be confused with their basic character. We were tested in difficult conditions that do not affect our central purposes. Today relations with Europe and Japan are strong and improving. We have made progress in developing common positions on security, détente, and energy. The experience of the past year has demonstrated that there is no contradiction between vigorous, organic alliance relations and a more positive relationship with adversaries; indeed they are mutually reinforcing.

Third, the emergence of more normal relations with the Soviet Union must not undermine our resolve to maintain our national defense.

There is a tendency in democratic societies to relax as dangers seems to recede; there is an inclination to view the maintenance of strength as incompatible with relaxation of tensions, rather than its precondition. But this is primarily a question of leadership. We shall attempt to be vigilant to the dangers facing America. This administration will not be misled—or mislead—on issues of national defense. At the same time we do not accept the proposition that we need crises to sustain our defense. A society that needs artificial crises to do what is needed for survival will soon find itself in mortal danger.

Fourth, we must know what can and cannot be achieved in changing human conditions in the East.

The question of dealing with Communist governments has troubled the American people and the Congress since 1917. There has always been a fear that by working with a government whose internal policies differ so sharply with our own, we are in some manner condoning these policies or encouraging their continuation. Some argue that until there is a genuine "liberalization"—or signs of serious progress in this direction—all elements of conciliation in Soviet policy must be regarded as temporary and tactical. In that view, demands for internal changes must be the precondition for the pursuit of a relaxation of tensions with the Soviet Union.

Our view is different. We shall insist on responsible international behavior by the Soviet Union and use it as the primary index of our relationship. Beyond this we will use our influence to the maximum to alleviate suffering and to respond to humane appeals. We know what we stand for, and we shall leave no doubt about it.

Both as a government and as a people we *have* made the attitude of the American people clear on countless occasions, in ways that have produced results. I believe that both the Executive and the Congress, each playing its proper role, have been effective. With respect to the specific issue of emigration:

· The education exit tax of 1971 is no longer being collected. We have been assured that it will not be reapplied.

· Hardship cases submitted to the Soviet Government have been given increased attention, and remedies have been forthcoming in many well-known instances.

· The volume of Jewish emigration has increased from a trickle to tens of thousands.

· And we are now moving toward an understanding that should significantly diminish the obstacles to emigration and ease the hardship of prospective emigrants.

We have accomplished much. But we cannot demand that the Soviet Union, in effect, suddenly reverse five decades of Soviet, and centuries of Russian, history. Such an attempt would be futile and at the same time hazard all that has already been achieved. Changes in Soviet society have already occurred, and more will come. But they are most likely to develop through an evolution that can best go forward in an environment of decreasing international tensions. A renewal of the Cold War will hardly encourage the Soviet Union to change its emigration policies or adopt a more benevolent attitude toward dissent.

V. AGENDA FOR THE FUTURE

DÉTENTE IS a process, not a permanent achievement. The agenda is full and continuing. Obviously, the main concern must be to reduce the sources of potential conflict. This requires efforts in several interrelated areas:

· The military competition in all its aspects must be subject to increasingly firm restraints by both sides.

· Political competition, especially in moments of crisis, must be guided by the principles of restraint set forth in the documents described earlier. Crises there will be, but the United States and the Soviet Union have a special obligation deriving from the unimaginable military power that they wield and represent. Exploitation of crisis situations for unilateral gain is not acceptable.

· Restraint in crises must be augmented by cooperation in removing the causes of crises. There have been too many instances, notably in the Middle East, which demonstrate that policies of unilateral advantage sooner or later run out of control and lead to the brink of war, if not beyond.

· The process of negotiations and consultation must be continuous and intense. But no agreement between the nuclear superpowers can be durable if made over the heads of other nations which have a stake in the outcome. We should not seek to impose peace; we can, however, see that our own actions and conduct are conducive to peace.

In the coming months we shall strive:

· to complete the negotiations for comprehensive and equitable limitations on strategic arms until at least 1985;

· to complete the multilateral negotiations on mutual force reductions in Central Europe, so that security will be enhanced for all the countries of Europe;

· to conclude the Conference of European Security and Cooperation in a manner that promotes both security and human aspirations;

· to continue the efforts to limit the spread of nuclear weapons to additional countries without depriving those countries of the peaceful benefits of atomic energy;

· to complete ratification of the recently negotiated treaty banning underground nuclear testing by the U.S. and U.S.S.R. above a certain threshold;

· to begin negotiations on the recently agreed effort to overcome the possible dangers of environmental modification techniques for military purposes;

· to resolve the long-standing attempts to cope with the dangers of chemical weaponry.

We must never forget that the process of détente depends ultimately on habits and modes of conduct that extend beyond the letters of agreements to the spirit of relations as a whole. This is why the whole process must be carefully nurtured.

In cataloging the desirable, we must take care not to jeopardize what is attainable. We must consider what alternative policies are available, and what their consequences would be. And, the implications of alternatives must be examined, not just in terms of a single issue, but for how they might affect the entire range of Soviet-American relations and the prospects for world peace.

We must assess not only individual challenges to détente, but also their cumulative impact:

If we justify each agreement with Moscow only when we can show unilateral gain;

If we strive for an elusive strategic "superiority";

If we systematically block benefits to the Soviet Union;

If we try to transform the Soviet system by pressure;

If, in short, we look for final results before we agree to any results, then we would be reviving the doctrines of liberation and massive retaliation of the 1950s. And we would do so at a time when Soviet physical power and influence in the world are greater than a quarter-century ago when those policies were devised and failed. The futility of such a course is as certain as its danger.

Let there be no question, however, that Soviet actions could destroy détente, as well:

If the Soviet Union uses détente to strengthen its military capacity in all fields;

If in crises it acts to sharpen tension;

If it does not contribute to progress toward stability;

If it seeks to undermine our alliances;

If it is deaf to the urgent needs of the least developed and the emerging issues of interdependence, then it in turn tempts a return to the tensions and conflicts we have made such efforts to overcome. The policy of confrontation has worked for neither of the superpowers.

We have insisted toward the Soviet Union that we cannot have the atmosphere of détente without the substance. It is equally clear that the substance of détente will disappear in an atmosphere of hostility.

We have profound differences with the Soviet Union—in our

values, our methods, our vision of the future. But it is these very differences which compel any responsible administration to make a major effort to create a more constructive relationship.

We face an opportunity that was not possible twenty-five years, or even a decade, ago. If that opportunity is lost, its moment will not quickly come again. Indeed, it may not come at all.

As President Kennedy pointed out: "For in the final analysis our most basic common link is that we all inhabit this small planet. We all breathe the same air. We all cherish our children's future. And we are all mortal."

SEVEN

FROM COEXISTENCE
TO WORLD COMMUNITY

*Address to the Twenty-ninth United Nations
General Assembly, September 23, 1974*

Mr. PRESIDENT, Mr. Secretary-General, distinguished delegates, ladies and gentlemen:

Last year, in my first address as Secretary of State, I spoke to this Assembly about American purposes. I said that the United States seeks a comprehensive, institutionalized peace, not an armistice. I asked other nations to join us in moving the world from détente to cooperation, from coexistence to community.

In the year that has passed some progress has been made in dealing with particular crises. But many fundamental issues persist and new issues threaten the very structure of world stability.

Our deepest problem—going far beyond the items on our agenda—is whether our vision can keep pace with our challenges. Will history recall the twentieth century as a time of mounting global conflict or as the beginning of a global conception? Will our age of interdependence spur joint progress or common disaster?

The answer is not yet clear. We are delicately poised. New realities have not yet overcome old patterns of thought and action. Traditional concepts—of national sovereignty, social struggle, and the relation between the old and the new nations

—too often guide our course. And so we have managed but not advanced; we have endured but not prospered; and we have continued the luxury of political contention.

This condition has been dramatized in the brief period since last fall's regular session. War has ravaged the Middle East and Cyprus. The technology of nuclear explosives has resumed its dangerous spread. Inflation—and the threat of global decline—hang over the economies of rich and poor alike.

We cannot permit this trend to continue. Conflict between nations once devastated continents; the struggle between blocs may destroy humanity. Ideologies and doctrines drawn from the last century do not even address, let alone solve, the unprecedented problems of today. As a result, events challenge habits; a gulf grows between rhetoric and reality.

The world has dealt with local conflicts as if they were perpetually manageable. We have permitted too many of the underlying causes to fester unattended, until the parties believed that their only recourse was war. And because each crisis ultimately has been contained we have remained complacent. But tolerance of local conflict tempts world holocaust. We have no guarantee that some local crisis—perhaps the next—will not explode beyond control.

The world has dealt with nuclear weapons as if restraint were automatic. Their very awesomeness has chained these weapons for almost three decades; their sophistication and expense have helped to keep constant for a decade the number of states who possess them. Now—as was quite foreseeable—political inhibitions are in danger of crumbling. Nuclear catastrophe looms more plausible—whether through design or miscalculation, accident, theft, or blackmail.

The world has dealt with the economy as if its constant advance were inexorable. While postwar growth has been uneven and some parts of the world have lagged, our attention was focussed on how to increase participation in a general advance. We continue to deal with economic issues on a national, regional, or bloc basis at the precise moment that our interdependence is multiplying. Strains on the fabric and institutions of the world economy threaten to engulf us all in a general depression.

The delicate structure of international cooperation, so laboriously constructed over the last quarter-century, can hardly survive—and certainly cannot be strengthened—if it is continually subjected to the shocks of political conflict, war and economic crisis.

The time has come, then, for the nations assembled here to act on the recognition that continued reliance on old slogans and traditional rivalries will lead us towards:

· a world ever more torn between rich and poor, East and West, producer and consumer;

· a world where local crises threaten global confrontation and where the spreading atom threatens global peril;

· a world of rising costs and dwindling supplies, of growing populations and declining production.

There is another course. Last week, before this Assembly, President Ford dedicated our country to a cooperative, open approach to build a more secure and prosperous world. The United States will assume the obligations that our values and strength impose upon us.

But the building of a cooperative world is beyond the grasp of any one nation. An interdependent world requires not merely the resources but the vision and creativity of us all. Nations cannot simultaneously confront and cooperate with one another. We can no longer afford to pursue our national, or regional, or bloc self-interest—except in a global context.

We must recognize that the common interest is the only valid test of the national interest.

It is in the common interest, and thus in the interest of each nation:

· that local conflicts be resolved short of force and their root causes removed by political means;

· that the spread of nuclear technology be achieved without the spread of nuclear weapons;

· that growing economic interdependence lift all nations and not drag them down together.

We will not solve these problems during this session, or any one session, of the General Assembly.

But we must at least begin:

· to remedy problems, not just manage them;

· to shape events, rather than endure them;

· to confront our challenges instead of one another.

I. THE POLITICAL DIMENSION

THE URGENT political responsibility of our era is to resolve conflicts without war. History is replete with examples of the tragedy that sweeps nations when ancient enmities and the inertia of habit freeze the scope for decision. Equally, history is marked by brief moments when an old order is giving way to a pattern new and unforeseen; these are times of potential disorder and danger but also of opportunity for fresh creation.

We face such a moment today. Together let us face its realities:

First, a certain momentum towards peace has been created —in East-West relations, and in certain regional conflicts. It must be maintained. But we are only at the beginning of the process. We have eased tensions; we are far from reconcilia-tion. If we do not continue to advance, we will slip back.

Second, progress in negotiation of difficult issues comes only through patience, perseverance, and recognition of the toler-able limits of the other side. Peace is a process, not a condition. It can only be reached in steps.

Third, failure to recognize and grasp the attainable will prevent the achievement of the ideal. Attempts to resolve all issues at one time are a certain prescription for stagnation. Progress towards peace can be thwarted by asking too much as surely as by asking too little.

Fourth, the world community can help resolve chronic con-flicts, but exaggerated expectations will prevent essential ac-commodation among the parties. This Assembly can help or hinder the negotiating process. It can seek a scapegoat or a solution. It can offer the parties an excuse to escape reality or sturdy support in the search for compromise. It can decide on propaganda or contribute to realistic solutions that are re-sponsive to man's yearning for peace.

The Middle East starkly demonstrates these considerations. In the past year we have witnessed both the fourth Arab-Israeli war in a generation and the hopeful beginnings of a political process towards a lasting and just peace.

We have achieved the respite of a cease fire and of two dis-engagement agreements, but the shadow of war remains. The legacy of hatred and suffering, the sense of irreconcilability, have begun to yield—however haltingly—to the process of negotiation. But we still have a long road ahead.

One side seeks the recovery of territory and justice for a dis-placed people. The other side seeks security and recognition by its neighbors of its legitimacy as a nation. In the end, the common goal of peace surely is broad enough to embrace all these aspirations.

Let us be realistic about what must be done. The art of negotiation is to set goals that can be achieved at a given time and to reach them with determination. Each step forward modifies old perceptions and brings about a new situation that improves the chances of a comprehensive settlement.

Because these principles were followed in the Middle East, agreements have been reached in the past year which many thought impossible. They were achieved, above all, because of the wisdom of the leaders of the Middle East who decided that there had been enough stalemate and war; that more might be gained by testing each other in negotiation than by testing each other on the battlefield.

The members of this body, both collectively and individually, have a solemn responsibility to encourage and support the parties in the Middle East on their present course. We have as well an obligation to give our support to the United Nations peacekeeping forces in the Middle East and elsewhere. The United States applauds their indispensable role, as well as the outstanding contribution of Secretary-General Waldheim in the cause of peace.

During the past year my country has made a major effort to promote peace in the Middle East. President Ford has asked me to reaffirm today that we are determined to press forward with these efforts. We will work closely with the parties and we will cooperate with all interested countries within the framework of the Geneva Conference.

The tormented island of Cyprus is another area where peace requires a spirit of compromise, accommodation, and justice. The United States is convinced that the sovereignty, political independence, and territorial integrity of Cyprus must be maintained. It will be up to the parties to decide on the form of government they believe best suited to the particular conditions of Cyprus. They must reach accommodation on the areas to be administered by the Greek and Turkish Cypriot communities as well as on the conditions under which refugees can return to their homes and reside in safety. Finally, no lasting peace is possible unless provisions are agreed upon which will lead to the timely and phased reduction of armed forces and armaments and other war materiel.

The United States is prepared to play an even more active role than in the past in helping the parties find a solution to the centuries-old problem of Cyprus. We will do all we can but it is those most directly concerned whose effort is most crucial. Third parties should not be asked to produce miraculous outcomes not anchored in reality. Third parties *can* encourage those directly involved to perceive their broader interests; they can assist in the search for elements of agreement by interpreting each side's views and motives to the other. But no mediator can succeed unless the parties genuinely want his mediation and are ready to make the difficult decisions needed for a solution.

The United States is already making a major contribution to help relieve the human suffering of the people of Cyprus. We urge the international community to continue and, if possible, to increase its own humanitarian relief effort.

II. THE NUCLEAR DIMENSION

THE SECOND new dimension on our agenda concerns the problem of nuclear proliferation.

The world has grown so accustomed to the existence of

nuclear weapons that it assumes they will never be used. But today, technology is rapidly expanding the number of nuclear weapons in the hands of major powers and threatens to put nuclear explosive technology at the disposal of an increasing number of other countries.

In a world where many nations possess nuclear weapons, dangers would be vastly compounded. It would be infinitely more difficult, if not impossible, to maintain stability among a large number of nuclear powers. Local wars would take on a new dimension. Nuclear weapons would be introduced into regions where political conflict remains intense and the parties consider their vital interests overwhelmingly involved. There would, as well, be a vastly heightened risk of direct involvement of the major nuclear powers.

This problem does not concern one country, one region, or one bloc alone. No nation can be indifferent to the spread of nuclear technology; every nation's security is directly affected.

The challenge before the world is to realize the peaceful benefits of nuclear technology without contributing to the growth of nuclear weapons or to the number of states possessing them.

As a major nuclear power, the United States recognizes its special responsibility. We realize that we cannot expect others to show restraint if we do not ourselves practice restraint. Together with the Soviet Union we are seeking to negotiate new quantitative and qualitative limitations on strategic arms. Last week our delegations reconvened in Geneva, and we intend to pursue these negotiations with the seriousness of purpose they deserve. The United States has no higher priority than controlling and reducing the levels of nuclear arms.

Beyond the relations of the nuclear powers to each other, lies the need to curb the spread of nuclear explosives. We must take into account that plutonium is an essential ingredient of nuclear explosives and that in the immediate future the amount of plutonium generated by peaceful nuclear reactors will be multiplied many times. Heretofore, the United States and a number of other countries have widely supplied nuclear fuels and other nuclear materials in order to promote the use of nuclear energy for peaceful purposes. This policy cannot continue if it leads to the proliferation of nuclear explosives. Sales of these materials can no longer be treated as a purely commercial competitive enterprise.

The world community, therefore, must work urgently toward a system of effective international safeguards against the diversion of plutonium or its by-products to the manufacture of nuclear explosives. The United States is prepared to join with others in a comprehensive effort.

Let us together agree on the practical steps which must be taken to assure the benefits of nuclear energy free of its terrors:

· The United States will shortly offer specific proposals to strengthen safeguards to the other principal supplier countries.

· We shall intensify our efforts to gain the broadest possible acceptance of International Atomic Energy Agency safeguards, to establish practical controls on the transfer of nuclear materials, and to ensure the effectiveness of these procedures.

· The United States will urge the IAEA to draft an international convention for enhancing physical security against theft or diversion of nuclear material. Such a convention should set forth specific standards and techniques for protecting materials while in use, storage and transfer.

· The Treaty on the Non-Proliferation of Nuclear Weapons, which this Assembly has endorsed, warrants full and continuing support. The Treaty contains not only a broad commitment to limit the spread of nuclear explosives, but specific obligations to accept and implement IAEA safeguards and to control the transfer of nuclear materials.

Mr. President, whatever advantages seem to accrue from the acquisition of nuclear explosive technology will prove to be ephemeral. When Pandora's box has been opened no country will be the beneficiary and all mankind will have lost. For then we will be living in a world in which stability has been relegated to history and fear has become the pervasive reality.

This is not inevitable. If we act decisively now, we can still control our future.

III. THE ECONOMIC DIMENSION

LORD KEYNES wrote: "The power to become habituated to his surroundings is a marked characteristic of mankind. Very few of us realize with conviction the intensely unusual, unstable, complicated, unreliable, temporary nature of the economic organization."

The economic history of the postwar period has been one of sustained growth—for developing as well as developed nations. The universal expectation of our peoples, the foundation of our political institutions, and the assumption underlying the evolving structure of peace are all based on the belief that this growth will continue.

But will it? The increasingly open and cooperative global economic system that we have come to take for granted is now under unprecedented attack. The world is poised on the brink of a return to the unrestrained economic nationalism which accompanied the collapse of economic order in the

Thirties. And should that occur, all would suffer—poor as well as rich, producer as well as consumer.

So let us no longer fear to confront in public the facts which have come to dominate our private discussions and concerns.

The early warning signs of a major economic crisis are evident. Rates of inflation unprecedented in the past quarter-century are sweeping developing and developed nations alike. The world's financial institutions are staggering under the most massive and rapid movements of reserves in history. And profound questions have arisen about meeting man's most fundamental needs for energy and food.

While the present situation threatens every individual and nation, it is the poor who suffer the most. While the wealthier adjust their living standards, the poor see the hopes of a lifetime collapse around them. While others tighten their belts, the poor starve. While others can hope for a better future, the poor see only despair ahead.

It can be in the interest of no country or group of countries to base policies on a test of strength, for a policy of confrontation would end in disaster for all. Meeting man's basic needs for energy and food, and assuring economic growth while mastering inflation require international cooperation to an unprecedented degree.

Let us apply these principles first to the energy situation.

· Oil producers seek a better life for their peoples and a just return for their diminishing resources.

· The developing nations less well endowed by nature face the disintegration of the results of decades of striving for development as a result of a price policy over which they have no control.

· The developed nations find the industrial civilization built up over centuries in jeopardy.

Thus both producers and consumers have legitimate claims. The problem is to reconcile them for the common good.

The United States is working closely with several oil producers to help diversify their economies. We have established commissions to facilitate the transfer of technology and to assist with industrialization. We are prepared to accept substantial investments in the United States and we welcome a greater role for the oil producers in the management of international economic institutions.

The investment of surplus oil revenues presents a great challenge. The countries which most need these revenues are generally the least likely to receive them. The world's financial institutions have coped thus far but ways must be found to assure assistance for those countries most in need of it. And the full brunt of the surplus revenues is yet to come.

But despite our best efforts to meet the oil producers' legitimate needs and to channel their resources into constructive uses, the world cannot sustain even the present level of prices, much less continuing increases. The prices of other commodities will inevitably rise is a never-ending inflationary spiral. Nobody will benefit from such a race. The oil producers will be forced to spend more for their own imports. Many nations will not be able to withstand the pace and the poorer could be overwhelmed. The complex, fragile structure of global economic cooperation required to sustain national economic growth stands in danger of being shattered.

The United States will work with other consuming nations on means of consumer conservation and on ways to cushion the impact of massive investments from abroad. The preliminary agreement on a program of solidarity and cooperation signed a few days ago in Brussels by the major consumer countries is an encouraging first step.

But the long-range solution requires a new understanding

between consumers and producers. Unlike food prices, the high cost of oil is not the result of economic factors, of an actual shortage of capacity or of the free play of supply and demand. Rather it is caused by deliberate decisions to restrict production and maintain an artificial price level. We recognize that the producers should have a fair share; the fact remains that present prices even threaten the economic well-being of producers. Ultimately they depend upon the vitality of the world economy for the security of their markets and their investments. And it cannot be in the interest of any nation to magnify the despair of the least developed who are uniquely vulnerable to exorbitant prices and who have no recourse but to pay.

What has gone up by political decision can be reduced by political decision.

Last week President Ford called upon the oil producers to join with consumers in defining a strategy which will meet the world's long-term need for both energy and food at reasonable prices. He set forth the principles which should guide such a policy. And he announced to this Assembly America's determination to meet our responsibilities to help alleviate another grim reality—world hunger.

At a time of universal concern for justice and in an age of advanced technology, it is intolerable that millions are starving and hundreds of millions remain undernourished.

The magnitude of the long-term problem is clear. At present rates of population growth, world food production must double by the end of this century to maintain even the present inadequate dietary level. And an adequate diet for all would require that we triple world production. If we are true to our principles, we have an obligation to strive for an adequate supply of food to every man, woman, and child in the world. This is a technical possibility, a political necessity and a moral imperative.

The United States is prepared to join with all nations at the World Food Conference in Rome to launch the truly massive effort which is required. We will present a number of specific proposals:

· To help developing nations. They have the lowest yields and the largest amounts of unused land and water; their potential in food production must be made to match their growing need.

· To increase substantially global fertilizer production. We must end once and for all the world's chronic fertilizer shortage.

· To expand international, regional, and national research programs. Scientific and technical resources must be mobilized now to meet the demands of the year 2000 and beyond.

· To rebuild the world's food reserves. Our capacity for dealing with famine must be freed from the vagaries of weather.

· To provide a substantial level of concessionary food aid. We must prevent the poorest nations from being overwhelmed and enable them to build the social, economic, and political base for self-sufficiency.

The hopes of every nation for a life of peace and plenty rest on an effective international resolution of the crises of inflation, fuel and food. We must act now and we must act together.

IV. THE HUMAN DIMENSION

Mr. President, let us never forget that all of our political endeavors are ultimately judged by one standard—to translate our actions into human concerns.

The United States will never be satisfied with a world where man's fears overshadow his hopes. We support the United Nations' efforts in the fields of international law and human rights. We approve of the activities of the United Nations in social, economic, and humanitarian realms around the world. The United States considers the United Nations World Population Conference last month, the World Food Conference a month from now and the continuing Law of the Sea conference of fundamental importance to our common future.

In coming months the United States will make specific proposals for the United Nations to initiate: a major international effort to prohibit torture in international law; a concerted campaign to control the disease which afflicts and debilitates over two hundred million people in seventy countries—schistosomiasis; and a substantial strengthening of the world's capacity to deal with natural disaster, especially the improvement of the United Nations Disaster Relief Organization.

CONCLUSION

MR. PRESIDENT, we have long lived in a world where the consequences of our failures were manageable—a world where local conflicts were contained, nuclear weapons threatened primarily those nations which possessed them, and the cycle of economic growth and decline seemed principally a national concern.

But that is no longer the case; we confront a fundamentally

changed situation. It is no longer possible to imagine that conflicts, weapons and recession will not spread.

We must now decide. The problems we face will be with us the greater part of the century. But will they be with us as challenges to be overcome or as adversaries that have vanquished us?

It is easy to agree to yet another set of principles or to actions *other* nations should take. But the needs of the poor will not be met by slogans, the needs of an expanding global economy will not be met by new restrictions, the search for peace cannot be conducted on the basis of confrontation. So each nation must ask what *it* can do, what contribution *it* is finally prepared to make to the common good.

Mr. President, beyond peace, beyond prosperity, lie man's deepest aspirations for a life of dignity and justice. And beyond our pride, beyond our concern for the national purpose we are called upon to serve, there must be a concern for the betterment of the human condition. While we cannot, in the brief span allowed to each of us, undo the accumulated problems of centuries, we dare not do less than try. So let us now get on with our tasks.

Let us act in the spirit of Thucydides that "the bravest are surely those who have the clearest vision of what is before them, glory and danger alike, and yet notwithstanding go out to meet it."

There is hope now because our necessity is compelling if we but recognize it.

EIGHT

THE MORAL FOUNDATIONS
OF FOREIGN POLICY

*Address delivered at a meeting sponsored
by the Upper Midwest Council and other
organizations, Bloomington (Minneapolis),
July 15, 1975*

AMERICA has now entered upon its two hundredth year as a free nation. In those two centuries our country has grown from a small agricultural nation with very few responsibilities beyond its borders to a world power with global responsibilities. Yet, while the range of interests has changed massively, our commitment to the values that gave birth to our nation has remained unaltered.

These are the aspects of our national experience I would like to address today: the pursuit of America's values as a humane and just example to others, and the furthering of America's interests in a world where power remains the ultimate arbiter. How do we reconcile and advance both aspects of our national purpose? What, in our time, is the significance of the age-old quandary of the relationship between principle and power?

Through the greater part of our history we have been able to avoid the issue. A fortunate margin of safety and an unexplored continent produced the impression that principle and power automatically coalesced, that no choice was necessary, or that only one choice was possible.

But now for nearly a decade our nation has been weighed down by uncertainty and discord. We have found ourselves doubtful of our virtue and uncertain of our direction, largely because we have suddenly realized that, like other nations before us, we must now reconcile our principles with our necessities. Amid frustration, many Americans questioned the validity of our involvement in the international arena; in the wake of our disappointments, some abroad now doubt our resolve.

We are, I believe, emerging from this period with a renewed sense of confidence. Recent events have brought home to us—and to the rest of the world—that a purposeful, strong, and involved America is essential to peace and progress. These same events have also reminded us of the contribution this country made in the thirty years since World War II and what is at stake in the next thirty years.

The United States can look back on an extraordinary generation of achievement. We have maintained a stable balance of power in the world. We have preserved peace and fostered the growth of the industrial democracies of North America, Western Europe, and Japan. We helped shape the international trade and monetary system which has nourished global prosperity. We promoted decolonization and pioneered in development assistance for the new nations. We have taken major initiatives to forge more reliable and positive relationships with the major Communist powers.

In a planet shrunk by communications and technology, in a world either devastated by war or struggling in the first steps of nationhood, in an international system not of empire but of scores of independent states, the global contribution of one nation—the United States—has been without precedent in human history. Only a nation of strong conviction and great idealism could have accomplished these efforts.

We shall not turn our backs on this legacy.

The Modern Agenda. Today we face a new agenda. Our accomplishments over the past generation have changed the world and defined our tasks for the coming decades:

· Our allies, the major industrial democracies, have recovered their vigor and influence. We are transforming our alliances into more equal partnerships. We shall act in harmony with friends whose security and prosperity are indispensable to our own and whose cooperation is essential for progress and justice.

· The incredible destructiveness of modern weapons has transformed international politics. We must maintain our military strength. But we have an obligation, in our own interest as well as the world's, to work with other nations to control both the growth and the spread of nuclear weapons.

· In our relations with the Communist powers we must never lose sight of the fact that in the thermonuclear age general war would be disastrous to mankind. We have an obligation to seek a more productive and stable relationship despite the basic antagonism of our values.

· Thirty years of economic and political evolution have brought about a new diffusion of power and initiative. At the same time, interdependence imposes upon all nations the reality that they must prosper together or suffer together. The destinies of the world's nations have become inevitably intertwined. Thus, the capacity of any one nation to shape events is more limited, and consequently our own choices are more difficult and complex.

The Legacy of Our Past. To deal with this agenda we require strength of purpose and conviction. A nation unsure of its values cannot shape its future. A people confused about its direction will miss the opportunity to build a better and more peaceful world. This is why perhaps our deepest challenge is our willingness to face the increasing ambiguity of the problem of ends and means.

We start with strong assets. Throughout our history, we have sought to define and justify our foreign policy in terms of principle. We have never seen ourselves as just another nation-state pursuing selfish aims. We have always stood for something beyond ourselves—a beacon to the oppressed from other lands, from the first settlers to the recent refugees from Indochina. This conviction of our uniqueness contributed to our unity, gave focus to our priorities, and sustained our confidence in ourselves. It has been, and is, a powerful force.

But the emphasis on principle has also produced a characteristic American ambivalence. Relations with a world of nations falling short of our ideal has always presented us with dilemmas. As a people, we have oscillated between insistence on our uniqueness and the quest for broad acceptance of our values, between trying to influence international developments and seeking to isolate ourselves from them, between expecting too much of our power and being ashamed of it, between optimistic exuberance and frustration with the constraints practicality imposes.

Through most of our history, we have sought to shield our country and hemisphere from outside intrusion, to shun involvement in balance-of-power politics. Soldiers and diplomats —the practitioners of power—have always been looked upon with suspicion. We considered generosity in relief efforts, the encouragement of free international trade, and the protection of our economic interests abroad as the only wholesome forms of international involvement.

Our Founding Fathers were sophisticated men who understood the European balance of power and knew how to profit from it. For the succeeding century and a half, our security was assured by favorable circumstances over which we had little influence. Shielded by two oceans and enriched by a bountiful nature, we proclaimed our special situation as universally valid to nations whose narrower margin of survival meant that their range of choices was far more limited than our own.

Indeed, the concern of other nations for security reinforced our sense of uniqueness. We were a haven for millions. a place where the injustices, inequities, privations, and abridgements of human dignity which the immigrants had suffered were absent or amenable to rapid redress.

As our strength and size expanded, we remained uncomfortable with the uses and responsibilities of power and involvement in day-to-day diplomacy. At the turn of the century, for example, there were soul-searching debates over the Spanish-American War and our first acquisition of noncontiguous territories. While many saw our policies as dictated by our interests, others considered them our entrance into a morally questionable world.

Our tradition of law encouraged repeated attempts to legislate solutions to international conflicts. Arbitration, conciliation, international legal arrangements, neutrality legislation, collective security systems—all these were invoked to banish the reality of power. And when our involvement in conflict became unavoidable in 1917, Woodrow Wilson translated our geopolitical interest in preventing any nation's hegemony in Europe into a universal moral objective; we fought to "make the world safe for democracy."

The inevitable disillusionment with an imperfect outcome led to a tide of isolationist sentiment. The Great Depression drew our energies further inward, as we sought to deal with the problems of our own society—even as that same depression simultaneously generated real dangers abroad.

We were stirred from isolation only by external attack, and

we sustained our effort because of the obvious totalitarian evil. We had opposed all-out war, and total victory further strengthened our sense of moral rectitude—and ill prepared us for the aftermath. Of all the nations involved, we alone emerged essentially unscathed from the ravages of conflict, our military power, economic strength, and political confidence intact. And in the postwar bipolar world of cold war confrontation, we believed we faced a reincarnation of the just-defeated foe—an apparently monolithic and hostile ideological empire whose ambitions and values were antithetical to our own.

Our success and the preeminent position it brought convinced us that we could shape the globe according to American design. Our preponderant power gave us a broad margin for error, so we believed that we could overwhelm problems through the sheer weight of resources. No other nation possessed so much insurance against so many contingencies; we could afford to be imprecise in the definition of our interests. Indeed, we often imagined that we had nothing so selfish as interests, only obligations and responsibilities. In a period of seemingly clear-cut black-and-white divisions, we harbored few doubts about the validity of our cause.

America's Role. We no longer live in so simple a world. We remain the strongest nation and the largest single factor in international affairs. Our leadership is perhaps even more essential than before. But our strategic superiority has given way to nuclear balance. Our political and economic predominance has diminished as others have grown in strength, and our dependence on the world economy has increased. Our margin of safety has shrunk.

Today we find that—like most other nations in history—we can neither escape from the world nor dominate it. Today, we must conduct diplomacy with subtlety, flexibility, maneuver, and imagination in the pursuit of our interests. We must be thoughtful in defining our interests. We must prepare against the worst contingency and not plan only for the best. We must pursue limited objectives and many objectives simultaneously. In this effort, the last decade has taught us:

· That our power will not always bring preferred solutions; but we are still strong enough to influence events, often decisively.

· That we cannot remedy all the world's ills; but we can help build an international structure that will foster the initiative and cooperation of others.

· That we can no longer expect that moral judgments expressed in absolute terms will command broad acceptance; but as the richest and most powerful nation, we still have a special responsibility to look beyond narrow definitions of our national interests and to serve as a sponsor of world order.

· That we cannot banish power politics from international affairs; but we can promote new and wider communities of interest among nations; we can mute the use and threat of force; we can help establish incentives for restraint and penalties for its absence; we can encourage the resolution of disputes through negotiation; and we can help construct a more equitable pattern of relations between developed and developing nations.

This new complexity has produced in some a rebellion against contemporary foreign policy. We are told that our foreign policy is excessively pragmatic, that it sacrifices virtue in the mechanical pursuit of stability. Once attacked as cold-war-oriented, we are now criticized by some as insentive to moral values. Once regarded as naive in the use of power, we are now alleged to rely too much on the efficacy of force. Once viewed as the most generous of nations, we now stand accused by some of resisting a more equitable international economic system.

It is time to face the reality of our situation. Our choice is not between morality and pragmatism. We cannot escape either, nor are they incompatible. This nation must be true to its own beliefs, or it will lose its bearings in the world. But at the same time it must survive in a world of sovereign nations and competing wills.

We need moral strength to select among often agonizing choices and a sense of purpose to navigate between the shoals of difficult decisions. But we need as well a mature sense of means lest we substitute wishful thinking for the requirements of survival.

Clearly we are in need of perspective. Let me state some basic principles:

· *Foreign policy must start with security.* A nation's survival is at its first and ultimate responsibility; it cannot be compromised or put to risk. There can be no security for us or for others unless the strength of the free countries is in balance with that of potential adversaries, and no stability in power relationships is conceivable without America's active participation in world affairs.

The choices in foreign policy are often difficult and the margins are frequently narrow; imperfect solutions are sometimes unavoidable. In the Second World War, for example, we joined forces with countries whose values we did not share, in order to accomplish the morally worthy objective of defeating Nazism. Today we cooperate with many nations for the purpose of regional stability and global security, even though we disapprove of some of their internal practices. These choices are made consciously and are based on our best assessment of what is necessary.

· *At the same time, security is a means, not an end.* The purpose of security is to safeguard the values of our free society. And our survival is not always at stake in international issues. Many of our decisions are not imposed on us by events. Where we have latitude, we must seize the moral opportunity for humanitarian purposes.

Our assistance to developing nations, for example, serves both foreign policy and humanitarian ends. It strengthens political ties to other nations. It contributes to expanded trade; close to 90 percent of our foreign assistance is eventually spent in this country. And our assistance reflects our values as a people, because we cannot close our eyes to the suffering of others. Because of history and moral tradition, we cannot live with ourselves as an island of plenty in a world of deprivation.

In the whole field of foreign aid, and particularly in food aid, America's record is unsurpassed. We and the world owe much to leaders with vision and compassion like Senator Humphrey who drafted the Food for Peace legislation some twenty years ago.

· *Finally, our values link the American people and their government.* In a democracy, the conduct of foreign policy is possible only with public support. Therefore your government owes you an articulation of the purposes which its policies are designed to serve—to make clear our premises, to contribute to enlightened debate, and to explain how our policies serve the American people's objectives. And those principles —freedom, the dignity of the individual, the sanctity of law— are at the heart of our policy; they are also the foundation of our most basic and natural partnerships with the great industrial democracies, which are essential to our safety and well-being.

Morality and Policy. The relation of morality to policy is thus not an abstract philosophical issue. It applies to many topics of the current debate. It applies to relations with the Communist powers, where we must manage a conflict of moral purposes and interests in the shadow of nuclear peril; and it applies in our political ties with nations whose domestic practices are inconsistent with our own.

Our relationship with the Communist powers has raised difficult questions for Americans since the Bolshevik Revolution. It was understood very early that the Communist system and ideology were in conflict with our own principles. Sixteen years passed before President Franklin Roosevelt extended diplomatic recognition to the Soviet Government. He did so in the belief, as he put it, that "through the resumption of normal relations the prospects of peace over all the world are greatly strengthened."

Today again courageous voices remind us of the nature of the Soviet system and of our duty to defend freedom. About this there is no disagreement.

There is, however, a clear conflict between two moral imperatives which is at the heart of the problem. Since the dawn of the nuclear age, the world's fears of holocaust and its hopes for a better future have both hinged on the relationship between the two superpowers. In an era of strategic nuclear balance—when both sides have the capacity to destroy civilized life—there is no alternative to coexistence.

In such conditions the necessity of peace is itself a moral imperative. As President Kennedy pointed out: . . . in the final analysis our most basic common link is that we all inhabit this small planet. We all breathe the same air. We all cherish our children's future. And we are all mortal.

It is said, correctly, that the Soviet perception of "peaceful coexistence" is not the same as ours, that Soviet policies aim at the furthering of Soviet objectives. In a world of nuclear weapons capable of destroying mankind, in a century which has seen resort to brutal force on an unprecedented scale and intensity, in an age of ideology which turns the domestic policies of nations into issues of international contention, the problem of peace takes on a profound moral and practical difficulty. But the issue, surely, is not whether peace and stability serve Soviet purposes, but whether they also serve our own. Constructive actions in Soviet policy are desirable whatever the Soviet motives.

This government has stated clearly and constantly the principles which we believe must guide U.S.-Soviet relations and international conduct and which are consistent with both our values and our interests:

· We will maintain a strong and flexible military posture to preserve our security. We will as a matter of principle and national interest oppose any attempts by any country to achieve global or regional predominance.

· We will judge the state of U.S.-Soviet relations not by atmospherics, but by whether concrete problems are successfully resolved.

· All negotiations will be a two-way street, based on reciprocity of benefit and reliable observance of agreements.

· We will insist as we always have, that progress in U.S.-Soviet economic relations must reflect progress toward stable political relationships.

· We will never abandon our ideals or our friends. We will not negotiate over the heads of, or against the interests of, other nations.

· We will respond firmly to attempts to achieve unilateral advantage or to apply the relaxation of tensions selectively.

Beyond the necessities of coexistence there is the hope of a more positive relationship. The American people will never be satisfied with simply reducing tension and easing the danger of nuclear holocaust. Over the longer term, we hope that firmness in the face of pressure and the creation of incentives for cooperative action may bring about a more durable pattern of stability and responsible conduct.

Today's joint manned mission in space—an area in which fifteen years ago we saw ourselves in almost mortal rivalry— is symbolic of the distance we have traveled. Practical progress has been made on a wide range of problems. Berlin has been removed as a source of conflict between East and West; crises have been dampened; the frequency of U.S.-Soviet consultation on bilateral and multilateral problems is unprecedented; the scope of bilateral exchanges and cooperation in many fields is in dramatic contrast to the state of affairs ten, even five, years ago. The agreements already achieved to limit strategic armament programs—the central weapons of our respective military arsenals—are unparalleled in the history of diplomacy.

Our immediate focus is on the international actions of the Soviet Union not because it is our only moral concern, but because it is the sphere of action that we can most directly and confidently affect. As a consequence of improved foreign policy relationships, we have successfully used our influence to promote human rights. But we have done so quietly, keeping in mind the delicacy of the problem and stressing results rather than public confrontation.

Therefore critics of détente must answer: What is the alternative that they propose? What precise policies do they want us to change? Are they prepared for a prolonged situation of dramatically increased international danger? Do they wish to return to the constant crises and high arms budgets of the cold war? Does détente encourage repression—or is it détente that has generated the ferment and the demands for openness that we are now witnessing? Can we ask our people to support confrontation unless they know that every reasonable alternative has been explored?

In our relations with the Soviet Union, the United States will maintain its strength, defend its interests, and support its friends with determination and without illusion. We will speak up for our beliefs with vigor and without self-deception. We consider détente a means to regulate a competitive relationship—not a substitute for our own efforts in building the strength of the free world. We will continue on the course on which we are embarked, because it offers hope to our children of a more secure and a more just world.

These considerations raise a more general question: To what extent are we able to affect the internal policies of other governments and to what extent is it desirable?

There are some 150 nations in the world, and barely a score of them are democracies in any real sense. The rest are nations whose ideology or political practices are inconsistent with our own. Yet we have political relations and often alliances with some of these countries in Asia, Latin America, Africa, and Europe.

We do not and will not condone repressive practices. This is not only dictated by our values but is also a reflection of the reality that regimes which lack legitimacy or moral authority are inherently vulnerable. There will therefore be limits to the degree to which such regimes can be congenial partners. We have used, and we will use, our influence against repressive practices. Our traditions and our interests demand it.

But truth compels also a recognition of our limits. The question is whether we promote human rights more effectively by counsel and friendly relations where this serves our interest or by confrontational propaganda and discriminatory legislation. And we must also assess the domestic performance of foreign governments in relation to their history and to the threats they face. We must have some understanding for the dilemmas of countries adjoining powerful, hostile, and irreconcilable totalitarian regimes.

Our alliances and political relationships serve mutual ends; they contribute to regional and world security and thus support the broader welfare. They are not favors to other governments, but reflect a recognition of mutual interests. They should be withdrawn only when our interests change and not as a punishment for some act with which we do not agree.

In many countries, whatever the internal structure, the populations are unified in seeking our protection against outside aggression. In many countries our foreign policy relationships have proved to be no obstacle to the forces of change. And in many countries, especially in Asia, it is the process of American disengagement that has eroded the sense of security and created a perceived need for greater internal discipline—and at the same time diminished our ability to influence domestic practices.

The attempt to deal with those practices by restrictive American legislation raises a serious problem not because of the moral view it expresses—which we share—but because of the mistaken impression it creates that our security ties are acts of charity. And beyond that, such acts—because they are too public, too inflexible, and too much a stimulus to nationalistic resentment—are almost inevitably doomed to fail.

There are no simple answers. Painful experience should have taught us that we ought not exaggerate our capacity to foresee, let alone to shape, social and political change in other societies. Therefore let me state the principles that will guide our action:

· Human rights are a legitimate international concern and

have been so defined in international agreements for more than a generation.

· The United States will speak up for human rights in appropriate international forums and in exchanges with other governments.

· We will be mindful of the limits of our reach; we will be conscious of the difference between public postures that satisfy our self-esteem and policies that bring positive results.

· We will not lose sight of either the requirements of global security or what we stand for as a nation.

The Domestic Dimension. For Americans, then, the question is not whether our values should affect our foreign policy, but how. The issue is whether we have the courage to face complexity and the inner conviction to deal with ambiguity, whether we will look behind easy slogans and recognize that our great goals can only be reached by patience and in imperfect stages.

The question is also whether we will use our moral convictions to escape reality or as a source of courage and self-confidence. We hear too often assertions that were a feature of our isolationist period: that a balance of power is a cynical game; that secret conspiratorial intentions lurk behind open public policies; that weapons are themselves the sources of conflict; that intelligence activities are wicked; that humanitarian assistance and participation in the economic order are an adequate substitute for political engagement.

These are the counsels of despair. I refuse to accept the premise that our moral values and policy objectives are irreconcilable. The ends we seek in our foreign policy must have validity in the framework of our beliefs, or we have no meaningful foreign policy. The maintenance of peace is a moral as well as a practical objective; measures to limit armaments serve a moral as well as practical end; the cohesion of our alliances with the great industrial democracies makes our way of life and our principles more secure; cooperation to improve the world economic system enhances the well-being of peoples; policies to reconcile the rich nations and the poor, and to enhance the progress of both, serve a humane as well as a political end.

We live in a secular age which prides itself on its realism. Modern society is impersonal and bureaucratized. The young, who in every generation crave a sense of purpose, are too often offered cynicism and escapism instead of a faith that truly inspires. All modern democracies are beset by problems beyond the margin of governments' ability to control. Debunking of authority further drains democratic government of the ability to address the problems that beset it. A world of turmoil and danger cries out for structure and leadership. The opportunities that we face as a nation to help shape a more just international order depend more than ever on a steady, resolute, and self-assured America.

This requires confidence—the leaders' confidence in their values, the public's confidence in its government, and the nation's collective confidence in the worth of its objectives.

Thus, for this nation to contribute truly to peace in the world it must make peace with itself. It is time to put aside the cynicism and distrust that have marked—and marred—our political life for the better part of the past decade. It is time to remind ourselves that, while we may disagree about means, as Americans we all have the same ultimate objective —the peace, prosperity, and tranquility of our country and of the world.

And most of all, it is time we recognized that as the greatest democracy the world has ever known, we are a living reminder that there is an alternative to tyranny and oppression.

The revolution that we began two hundred years ago goes on, for most of the world still lives without the freedom that has for so long been ours. To them we remain a beacon of hope and an example to be emulated.

So let us come together for the tasks that our time demands. We have before us an opportunity to bring peace to a world that awaits our leadership.

NINE

INTERNATIONAL LAW, WORLD ORDER, AND HUMAN PROGRESS

Address to the American Bar Association
Annual Convention, Montreal,
August 11, 1975

My FRIENDS in the legal profession like to remind me of a comment by a British judge on the difference between lawyers and professors. "It's very simple," said Lord Denning. "The function of lawyers is to find a solution to every difficulty presented to them, whereas the function of professors is to find a difficulty with every solution." Today the number of difficulties seems to be outpacing the number of solutions—either because my lawyer friends are not working hard enough, or because there are too many professors in government.

Law and lawyers have played a seminal role in American public life since the founding of the Republic. In this century lawyers have been consistently at the center of our diplomacy, providing many of our ablest Secretaries of State and diplomats, and often decisively influencing American thinking about foreign policy.

This is no accident. The aspiration to harness the conflict of nations by standards of order and justice runs deep in the American tradition. In pioneering techniques of arbitration, conciliation, and adjudication, in developing international institutions and international economic practices, and in creating a body of scholarship sketching visions of world order, American legal thinking has reflected both American idealism and American pragmatic genius.

The problems of the contemporary world structure summon these skills and go beyond them. The rigid international structure of the cold war has disintegrated. We have entered an era of diffused economic power, proliferating nuclear weaponry, and multiple ideologies and centers of initiative. The challenge of our predecessors was to fashion stability from chaos. The challenge of our generation is to go from the building of national and regional institutions and the management of crises to the building of a new international order which offers a hope of peace, progress, well-being, and justice for the generations to come.

Justice Holmes said of the common law that it "is not a brooding omnipresence in the sky but the articulate voice of some sovereign or quasi-sovereign that can be identified." But international politics recognizes no sovereign or even quasi-sovereign power beyond the nation-state.

Thus in international affairs the age-old struggle between order and anarchy has a political as well as a legal dimension. When competing national political aims are pressed to the point of unrestrained competition, the precept of laws proves fragile. The unrestrained quest for predominance brooks no legal restraints. In a democratic society law flourishes best amidst pluralistic institutions. Similarly in the international arena stability requires a certain equilibrium of power. Our basic foreign policy objective inevitably must be to shape a stable and cooperative global order out of diverse and contending interests.

But this is not enough. Preoccupation with interests and power is at best sterile and at worst an invitation to a constant test of strength. The true task of statesmanship is to draw from the balance of power a more positive capacity to better the human condition—to turn stability into creativity, to transform the relaxation of tensions into a strengthening of freedoms, to turn man's preoccupations from self-defense to human progress.

An international order can be neither stable nor just without accepted norms of conduct. International law both provides a means and embodies our ends. It is a repository of our experience and our idealism—a body of principles drawn from the practice of states and an instrument for fashioning new patterns of relations between states. Law is an expression of our own culture and yet a symbol of universal goals. It is the heritage of our past and a means of shaping our future.

The challenge of international order takes on unprecedented urgency in the contemporary world of interdependence. In an increasing number of areas of central political relevance, the legal process has become of major concern. Technology has driven us into vast new areas of human activity and opened up new prospects of either human progress or international contention. The use of the oceans and of outer space, the new excesses of hijacking, terrorism, and warfare, the expansion of multinational corporations will surely become areas of growing dispute if they are not regulated by a legal order.

The United States will not seek to impose a parochial or self-serving view of the law on others. But neither will we carry the quest for accommodation to the point of prejudicing our own values and rights. The new corpus of the law of nations must benefit all peoples equally; it cannot be the preserve of any one nation or group of nations.

The United States is convinced in its own interest that the extension of legal order is a boon to humanity and a necessity. The traditional aspiration of Americans takes on a new relevance and urgency in contemporary conditions. On a planet marked by interdependence, unilateral action and unrestrained pursuit of the national advantage inevitably provoke counter-action and therefore spell futility and anarchy. In an age of awesome weapons of war, there must be accommodation or there will be disaster.

Therefore there must be an expansion of the legal consensus, in terms both of subject matter and participation. Many new and important areas of international activity, such as new departures in technology and communication, cry out for agreed international rules. In other areas, juridical concepts have advanced faster than the political will that is indispensable to assure their observance—such as the U.N. Charter provisions governing the use of force in international relations. The pace of legal evolution cannot be allowed to lag behind the headlong pace of change in the world at large. In a world of 150 nations and competing ideologies, we cannot afford to wait upon the growth of customary international law. Nor can we be content with the snail's pace of treaty-making as we have known it in recent years in international forums.

We are at a pivotal moment in history. If the world is in flux, we have the capacity and hence the obligation to help shape it. If our goal is a new standard of international restraint and cooperation, then let us fashion the institutions and practices that will bring it about.

This morning I would like to set forth the American view on some of those issues of law and diplomacy whose solution can move us toward a more orderly and lawful world. These issues emphasize the contemporary international challenge: In the oceans where traditional law has been made obsolete by modern technology; in outer space where endeavors undreamed of a generation ago impinge upon traditional concerns for security and for sovereignty; in the laws of war where new practices of barbarism challenge us to develop new social and international restraints; and in international economics where transnational enterprises conduct their activities beyond the frontier of traditional political and legal regulation.

I shall deal in special detail with the Law of the Sea, in an effort to promote significant and rapid progress in this vitally important negotiation.

The Law of the Sea. The United States is now engaged with some 140 nations in one of the most comprehensive and critical negotiations in history—an international effort to devise rules to govern the domain of the oceans. No current international negotiation is more vital for the long-term stability and prosperity of our globe.

One need not be a legal scholar to understand what is at stake. The oceans cover 70 percent of the earth's surface. They both unite and divide mankind. The importance of free navigation for the security of nations, including our country, is traditional; the economic significance of ocean resources is becoming enormous.

From the seventeenth century until now, the law of the seas has been founded on a relatively simple precept: freedom of the seas, limited only by a narrow belt of territorial waters generally extending three miles offshore. Today, the explosion of technology requires new and more sophisticated solutions.

· In a world desperate for new sources of energy and minerals, vast and largely untapped reserves exist in the oceans.

· In a world that faces widespread famine and malnutrition, fish have become an increasingly vital source of protein.

· In a world clouded by pollution, the environmental integrity of the oceans turns into a critical international problem.

· In a world where 95 percent of international trade is carried on the seas, freedom of navigation is essential.

Unless competitive practices and claims are soon harmonized, the world faces the prospect of mounting conflict. Shipping tonnage is expected to increase fourfold in the next thirty years. Large, self-contained factory vessels already circle the globe and dominate fishing areas that were once the province of small coastal boats. The worldwide fish harvest is increasing dramatically, but without due regard to sound management or the legitimate concerns of coastal states. Shifting population patterns will soon place new strains on the ecology of the world's coastlines.

The current negotiation may thus be the world's last chance. Unilateral national claims to fishing zones and territorial seas extending from fifty to two hundred miles have already resulted in seizures of fishing vessels and constant disputes over rights to ocean space. The breakdown of the current negotiation, a failure to reach a legal consensus, will lead to unrestrained military and commercial rivalry and mounting political turmoil.

The United States strongly believes that law must govern the oceans. In this spirit, we welcomed the U.N. mandate in 1970 for a multilateral conference to write a comprehensive treaty governing the use of the oceans and their resources. We contributed substantially to the progress that was made at Caracas last summer and at Geneva this past spring which produced a "single negotiating text" of a draft treaty. This will focus the work of the next session, scheduled for March 1976, in New York. The United States intends to intensify its efforts.

The issues in the Law of the Sea negotiation stretch from the shoreline to the farthest deep seabed. They include:

· The extent of the territorial sea and the related issues of guarantees of free transit through straits;

· The degree of control that a coastal state can exercise in an offshore economic zone beyond its territorial waters; and

· The international system for the exploitation of the resources of the deep seabeds.

If we move outward from the coastline, the first issue is the extent of the territorial sea—the belt of ocean over which the coastal state exercises sovereignty. Historically, it has been recognized as three miles; that has been the long-established U.S. position. Increasingly, other states have claimed twelve miles or even two hundred.

After years of dispute and contradictory international practice, the Law of the Sea Conference is approaching a consensus on a twelve-mile territorial limit. We are prepared to accept this solution, provided that the unimpeded transit rights through and over straits used for international navigation are guaranteed. For without such guarantees, a twelve-mile territorial sea would place over one hundred straits—including the Straits of Gilbraltar, Malacca, and Bab el Mandeb—now free for international sea and air travel under the jurisdictional control of coastal states. This the United States cannot accept. Freedom of international transit through these and other straits is for the benefit of all nations, for trade and for security. We will not join in an agreement which leaves any uncertainty about the right to use world communication routes without interference.

Within two hundred miles of the shore are some of the world's most important fishing grounds as well as substantial deposits of petroleum, natural gas, and minerals. This has led some coastal states to seek full sovereignty over this zone. These claims, too, are unacceptable to the United States. To accept them would bring 30 percent of the oceans under national territorial control—in the very areas through which most of the world's shipping travels.

The United States joins many other countries in urging

international agreement on a two-hundred-mile offshore *economic zone*. Under this proposal, coastal states would be permitted to control fisheries and mineral resources in the economic zone, but freedom of navigation and other rights of the international community would be preserved. Fishing within the zone would be managed by the coastal state, which would have an international duty to apply agreed standards of conservation. If the coastal state could not harvest all the allowed yearly fishing catch, other countries would be permitted to do so. Special arrangements for tuna and salmon, and other fish which migrate over large distances, would be required. We favor also provisions to protect the fishing interests of land-locked and other geographically disadvantaged countries.

In some areas the *continental margin* extends beyond two hundred miles. To resolve disagreements over the use of this area, the United States proposes that the coastal states be given jurisdiction over continental margin resources beyond 200 miles, to a precisely defined limit, and that they share a percentage of financial benefit from mineral exploitation in that area with the international community.

Beyond the territorial sea, the offshore economic zone, and the continental margin lie the *deep seabeds*. They are our planet's last great unexplored frontier. For more than a century we have known that the deep seabeds hold vast deposits of manganese, nickel, cobalt, copper, and other minerals, but we did not know how to extract them. New modern technology is rapidly advancing the time when their exploration and commercial exploitation will become a reality.

The United Nations has declared the deep seabed to be the "common heritage of mankind." But this only states the problem. How will the world community manage the clash of national and regional interests, or the inequality of technological capability? Will we reconcile unbridled competition with the imperative of political order?

The United States has nothing to fear from competition. Our technology is the most advanced, and our Navy is adequate to protect our interests. Ultimately, unless basic rules regulate exploitation, rivalry will lead to tests of power. A race to carve out exclusive domains of exploration on the deep seabed, even without claims of sovereignty, will menace freedom of navigation, and invite a competition like that of the colonial powers in Africa and Asia in the last century.

This is not the kind of world we want to see. Law has an opportunity to civilize us in the early stages of a new competitive activity.

We believe that the Law of the Sea treaty must preserve the right of access presently enjoyed by states and their citizens under international law. Restrictions on free access will retard the development of seabed resources. Nor is it feasible, as some developing countries have proposed, to reserve to a new international seabed organization the sole right to exploit the seabeds.

Nevertheless, the United States believes strongly that law must regulate international activity in this area. The world community has an historic opportunity to manage this new wealth cooperatively and to dedicate resources from the exploitation of the deep seabeds to the development of the poorer countries. A cooperative and equitable solution can lead to new patterns of accommodation between the developing and industrial countries. It could give a fresh and conciliatory cast to the dialogue between the industrialized and so-called Third World. The legal regime we establish for the deep seabeds can be a milestone in the legal and political development of the world community.

The United States has devoted much thought and consideration to this issue. We offer the following proposals:

· An international organization should be created to set rules for deep seabed mining.

· This international organization must preserve the rights of all countries and their citizens directly to exploit deep seabed resources.

· It should also insure fair adjudication of conflicting interests and security of investmen.

· Countries and their enterprises mining deep seabed resources should pay an agreed portion of their revenues to the international organization, to be used for the benefit of developing countries.

· The management of the organization and its voting procedures must reflect and balance the interests of the participating states. The organization should not have the power to control prices or production rates.

· If these essential U.S. interests are guaranteed, we can agree that this organization will also have the right to conduct mining operations on behalf of the international community primarily for the benefit of developing countries.

· The new organization should serve as a vehicle for cooperation between the technologically advanced and the developing countries. The United States is prepared to explore ways of sharing deep seabed technology with other nations.

· A balanced commission of consumers, seabed producers, and land-based producers could monitor the possible adverse effects of deep seabed mining on the economies of those developing countries which are substantially dependent on the export of minerals also produced from the deep seabed.

The United States believes that the world community has before it an extraordinary opportunity. The regime for the deep seabeds can turn interdependence from a slogan into reality. The sense of community which mankind has failed to achieve on land could be realized through a regime for the ocean.

The United States will continue to make determined efforts to bring about final progress when the Law of the Sea Conference reconvenes in New York next year. But we must be clear on one point: The United States cannot indefinitely sacrifice its own interest in developing an assured supply of critical resources to an indefinitely prolonged negotiation. We prefer a generally acceptable international agreement that provides a stable legal environment *before* deep seabed mining actually begins. The responsibility for achieving an agreement before actual exploitaion begins is shared by all nations. We cannot defer our own deep seabed mining for too much longer. In this spirit, we and other potential seabed producers can consider appropriate steps to protect current investment, and to insure that this investment is also protected in the treaty.

The Conference is faced with other important issues:

· Ways must be found to encourage marine scientific research for the benefit of all mankind while safeguarding the legitimate interests of coastal states in their economic zones.

· Steps must be taken to protect the oceans from pollution. We must establish uniform international controls on pollution from ships and insist upon universal respect for environmental standards for continental shelf and deep seabed exploitation.

· Access to the sea for land-locked countries must be assured.

· There must be provisions for compulsory and impartial third-party settlement of disputes. The United States cannot accept unilateral interpretation of a treaty of such scope by individual states or by an international seabed organization.

The pace of technology, the extent of economic need, and

the claims of ideology and national ambition threaten to submerge the difficult process of negotiation. The United States therefore believes that a just and beneficial regime for the oceans is essential to world peace, for the self-interest of every nation is heavily engaged. Failure would seriously impair confidence in global treaty-making and in the very process of multilateral accommodation. The conclusion of a comprehensive Law of the Sea treaty on the other hand would mark a major step toward a new world community.

The urgency of the problem is illustrated by disturbing developments which continue to crowd upon us. Most prominent is the problem of fisheries.

The United States cannot indefinitely accept unregulated and indiscriminate foreign fishing off its coasts. Many fish stocks have been brought close to extinction by foreign overfishing. We have recently concluded agreements with the Soviet Union, Japan, and Poland which limit their catch and we have a long and successful history of conservation agreements with Canada. But much more needs to be done.

Many within Congress are urging us to solve this problem unilaterally. A bill to establish a two-hundred-mile fishing zone passed the Senate last year; a new one is currently before the House.

The Administration shares the concern which has led to such proposals. But unilateral action is both extremely dangerous and incompatible with the thrust of the negotiations described here. The United States has consistently resisted the unilateral claims of other nations, and others will almost certainly resist ours. Unilateral legislation on our part would almost surely prompt others to assert extreme claims of their own. Our ability to negotiate an acceptable international consensus on the economic zone will be jeopardized. If every state proclaims its own rules of law and seeks to impose them on others, the very basis of international law will be shaken, ultimately to our own detriment.

We warmly welcome the recent statement by Prime Minister Trudeau reaffirming the need for a solution through the Law of the Sea Conference rather than through unilateral action. He said, "Canadians at large should realize that we have very large stakes indeed in the Law of the Sea Conference and we would be fools to give up those stakes by an action that would be purely a temporary, paper success."

That attitude will guide our actions as well. To conserve the fish and protect our fishing industry while the treaty is being negotiated, the United States will negotiate interim arrangements with other nations to conserve the fish stocks, to insure effective enforcement, and to protect the livelihood of our coastal fishermen. These agreements will be a transition to the eventual two-hundred-mile zone. We believe it is in the interests of states fishing off our coasts to cooperate with us in this effort. We will support the efforts of other states, including our neighbors, to deal with their problems by similar agreements. We will consult fully with Congress, our States, the public, and foreign governments on arrangements for implementing a two-hundred-mile zone by virtue of agreement at the Law of the Sea Conference.

Unilateral legislation would be a last resort. The world simply cannot afford to let the vital questions before the Law of the Sea Conference be answered by default. We are at one of those rare moments when mankind has come together to devise means of preventing future conflict and shaping its destiny, rather than to solve a crisis that has occurred or to deal with the aftermath of war. It is a test of vision and will, and of statesmanship. It must succeed. The United States is resolved to help conclude the conference in 1976—before the pressure of events and contention places international consensus irretrievably beyond our grasp.

Outer Space and the Law of Nations. The oceans are not the only area in which technology drives man in directions he has not foreseen and toward solutions unprecedented in history. No dimension of our modern experience is more a source of wonder than the exploration of space. Here, too, the extension of man's reach has come up against national sensitivities and concerns for sovereignty. Here, too, we confront the potential for conflict or the possibility for legal order. Here, too, we have an opportunity to substitute law for power in the formative stage of an international activity.

Space technologies are directly relevant to the well-being of all nations. Earth-sensing satellites, for example, can dramatically help nations to assess their resources and to develop their potential. In the Sahel region of Africa we have seen the tremendous potential of this technology in dealing with natural disasters. The United States has urged in the United Nations that the new knowledge be made freely and widely available.

The use of satellites for broadcasting has a great potential to spread educational opportunities, and to foster the exchange of ideas.

In the nearly two decades since the first artificial satellite, remarkable progress has been made in extending the reach of law to outer space. The Outer Space Treaty of 1967 placed space beyond national sovereignty and banned weapons of mass destruction from earth orbit. The treaty also established the principle that the benefits of space exploration should be shared. Supplementary agreements have provided for the registry of objects placed in space, for liability for damage caused by their return to earth, and for international assistance to astronauts in emergencies. Efforts are underway to develop further international law governing man's activities on the moon and other celestial bodies.

Earth-sensing and broadcasting satellites, and conditions of their use, are a fresh challenge to international agreement. The U.N. Committee on the Peaceful Uses of Outer Space is seized with the issue, and the United States will cooperate actively with it. We are committed to the wider exchange of communication and ideas. But we recognize that there must be full consultation among the countries directly concerned. While we believe that knowledge of the earth and its environment gained from outer space should be broadly shared, we recognize that this must be accompanied by efforts to insure that all countries will fully understand the significance of this new knowledge.

The United States stands ready to engage in a cooperative search for agreed international ground rules for these activities.

Hijacking, Terrorism, and War. The modern age has not only given us the benefits of technology; it has also spawned the plagues of aircraft hijacking, international terrorism, and new techniques of warfare. The international community cannot ignore these affronts to civilization; it must not allow them to spread their poison; it has a duty to act vigorously to combat them.

Nations already have the legal obligation, recognized by unanimous resolution of the U.N. General Assembly, "to refrain from organizing, instigating, assisting, participating [or] acquiescing in" terrorist acts. Treaties have been concluded to combat hijacking, sabotage of aircraft, and attacks on diplomats. The majority of states observe these rules; a minority do not. But events even in the last few weeks dramatize that present restraints are inadequate.

The United States is convinced that stronger international

steps must be taken—and urgently—to deny skyjackers and terrorists a safe haven and to establish sanctions against states which aid them, harbor them, or fail to prosecute or extradite them.

The United States in 1972 proposed to the United Nations a new international Convention for the Prevention or Punishment of Certain Acts of International Terrorism, covering kidnapping, murder, and other brutal acts. This convention regrettably was not adopted—and innumerable innocent lives have been lost as a consequence. We urge the United Nations once again to take up and adopt this convention or other similar proposals as a matter of the highest priority.

Terrorism, like piracy, must be seen as outside the law. It discredits any political objective that it purports to serve and any nations which encourage it. If all nations deny terrorists a safe haven, terrorist practices will be substantially reduced— just as the incidence of skyjacking has declined sharply as a result of multilateral and bilateral agreements. All governments have a duty to defend civilized life by supporting such measures.

The struggle to restrain violence by law meets one of its severest tests in the law of war. Historically, nations have found it possible to observe certain rules in their conduct of war. This restraint has been extended and codified, especially in the past century. In our time new, ever more awesome tools of warfare, the bitterness of ideologies and civil warfare, and weakened bonds of social cohesion have brought an even more brutal dimension to human conflict.

At the same time our century has also witnessed a broad effort to ameliorate some of these evils by international agreements. The most recent and comprehensive is the four Geneva Conventions [of 1949] for the Protection of War Victims.

But the law in action has been less impressive than the law

on the books. Patent deficiencies in implementation and compliance can no longer be ignored. Two issues are of paramount concern: First, greater protection for civilians and those imprisoned, missing, and wounded in war; and, second, the application of international standards of humane conduct in civil wars.

An international conference is now underway to supplement the 1949 Geneva Conventions on the law of war. We will continue to press for rules which will prohibit nations from barring a neutral country, or an international organization such as the International Committee of the Red Cross, from inspecting its treatment of prisoners. We strongly support provisions requiring full accounting for the missing in action. We will advocate immunity for aircraft evacuating the wounded. And we will seek agreement on a protocol which demands humane conduct during civil war, which bans torture, summary execution, and the other excesses which too often characterize civil strife.

The United States is committed to the principle that fundamental human rights require legal protection under all circumstances; that some kinds of individual suffering are intolerable no matter what threat nations may face. The American people and Government deeply believe in fundamental standards of humane conduct; we are committed to uphold and promote them; we will fight to vindicate them in international forums.

Multinational Enterprises. The need for new international regulation touches areas as modern as new technology and as old as war. It also reaches our economic institutions, where human ingenuity has created new means for progress while bringing new problems of social and legal adjustment.

Multinational enterprises have contributed greatly to economic growth in both their industrialized home countries, where they are most active, and in developing countries, where they conduct some of their operations. If these organizations are to continue to foster world economic growth, it is in the common interest that international law, not political contests, govern their future.

Some nations feel that multinational enterprises influence their economies in ways unresponsive to their national priorities. Others are concerned that these enterprises may evade national taxation and regulation through facilities abroad. And recent disclosures of improper financial relationships between these companies and government officials in several countries raise fresh concerns.

But it remains equally true that multinational enterprises can be powerful engines for good. They can marshal and organize the resources of capital, initiative, research, technology, and markets in ways which vastly increase production and growth. If an international consensus on the proper role and responsibilities of these enterprises could be reached, their vital contribution to the world economy could be further expanded. A multilateral treaty establishing binding rules for multinational enterprises does not seem possible in the near future. However, the United States believes an agreed statement of basic principles is achievable. We are prepared to make a major effort and invite the participation of all interested parties.

We are now actively discussing such guidelines and will support the relevant work of the U.N. Commission on Transnational Corporations. We believe that such guidelines must:

· Accord with existing principles of international law governing the treatment of foreigners and their property rights;

· Call upon multinational corporations to take account of national priorities, act in accordance with local law, and employ fair labor practices;

· Cover all multinationals, state-owned as well as private;

· Not discriminate in favor of host country enterprises, except under specifically defined and limited circumstances;

· Set forth not only the obligations of the multinationals, but also the host country's responsibilities to the foreign enterprises within their borders;

· Acknowledge the responsibility of governments to apply recognized conflict-of-laws principles in reconciling regulations applied by various host nations.

If multinational institutions become an object of economic warfare, it will be an ill omen for the global economic system. We believe that the continued operation of transnational companies, under accepted guidelines, can be reconciled with the claims of national sovereignty. The capacity of nations to deal with this issue constructively will be a test of whether the search for common solutions or the clash of ideologies will dominate our economic future.

Conclusion. Since the early days of the Republic, Americans have seen that their nation's self-interest could not be separated from a just and progressive international legal order. Our Founding Fathers were men of law, of wisdom, and of political sophistication. The heritage they left is an inspiration as we face an expanding array of problems that are at once central to our national well-being and soluble only on a global scale.

The challenge of the statesman is to recognize that a just international order cannot be built on power but only on restraint of power. As [Justice] Felix Frankfurter said, "Fragile as reason is and limited as law is as the institutionalized expression of reason, it is often all that stands between us and the tyranny of will, the cruelty of unbridled, unprincipled, undisciplined feeling." If the politics of ideological confrontation and strident nationalism become pervasive, broad and humane

international agreement will grow ever more elusive and unilateral actions will dominate. In an environment of widening
chaos, the stronger will survive and may even prosper temporarily. But the weaker will despair and the human spirit will
suffer.

The American people have always had a higher vision—a
community of nations that has discovered the capacity to act
according to man's more noble aspirations. The principles and
procedures of the Anglo-American legal system have proven
their moral and practical worth. They have promoted our
national progress and brought benefits to more citizens more
equitably than in any society in the history of man. They are
a heritage and a trust which we all hold in common. And
their greatest contribution to human progress may well lie
ahead of us.

The philosopher Kant saw law and freedom, moral principle and practical necessity, as parts of the same reality. He
saw law as the inescapable guide to political action. He believed that sooner or later the realities of human interdependence would compel the fulfillment of the moral imperatives of
human aspiration.

We have reached that moment in time where moral and
practical imperatives, law and pragmatism point toward the
same goals.

The foreign policy of the United States must reflect the
universal ideals of the American people. It is no accident that
a dedication to international law has always been a central
feature of our foreign policy. And so it is today—inescapably
—as for the first time in history we have the opportunity and
the duty to build a true world community.

TEN

GLOBAL CONSENSUS AND ECONOMIC DEVELOPMENT

*Address to the Seventh Special Session of
the United Nations General Assembly,
September 1, 1975*

WE ASSEMBLE here this week with an oportunity to improve the condition of mankind. We can let this opportunity slip away, or we can respond to it with vision and common sense.

The United States has made its choice. There are no panaceas available—only challenges. The proposals that I shall announce today on behalf of President Ford are a program of practical steps responding to the expressed concerns of developing countries. We have made a major effort to develop an agenda for effective international action; we are prepared in turn to consider the proposals of others. But the United States is committed to a constructive effort.

For some time the technical capacity has existed to provide a tolerable standard of life for the world's four billion people. But we, the world community, must shape the political will to do so. For man stands not simply at a plateau of technical ability; he stands at a point of moral choice. When the ancient dream of mankind—a world without poverty—becomes a possibility, our profound moral convictions make it also our duty. And the convening of this special session bears witness that economic progress has become a central and urgent concern of international relations.

The global order of colonial power that lasted through centuries has now disappeared; the cold war division of the world into two rigid blocs has now also broken down, and major changes have taken place in the international economy. We now live in a world of some 150 nations. We live in an environment of continuing conflicts, proliferating weapons, new ideological divisions and economic rivalry. The developing nations have stated their claim for a greater role, for more control over their economic destiny, and for a just share in global prosperity. The economically advanced nations have stated their claim for reliable supplies of energy, raw materials, and other products at a fair price; they seek stable economic relationships and expanding world trade, for these are important to the well-being of their own societies.

These economic issues have already become the subject of mounting confrontation—embargoes, cartels, seizures, countermeasures—and bitter rhetoric. Over the remainder of this century, should this trend continue, the division of the planet between North and South, between rich and poor, could become as grim as the darkest days of the cold war. We would enter an age of festering resentment, increased resort to economic warfare, a hardening of new blocs, the undermining of cooperation, the erosion of international institutions—and failed development.

Can we reconcile our competing goals? Can we build a better world, by conscious purpose, out of the equality and cooperation of states? Can we turn the energies of all nations to the tasks of human progress? These are the challenges of our time.

We profoundly believe that neither the poor nor the rich nations can achieve their purposes in isolation. Neither can extort them from the other—the developing countries least of all, for they would pay the greater cost of division of the planet, which would cut them off needlessly from sources of capital and markets essential to their own progress.

The reality is that ample incentives exist for cooperation on the basis of mutual respect. It is not necessarily the case that if some grow worse off, others will be worse off. But there is an opposite proposition, which we believe is true: that an economic system thrives if all who take part in it thrive. This is no theory; it is our own experience. And it is an experience that we, a people uniquely drawn from all the other peoples of the world, truly desire and hope to share with others.

Therefore it is time to go beyond the doctrines left over from a previous century that are made obsolete by modern reality.

History has left us the legacy of strident nationalism—discredited in this century by its brutal excesses a generation ago and by its patent inadequacy for the economic needs of our time. The economy is global. Recessions, inflation, trade relations, monetary stability, gluts and scarcities of products and materials, the growth of transnational enterprises—these are international phenomena and call for international responses.

History has also left us discredited doctrines of economic determinism and struggle. One of the ironies of our time is that systems based on the doctrine of materialism that promised economic justice have lagged in raising economic welfare.

And contrary to the ideologies of despair, many developing countries have been increasing their per capita incomes at far faster rates than obtained historically in Europe and North America in comparable stages of their growth.

It is also ironic that a philosophy of nonalignment, designed to allow new nations to make their national choices free from the pressure of competing blocs, now has produced a bloc of its own. Nations with radically different ecnomic interests and with entirely different political concerns are combined in a kind of solidarity that often clearly sacrifices practical interests. And it is ironic also that the most devastating blow to economic development in this decade came not from "imperialist rapacity" but from an arbitrary, monopolistic price increase by the cartel of oil exporters.

The reality is that the world economy is a single global system of trade and monetary relations on which hinges the development of all our economies. The advanced nations have an interest in the growth of markets and production in the developing world; with equal conviction we state that the developing countries have a stake in the markets, technological innovation, and capital investment of the industrial countries.

Therefore the nations assembled here have a choice. We can offer our people slogans, or we can offer them solutions. We can deal in rhetoric, or we can deal in reality. My government has made its choice.

The United States firmly believes that the economic challenges of our time must unite us, and not divide us.

So let us get down to business. Let us put aside the sterile debate over whether a new economic order is required or whether the old economic order is adequate. Let us look forward and shape the world before us. Change is inherent in what we do and what we seek. But one fact does not change: that without a consensus on the realities and principles of the development effort, we will achieve nothing.

· There must be consensus, first and foremost, on the principle that our common development goals can be achieved only by cooperation, not by the politics of confrontation.

· There must be consensus that acknowledges our respective concerns and our mutual responsibilities. All of us have rights, and all of us have duties.

· The consensus must embrace the broadest possible participation in international decisions. The developing countries must have a role and voice in the international system, especially in decisions that affect them. But those nations who are asked to provide resources and effort to carry out the decisions must be accorded a commensurate voice.

We have learned from experience that the methods of development assistance of the 1950s and 1960s are no longer adequate. Not only did the technical accomplishments of many programs fall short of expectations; the traditional approaches are less acceptable to the industrialized world because they have seemed to become an endless and one-sided financial burden. And they are less acceptable to the developing world because they have seemed to create a relationship of charity and dependency, inconsistent with equality and self-respect.

Therefore we must find new means. The United States offers today concrete proposals for international actions to promote economic development. We believe that an effective development strategy should concentrate on five fundamental areas:

· First, we must apply international cooperation to the problem of insuring basic economic security. The United States proposes steps to safeguard against the economic shocks to which developing countries are particularly vulnerable: sharp declines in their export earnings from the cycle of world supply and demand, food shortages, and natural disasters.

· Second, we must lay the foundations for accelerated growth. The United States proposes steps to improve developing countries' access to capital markets, to focus and adapt new technology to specific development needs, and to reach consensus on the conditions for foreign investment.

· Third, we must improve the basic opportunities of the developing countries in the world trading system so they can make their way by earnings instead of aid.

· Fourth, we must improve the conditions of trade and investment in key commodities on which the economies of many developing countries are dependent, and we must set an example in improving the production and availability of food.

Fifth, let us address the special needs of the poorest countries, who are the most devastated by current economic conditions, sharing the responsibility among old and newly wealthy donors.

The determination of the developing nations to mobilize their own effort is indispensable. Without it, no outside effort will have effect. Government policies to call forth savings, to institute land reform, to use external aid and capital productively, to manage and allocate national resources wisely, to promote family planning—for these there are no substitutes.

But there must be international as well as national commitment. The United States is prepared to do its part. The senior economic officials of our government have joined with me in developing our approach. Treasury Secretary Simon, with whom I have worked closely on our program, will discuss it tomorrow in relation to the world economy. The large congressional delegation that will attend the session, and the seriousness with which they and the Executive branch have collaborated in preparing these proposals, are evidence of my country's commitment.

We ask in return for a serious international dialogue on the responsibilities which confront us all.

INSURING ECONOMIC SECURITY

OUR FIRST TASK is to insure basic economic security.

The swings and shocks of economic adversity are a global concern tearing at the fabric of developed and developing nations alike. The cycle of good times and bad, abundance and famine, does vast damage to lives and economies. Unemployment, falling standards of living, and the ravages of inflation fuel social and political discontent. We have recently seen the corrosive effects in many countries.

Developing economies are by far the most vulnerable to natural and manmade disasters—the vagaries of weather and of the business cycle. Sharp increases in the prices of oil and food have a devastating effect on their livelihood. Recessions in the industrial countries depress their export earnings.

Thus economic security is the minimum requirement of an effective strategy for development. Without this foundation, sound development programs cannot proceed and the great efforts that development requires from poor and rich alike cannot be sustained.

And because economic security is a global problem, it is a global challenge:

· The industrial nations must work together more effectively to restore and maintain their noninflationary expansion;

· Nations which supply vital products must avoid actions which disrupt that expansion; and

· The international community must undertake a new approach to reduce drastic fluctuations in the export earnings of the developing countries.

Since the economic health of the industrial countries is central to the health of the global economy, their efforts to avoid the extremes of recession and inflation become an international, as well as a national, responsibility.

In a new departure this past year, the leaders of the United States and its major trading partners have begun closer coordination of their national economic policies. A shared sense of urgency, and the exchange of information about trends and intentions, have already influenced important policy decisions. President Ford intends to continue and intensify consultations of this kind. The successful recovery of the industrial economies will be the engine of international stability and growth.

Global economic security depends, secondly, on the actions of suppliers of vital products.

Thus the United States has believed that the future of the world economy requires discussions on energy and other key issues among oil consuming and producing nations. The Government of France is inviting industrialized, oil-producing, and developing nations to relaunch a dialogue this fall on the problems of energy, development, raw materials, and related financial issues. The United States has supported this proposal and worked hard to establish the basis for successful meetings.

But this dialogue is based on an approach of negotiation and consensus, not the exercise of brute economic power to gain unilateral advantage. The enormous, arbitrary increases in the price of oil of 1973 and 1974 have already exacerbated both inflation and recession worldwide. They have shattered the economic planning and progress of many countries. Another increase would slow down or reverse the recovery and the development of nearly every nation represented in this Assembly. It would erode both the will and the capacity in the industrial world for assistance to developing countries. It would, in short, strike a serious blow at the hopes of hundreds of millions around the world.

The forthcoming dialogue among consumers and producers is a test. For its part, the United States is prepared for cooperation. We will work to make it succeed, in our own self-interest and in the interest of all nations. We hope to be met in that same spirit.

The third basic factor in economic security is the stability of export earnings. The development programs—indeed, the basic survival—of many countries rest heavily on earnings from exports of primary products which are highly vulnerable to fluctuations in worldwide demand. Countries which depend on one product can find their revenues reduced drastically if its price drops or if exports fall precipitously. Most have insufficient reserves to cushion against sharp declines in earnings, and they cannot quickly increase the exports of other products. Facing such economic problems, most cannot borrow to offset the loss or can only do so at extremely high interest rates. In such situations countries are frequently forced to cut back on the imports on which their growth and survival depend. Thus the unpredictability of export earnings can make a mockery of development planning.

The question of stabilization of income from primary products has become central in the dialogue on international economic concerns. Price stabilization is not generally a promising approach. For many commodities it would be difficult to achieve without severe restrictions on production or exports, extremely expensive buffer stocks, or price levels which could stimulate substitutes and thereby work to the long-range disadvantage of producers. Even the most ambitious agenda for addressing individual commodities would not result in stabilization arrangements for all of them in the near term. And focusing exclusively on stabilizing commodity prices would not provide sufficient protection to the many developing countries whose earnings also depend on the exports of manufactured goods.

The U.S. Government has recently completed a review of these issues. We have concluded that, because of the wide diversity among countries, commodities, and markets, a new, much more comprehensive approach is required—one which will be helpful to exporters of all commodities and manufactured goods as well.

Let me set forth our proposal. The United States proposes

creation in the International Monetary Fund (IMF) of a new development security facility to stabilize overall export earnings.

· The facility would give loans to sustain development programs in the face of export fluctuations; up to $2.5 billion, and possibly more, in a single year and a potential total of $10 billion in outstanding loans.

· Assistance would be available to all developing countries which need to finance shortfalls in export earnings, unless the shortfalls are caused by their own acts of policy.

· The poorest countries would be permitted to convert their loans into grants under prescribed conditions. These grants would be financed by the proceeds of sales of IMF gold channeled through the proposed $2 billion Trust Fund now under negotiation.

· Eligible countries could draw most, or under certain conditions all, of their IMF quotas in addition to their normal drawing rights. Much of that could be drawn in a single year, if necessary; part automatically, part subject to balance-of-payments conditions, and part reserved for cases of particularly violent swings in commodity earnings.

· Shortfalls would be calculated according to a formula geared to future growth as well as current and past exports. In this way the facility helps countries protect their development plans.

· This facility would replace the IMF's compensatory finance facility; it would not be available for industrial countries.

The United States will present its detailed proposals to the Executive Directors of the International Monetary Fund this month.

This development security facility would provide unprecedented protection against disruptions caused by reductions in earnings—both for countries whose exports consist of a few commodities and for those with diversified and manufactured exports, whose earnings also fluctuate with business cycles. In the great majority of countries, this new facility will cover nearly all the earnings shortfall.

This new source of funds also reinforces our more traditional types of assistance; without the stabilization of earnings, the benefits of concessional aid for developing countries are vitiated. For industrialized countries, it means a more steady export market. For developing countries, it helps assure that development can be pursued without disruption and makes them more desirable prospects in international capital markets. For consumers and producers, rich and poor alike, it buttresses economic security.

Thus the success of our efforts in this area will demonstrate that our interdependence can strengthen the foundations of prosperity for all while promoting progress in the developing countries.

ACCELERATING ECONOMIC GROWTH

IT IS NOT ENOUGH to insure the minimal economic security of the developing countries. Development is a process of growth, acceleration, greater productivity, higher living standards, and social change. This is a process requiring the infusion of capital, technology, and managerial skills on a massive scale.

Developing countries themselves will have to provide most of the effort, but international support is indispensable. Even a moderate acceleration of recent growth rates will require some $40 billion a year in outside capital by 1980. The requirement for technological innovation, though impossible to quantify, is similarly great.

How can these needs for capital, technology, and skills be met?

Bilateral concessional assistance from the industrialized countries has been one important source. Last year it amounted to some $7.2 billion. This must continue to grow. But realistically, we cannot expect the level to increase significantly over the coming years. To put it frankly, the political climate for bilateral aid has deteriorated. In the industrial countries, support for aid has been eroded by domestic economic slowdown, compounded by energy problems; in the developing countries, there is resentment at forms of assistance which imply dependence.

The oil exporters have only begun to meet their responsibility for assistance to the poorer countries. Last year their concessionary aid disbursements were roughly $2 billion; they could, and must, rise substantially this year.

But the industrial nations and the oil exporters cannot, even together, supply all the new resources needed to accelerate development. It follows inescapably that the remaining needs for capital and technology can only be met, directly or indirectly, from the vast pool of private sources. This investment will take place only if the conditions exist to attract or permit it. The United States therefore believes it is time for the world community to address the basic requirements for accelerating growth in developing countries:

· First, developing countries must have better access to capital markets.

· Second, we must promote the transfer of technology.

· Third, it is time to reach an international consensus on the principles to guide the beneficial operation of transnational enterprises.

Access to Capital Markets. First, access to capital markets: The private capital markets are already a major source of development funds, either directly or through intermediaries. The World Bank and the regional development banks borrow extensively to lend to developing nations. The United States urges the expansion of these programs. We are gratified that advanced countries outside of the Western Hemisphere are joining us shortly in a $6 billion expansion of the Inter-American Development Bank. We will participate in negotiations for replenishment of the Asian Development Bank, and we are seeking congressional authority to join the African Development Fund.

But the developing countries that have been most successful and that no longer require concessional aid, especially in Asia and Latin America, have relied heavily on borrowing in the capital markets. Their future access must be assured.

We must now find new ways to enhance the opportunities of developing countries in the competition for capital. And we need to match in new ways potential sources of capital with the investment needs of developing countries.

Several courses of action offer promise.

First, the United States will support a major expansion of the resources of the World Bank's International Finance Corporation, the investment banker with the broadest experience in supporting private enterprise in developing countries. We propose a large increase in the IFC's capital, from the present $100 million to at least $400 million.

Second, the United States proposes creation of an International Investment Trust to mobilize portfolio capital for investment in local enterprises. The trust would attract new capital by offering investors a unique opportunity: participation in a managed broad selection of investments in developing country firms, public, private, and mixed. The International

Finance Corporation would manage it and perhaps provide seed capital, but most of its funds would come from government and private investors. Investors would have their exposure to major losses limited by a $200 million loss reserve provided by governments of industrialized, oil-producing, and developing nations. This institution could be a powerful link between the capital markets and the developing world and could provide billions of dollars of essential resources.

Third, the United States will contribute actively to the work of the IMF-World Bank Development Committee to find ways to assist developing countries in their direct borrowing in the capital markets. It is encouraging that the Latin American countries are considering a regional financial safety net to underpin their access to capital markets by mutual commitments of financial backing.

Finally, we believe that all industrial countries should systematically review the conditions for developing-country access to their national markets to assure that they offer fair and open opportunity. The United States is prepared to provide technical assistance and expertise to developing countries ready to enter long-term capital markets, and we ask others to join us.

Transfer of Technology. Developing countries need not only new funds but also new technology. Yet the mechanisms for the transfer of technology and for its local development are limited and are seldom at the sole command of national governments, and the technologies of industrial countries must often be adapted to local economic and social conditions. New institutions and new approaches are therefore required.

For technology to spur development, it must spur growth in priority areas: energy, food, other resources strategic to the developing economies, and industrialization itself.

First, *energy* is critical for both agricultural and industrial development. The enormous rise in the cost of oil in the last two years has more than wiped out the total of the foreign aid that developing countries have received. It has undermined their balance of payments and has mortgaged their future by forcing them into larger borrowing at higher interest rates. There is no easy short-term solution; but if energy dependence is to be reduced, efforts to exploit new and diversified sources must be intensified now.

The United States invites other nations to join us in an increase of bilateral support for training and technical assistance to help developing countries find and exploit new sources of fossil fuel and other forms of energy.

Methods of discovering and using less accessible or low-grade resources must be fully utilized. So must technology to produce solar and geothermal power. And these techniques must be suited to the conditions of the developing countries.

The United States believes the topic of energy cooperation should be high on the agenda for the forthcoming dialogue between consumers and producers. We will propose, in this dialogue, creation of an International Energy Institute bringing together developed and developing, consumer and producer, on the particular problem of energy development. The International Energy Agency and the International Atomic Energy Agency should both find ways to give technical assistance and support to this institute.

A second critical area for technological innovation is *food production and improvement of nutrition.*

During the past decade, a number of international agricultural research centers have been established to adapt techniques to local needs and conditions. In 1971 the Consultative Group for International Agricultural Research was formed to coordinate these efforts. The United States is prepared to expand the capacity of these institutions. In collaboration with national research organizations with more skilled manpower and funds, they could grow into a worldwide research network for development of agricultural technology.

We are also supporting legislation in the Congress to enable our universities to expand their technical assistance and research in the agricultural field.

Nonfood agricultural and forestry products are a third strategic area for technological assistance. The export earnings of many of the poorest countries—and the livelihood of many millions of their people—depend on such products as timber, jute, cotton, and natural rubber, some of which have encountered serious problems in the face of synthetics. They urgently need assistance to improve the productivity and competitiveness of these products and to diversify their economies.

The United States therefore proposes creation of an organization to coordinate and finance such assistance. Its task will be to attract manpower and capital for research. The financing of this effort should be a priority task for the new International Fund for Agricultural Development.

But developing countries' need for technology is not only for development of strategic sectors but for the broad *promotion of industrialization* itself. This requires the broadest application of skills, resources, and information.

This is not an easy task. The storehouse of technology is already huge and is growing geometrically. Developing practical devices to transfer technology beyond those which already exist will require careful thought. We are prepared to join with other nations in examining new initiatives.

To this end the United States supports creation of an International Industrialization Institute to sponsor and conduct research on industrial technology together with the governments, industries, and research facilities of developing countries.

We support creation of an international center for the exchange of technological information, as a clearinghouse for the sharing of ongoing research and new findings relevant to development.

We will expand our bilateral support of industrial technology appropriate to developing country needs.

We will work with others in this organization in preparing guidelines for the transfer of technology and in the planning of a conference on science and technology for development.

Transnational Enterprises. Access to capital markets and special programs to transfer new technology are but two factors of accelerated growth. There is a third—which may well be one of the most effective engines of development—the transnational enterprise.

Transnational enterprises have been powerful instruments of modernization both in the industrial nations—where they conduct most of their operations—and in the developing countries, where there is often no substitute for their ability to marshal capital, management skills, technology, and initiative. Thus the controversy over their role and conduct is itself an obstacle to economic development.

It is time for the world community to deal with the problems, real and perceived, that have arisen. If the nations assembled here cannot reach consensus on the proper role of these enterprises, the developing countries could lose an invaluable asset. Let us make this issue a test of our capacity to accommodate mutual concerns in practical agreement.

For our part, the United States is prepared to meet the proper concerns of governments in whose territories transnational enterprises operate. We affirm that enterprises must act in full accordance with the sovereignty of host governments and take full account of their public policy. Countries are entitled to regulate the operations of transnational enterprises within their borders. But countries wishing the benefits of these enterprises should foster the conditions that attract and maintain their productive operation.

The United States therefore believes that the time has come for the international community to articulate standards of conduct for both enterprises and governments. The United Nations Commission on Transnational Corporations and other international bodies have begun such an effort. We must reach agreement on balanced principles. These should apply to transnational enterprises in their relations with governments, and to governments in their relations with enterprises and with other governments. They must be fair principles, for failure to reflect the interests of all parties concerned would exacerbate rather than moderate the frictions which have damaged the environment for international investment. Specifically, the United States believes that:

· Transnational enterprises are obliged to obey local law and refrain from unlawful intervention in the domestic affairs of host countries. Their activities should take account of public policy and national development priorities. They should respect local customs. They should employ qualified local personnel, or qualify local people through training.

· Host governments in turn must treat transnational enterprises equitably, without discrimination among them, and in accordance with international law. Host governments should make explicit their development priorities and the standards which transnational enterprises are expected to meet, and maintain them with reasonable consistency.

· Governments and enterprises must both respect the contractual obligations that they freely undertake. Contracts should be negotiated openly, fairly, and with full knowledge of their implications. Greater assurance that contracts will be honored will improve the international commercial environment, increase the flow of investment, and expand economic transactions. Destructive and politically explosive investment disputes, which spoil the climate for large commitments and investment, will occur less frequently.

· Principles established for transnational enterprises should apply equally to domestic enterprises, where relevant. Standards should be addressed not only to privately owned corporations, but also to state-owned and mixed transnational enterprises, which are increasingly important in the world economy.

A statement of principles is not the only or necessarily a sufficient way of resolving many of the problems affecting transnational enterprises. We must develop others:

· Governments must harmonize their tax treatment of these enterprises. Without coordination, host-country and home-country policies may inhibit productive investment.

· Fact-finding and arbitral procedures must be promoted as means for settling investment disputes. The World Bank's International Center for the Settlement of Investment Disputes and other third-party facilities should be employed to settle the important disputes which inevitably arise.

· Laws against restrictive business practices must be developed, better coordinated among countries, and enforced. The United States has long been vigilant against such abuses in domestic trade, mergers, or licensing of technology. We stand by the same principles internationally. We condemn restrictive practices in setting prices or restraining supplies, whether by private or state-owned transnational enterprises or by the collusion of national governments.

· Insurance for foreign private investors should to the extent possible be multilateralized and should include financial participation by developing countries to reflect our mutual stake in encouraging foreign investment in the service of development.

· And there must be more effective bilateral consultation among governments to identify and resolve investment disputes before they become irritants in political relations.

The United States believes that just solutions are achievable—and necessary. If the world community is committed to economic development, it cannot afford to treat transnational enterprises as objects of economic warfare. The capacity of the international community to deal with this issue constructively will be an important test of whether the search for solutions or the clash of ideologies will dominate our economic future. The implications for economic development are profound.

TRADE AND DEVELOPMENT

THE THIRD BASIC AREA for our attention is trade. Improving the world trading system will magnify our success in every other sphere of the development effort.

Trade has been a driving force in the unprecedented expansion of the world economy over the last thirty years. Comparative advantage and specialization, the exchange of technology and the movement of capital, the spur to productivity that competition provides—these are central elements of efficiency and progress. Open trade promotes growth and combats inflation in all countries.

For developing nations, trade is perhaps the most important engine of development. Increased earnings from exports help pay for both the imports that are essential to expand production and the food for growing populations. These earnings reduce dependence on aid, limit the accumulation of debt, and help finance essential borrowing. Growing export industries can provide jobs and increase the government revenues necessary for development programs. It is no accident, therefore, that the success stories in development of the past three decades have been those very countries that have taken full advantage of the opportunities in world trade.

But today the global trading system is threatened by the most serious recession since the Second World War. We face the danger of proliferating artificial barriers and unfair competition reminiscent of the 1930s, which contributed to economic and political disaster. Every day that economic recovery is delayed, the temptation grows to restrict imports, subsidize exports, and control scarce commodities. Concerted action is necessary now to safeguard and improve the open trading system on which the future well-being of all our countries depends.

The multilateral trade negotiations now taking place in Geneva are central to this effort. They will have a profound impact on the future of the world economy and the prospects for development. If these negotiations fail, all countries risk a slide into an increasingly fragmented, closed world of nationalism, blocs, and mounting frictions. If they succeed, all countries will benefit and there will be major progress toward a cooperative and prosperous world.

Many of the less developed nations are emerging as important commercial powers. But developing countries need assistance to take better advantage of trading opportunities, especially to help them open up new markets. In revising rules to govern trade we must take account of their particular needs. In this connection, regional trading associations can help many small countries by providing the economies of scale which result from larger markets.

Thus success in the negotiations depends critically on promoting the interests of the developing countries. For if they do not help to make the rules, assume part of the responsibility to maintain a stable trade system, and share in the benefits of trade, the rules will be subject to increasing challenge, the stability of the system undermined, and the benefits for all nations jeopardized.

The United States therefore believes that a major goal of the multilateral trade negotiations should be to make the trading system better serve development goals. Let me briefly outline our policy.

· First, there must be fundamental structural improvement in the relationship of the developing countries to the world trading system. In the earlier stages of their development, they should receive special treatment through a variety of means—such as preferences, favorable concessions, and exceptions which reflect their economic status. But as they progress to a higher level of development, they must gradually accept the same obligations of reciprocity and stable arrangements that other countries undertake. At some point they must be prepared to compete on more equal terms, even as they derive growing benefits.

· Second, we must improve opportunities for the manufacturing sectors of developing countries. These provide the most promising new areas for exports at the critical stage in development, but the tariffs of industrial countries are a substantial obstacle. To ease this problem the United States has agreed to join other industrial countries in instituting generalized tariff preferences to permit developing countries enhanced access to the markets of industrialized nations.

I am pleased to announce today that the U.S. program will be put into effect on January 1, 1976. And before that date, we will begin consultations and practical assistance to enable exporting countries to benefit from the new trade opportunities in the American market, the largest single market for the manufactured goods of developing countries.

· Third, in keeping with the Tokyo Declaration, we should adapt rules of nontariff barriers to the particular situation of developing countries. In setting international standards for government procurement practices, for example, the United States will negotiate special consideration for the developing countries. We will also negotiate on the basis that under prescribed conditions, certain subsidies may be permitted without triggering countervailing duties for a period geared to achieving particular development objectives.

· Fourth, we will work for early agreement on tariffs for tropical products, which are a major source of earnings for the developing world. Moreover, the United States will implement its tariff for cuts on these products as soon as possible.

· Finally, we are ready to join with other participants in Geneva to negotiate changes in the system of protection in the industrialized countries that favors the import of raw materials over other goods. Many countries impose low or no duties on raw materials and high duties on manufactured or processed goods; the tariff protection increases or "escalates" with the degree of processing. Nothing could be better calculated to discourage and limit the growth of processing industries in developing countries. The United States will give high priority in the Geneva negotiations to reducing these barriers.

The developing countries have obligations in return. The world needs a system in which no nation, developed or developing, arbitrarily withholds or interferes with normal exports of materials. This practice—by depriving other countries of needed goods—can trigger unemployment, cut production, and fuel inflation. It is therefore as disruptive as any of the other trade barriers I have discussed. We urge negotiations on rules to limit and govern the use of export restraints, a logical extension of existing rules on imports. The United States will join others in negotiating supply-access commitments as part of the reciprocal exchange of concessions.

But commodities can be addressed only in part in the context of the trade negotiations. For some serious commodity problems, special arrangements and different institutional structures are required. Let me now turn to that subject.

COMMODITY TRADE
AND PRODUCTION

EXPORTS OF PRIMARY PRODUCTS—raw materials and other commodities—are crucial to the incomes of developing countries. These earnings can lift living standards above bare subsistence, generate profits to support the first steps of industrialization, and provide tax revenues for education, health and other social programs for development. This history of the United States—and many other countries—confirms the importance of commodities.

But this path can be precarious in an uncertain global environment. Those developing countries which are not oil exporters rely on primary commodities for nearly two-thirds of their export earnings. Yet their sales of raw materials and agricultural products have not grown as fast as those of industrial countries. Agricultural commodities, particularly, are vulnerable to the whims of weather and swings of worldwide demand. The market in minerals is especially sensitive to the pendulum of boom-and-bust in the industrial countries. The result is a cycle of scarcity and glut, of underinvestment and overcapacity.

Developing countries are hit hard by commodity cycles also as consumers; higher prices for energy imports, swings in the price and supply of food, and greater costs for other essential raw materials have been devastating blows, soaking up aid funds and the earnings by which they hoped to finance imports. All this can make a mockery of development plans.

But the problems of commodities are not the problems only of developing countries. The industrialized countries are in fact the largest exporters of food and most minerals. Gyrating prices complicate economic decisions in industrial countries. And consumers in industrial countries have painfully learned that high commodity prices leave their inflationary impact long after the commodity market has turned around.

Therefore both industrial and developing countries would benefit from more stable conditions of trade and an expansion of productive capacity in commodities.

Many solutions have been put forward to benefit producers of particular products: cartelization, price indexing, commodity agreements, and other methods. But reality demonstrates the interdependence of all our economies and therefore the necessity for approaches that serve global rather than narrow interests.

Food Security. The most vital commodity in the world is food. The United States is its largest producer and exporter. We recognize our responsibility. We have also sought to make international collaboration in food a model for realistic and cooperative approaches to other international economic issues.

The U.S. plicy is now one of maximum production. At home, we want a thriving farm economy and moderate prices for consumers. Internationally, we wish cooperative relations with nations that purchase from us, an open and growing market, and abundant supplies to meet the needs of the hungry through both good times and bad.

For hundreds of millions of people, food security is the single most critical need in their lives; for many it is a question of life itself. But food security means more than emergency relief to deal with crop failures, natural disasters, and pockets of famine. It means reasonable stability in the availability of food in commercial markets so that harvest failures in some parts of the world will not make food impossibly expensive elsewhere. We have seen with dramatic frequency in recent years how the international food market, strained to capacity, can shake the international economy. Its fluctuations have accelerated inflation, devastated development plans, and wreaked havoc with human lives. Yet in good times, the world community has not summoned the will to take obvious corrective steps to stabilize the market structure.

The United States believes that a global approach to food security, which contains elements that can apply to other commodities, should follow these basic principles:

· The problem must be approached globally, comprehensively, and cooperatively, by consultation and negotiation among all significant producers and consumers;

· Producers should recognize the global interest in stability of supply, and consumers should recognize the interest of producers in stability of markets and earnings;

· Special consideration should be given to the needs of developing countries; and

· Where volatile demand is combined with limited ability to make short-term increases in production, buffer stocks may be the best approach to achieving greater security for both consumers and producers.

At the World Food Conference last November, which was convened at our initiative, the United States proposed a comprehensive international cooperative approach to providing food security. We proposed an international system of nationally held grain reserves, to meet emergencies and improve the market. The United States has since then offered specific proposals and begun negotiations. But the international effort lagged when improved harvests seemed to diminish the immediate danger of worldwide shortage.

My government today declares that it is time to create this reserve system. If we do not, future crises are inevitable. Specifically, we propose:

· To meet virtually all potential shortfalls in food grains production, total world reserves must reach at least thirty million tons of wheat and rice. We should consider whether a similar reserve is needed in coarse grains.

· Responsibility for holding reserves should be allocated fairly, taking into account wealth, production, and trade. The United States is prepared to hold a major share.

· Acquisition and release of reserves should be governed by quantitative standards such as anticipated surpluses and shortfalls in production.

· Full participants in the system should receive assured access to supplies. Among major producers, full participation should require complete exchange of information and forecasts.

· Special assistance should be extended to developing countries that participate, to enable them to meet their obligation to hold a portion of global reserves.

The United States is ready to negotiate the creation of such a system. Let us move ahead rapidly.

Other Primary Commodities. And let us apply the same approach of cooperation to other primary commodities that are similarly beset by swings of price and supply—and that are similarly essential to the global economy.

There is no simple formula that will apply equally to all commodities. The United States therefore proposes to discuss new arrangements in individual commodities on a case-by-case basis.

Buffer stocks can be an effective technique to moderate instability in supplies and earnings. On the other hand, price-fixing arrangements distort the market, restrict production, and waste resources for everyone. It is developing countries that can least afford this waste. Restricted production idles the costly equipment and economic infrastructure that takes years to build. Artifically high prices lead consumers to make costly investment in domestic substitutes, ultimately eroding the market power of the traditional producers.

Accordingly, the United States proposes the following approach to commodity arrangements:

· We recommend that a consumer-producer forum be established for every key commodity to discuss how to promote the efficiency, growth, and stability of its market. This is particularly important in the case of grains, as I have outlined. It is also important in copper, where priority should be given to creating a forum for consumer-producer consultation.

· The first new formal international agreement being concluded is on tin. We have participated actively in its negotiation. President Ford has authorized me to announce that the United States intends to sign the tin agreement, subjec to congressional consultations and ratification. We welcome its emphasis on buffer stocks, its avoidance of direct price fixing, and its balanced voting system. We will retain our right to sell from our strategic stockpiles, and we recognize the right of others to maintain a similar program.

· We are participating actively in negotiations on coffee. We hope they will result in a satisfactory new agreement that reduces the large fluctuations in prices and supplies entering the market.

· We will also join in the forthcoming cocoa and sugar negotiations. Their objective will be to reduce the risks of investment and moderate the swings in prices and supplies.

· We will support liberalization of the International Monetary Fund's financing of buffer stocks, to assure that this facility is available without reducing other drawing rights.

Comprehensive Program of Investment. I have already announced my government's broad proposal of a development security facility, a more fundamental approach to stabilizing the overall earnings of countries dependent on commodities trade. My government also believes that an effective aproach to the commodities problem requires a comprehensive program of investment to expand worldwide capacity in minerals and other critical raw materials. This is basic to the health of both industrial and developing economies.

There are presently no shortages in most basic raw materials, nor are any likely in the next two or three years. But the adequacy of supplies in years to come will be determined by investment decisions taken now. Because the technology for processing lower grade ores is extremely complex and the financing requirements for major raw material investments are massive, new projects take several years to complete. In some countries the traditional source of funds—private foreign investment—is no longer as welcome, nor are investors as interested, as in the past.

The United States therefore proposes a major new international effort to expand raw material resources in developing countries.

The World Bank and its affiliates, in concert with private sources, should play a fundamental role. They can supply limited amounts of capital directly; more importantly, they can use their technical, managerial, and financial expertise to bring together funds from private and public sources. They can act as intermediary between private investors and host governments and link private and public effort by providing cross-guarantees on performance. World Bank loans could fund government projects, particularly for needed infrastructure, while the International Finance Corporation could join private enterprise in providing loans and equity capital. The World Bank Group should aim to mobilize $2 billion in private and public capital annually.

In addition, the United States will contribute to and actively support the new United Nations revolving fund for natural resources. This fund will encourage the worldwide exploration and exploitation of minerals and thus promote one of the most promising endeavors of economic development.

THE POOREST NATIONS

ANY STRATEGY for development must devote special attention to the needs of the poorest countries. The fate of one billion people—half the developing world and a quarter of mankind —will be affected by what we do or fail to do.

For the last four years, per capita income in the poorest countries—already below minimal standards for development—has declined. Their exports are most concentrated in the least dynamic sectors of world demand. It is they who have been most cruelly affected by the rise in the costs of oil, food, and other essential imports.

Whatever adversity the rest of mankind endures, it is these peoples who endure the most. Whatever problems we have, theirs are monumental. Whatever economic consequences flow from the decisions that we all make, the consequences are greatest for them. If global progress in economic development falters, they will be submerged.

This challenge transcends ideology and bloc politics. No international order can be considered just unless one of its fundamental principles is cooperation to raise the poorest of the world to a decent standard of life.

This challenge has two dimensions. We must look to elemental economic security and the immediate relief of suffering. And we must give preference to these countries' needs for future economic growth.

Elemental Economic Security. First, security means balance-of-payments support for the poorest countries during periods of adversity. For them global recessions and wide swings in prices of key commodities have a particularly disastrous impact. Yet these countries have very little access to short- and medium-term capital to help them weather bad times. The little finance to which they have access often involves interest rates that are too high considering their chronic debt-repayment problems.

To provide greater balance-of-payments support at more acceptable rates of interest for the poor nations, the United States last November proposed a Trust Fund in the International Monetary Fund of up to $2 billion for emergency relief. Although this proposal met with wide support, it has been stalled by a dispute over an unrelated issue: the role of gold in the international monetary system. We cannot let this delay continue. The United States is making a determined effort to move forward the monetary negotiations at the IMF meetings now underway. If others meet us in this same spirit, we could reach a consensus on the Trust Fund by the next meeting in January.

Second, security requires stable export earnings. The new approach that we are proposing today for earnings stabilization can provide major new economic insurance in the form of loans and grants for the poorest countries.

Third, security means having enough to eat. There must be determined international cooperation on food.

The World Food Conference set a target of ten million tons of food aid annually. This fiscal year the U.S. food aid budget provides for almost six million tons of food grains—60 percent of the world target, and a 20 percent increase over last year. Other producers must also provide their share.

Another priority in the poorest countries must be to reduce the tragic waste of losses after harvest from inadequate storage, transport, and pest control. There are often simple and inexpensive techniques to resolve these problems. Investment in such areas as better storage and pesticides could have a rapid and substantial impact on the world's food supply; indeed, the saving could match the total of all the food aid being given around the world. Therefore we urge that the Food and Agriculture Organization, in conjunction with the U.N. Development Program and the World Bank, set a goal of cutting in half these postharvest losses by 1985, and develop a comprehensive program to this end.

Finally, security means good health and easing the strains of population growth. Disease ravages the poorest countries most of all and exacts a devastating economic as well as human cost. At the same time we face the stark reality that there will be twice as many people to feed by the end of this century as there are today. One of the most promising approaches to these problems is the integrated delivery of basic health services at the community level, combining medical treatment, family planning, and nutritional information and using locally trained paramedical personnel. The United States will support a major expansion of the efforts already underway, including those in cooperation with the World Health Organization, to develop and apply these methods. We strongly urge the help of all concerned nations.

Future Economic Growth. Programs to achieve minimum security, however essential, solve only part of the problem. We must help the poorest nations break out of their present stagnation and move toward economic growth.

This means, first of all, that they should have preferential access to official, concessionary financial aid. They have the least dynamic exports, but they lack the capital to develop new ones. They have the direst need for financing, but they have no access to capital markets and little ability to carry greater debt.

If these countries themselves can summon the effort required, outside assistance can be productive. All nations with the financial capacity must share the responsibility. We will do our part. More than 70 percent of our development assistance goes to low-income countries. More than 60 percent of this year's proposed programs is devoted to food and nutrition, which are of particular importance to the poorest.

The special financial needs of the poorest countries can be met particularly well by expanded low-interest loans of the international financial institutions. The International Development Association of the World Bank Group is a principal instrument whose great potential has not been fully realized. After congressional consultations, the United States will join others in a substantial fifth replenishment of the resources of the International Development Association, provided that the oil-exporting countries also make a significant contribution.

An effective strategy for sustained growth in the poorest countries must expand their agricultural production, for external food aid cannot possibly fill their needs. The current gap between what the developing countries need and what they can produce themselves is fifteen million tons; at present rates of growth, the gap is expected to double or triple within the next decade. Failure to meet this challenge will doom much of the world to hunger and malnutrition and all of the world to periodic shortages and higher prices.

Traditional bilateral aid programs to boost agricultural production remain indispensable. President Ford is asking Congress for authorization to double our bilateral agricultural assistance this year to $582 million. We urge the other affluent nations to increase their contributions as well.

Clearly a massive program of international cooperation is also required. More research is needed to improve agricultural yields, make more efficient use of fertilizer, and find better farm management techniques. Technical assistance and information exchange are needed for training and for technological advance. Better systems of water control, transportation, and land management are needed to tap the developing countries' vast reserves of land, water, and manpower.

To mobilize massive new concessional resources for these purposes, the United States proposes the early establishment of the new International Fund for Agricultural Development. President Ford has asked me to announce that he will seek authorization of a direct contribution of $200 million to the Fund, provided that others will add their support for a combined goal of at least $1 billion.

The International Fund for Agricultural Development can be the major source of new capital to attack the most critical problems of the poorest developing countries. The United States urges the world community to give it prompt and major support.

THE POLITICAL DIMENSION

IN EVERY AREA of endeavor that I have described—economic security, growth, trade, commodities, and the needs of the poorest—the developing countries themselves want greater influence over the decisions that will affect their future. They are pressing for a greater role in the institutions and negotiations by which the world economic system is evolving.

The United States believes that participation in international decisions must be widely shared, in the name of both justice and effectiveness. We believe the following principles should apply:

The process of decision should be fair. No country or group of countries should have exclusive power in the areas basic to the welfare of others. This principle is valid for oil. It also applies to trade and finance.

The methods of participation must be realistic. We must encourage the emergence of real communities of interest between nations, whether they are developed or developing, producer or consumer, rich or poor. The genuine diversity of interests that exists among states must not be submerged by bloc discipline or in artificial, unrepresentative majorities. For only genuine consensus can generate effective action.

The process of decision should be responsive to change. On many issues developing countries have not had a voice that reflects their role. This is now changing. It is already the guiding principle of two of the most successful international bodies, the IMF and the World Bank, where the quotas of oil-producing states will soon be at least doubled—on the basis of objective criteria. Basic economic realities, such as the size of economies, participation in world trade, and financial contributions, must carry great weight.

Finally, participation should be tailored to the issues at hand. We can usefully employ many different institutions and procedures. Sometimes we should seek broad consensus in universal bodies, as we are doing this week in this Assembly; sometimes negotiations can more usefully be focused in more limited forums, such as the forthcoming consumer-producer dialogue; sometimes decisions are best handled in large specialized bodies such as the IMF and World Bank, where voting power is related to responsibility; and sometimes most effective action can be taken in regional bodies.

Most relevant to our discussion here is the improvement of the U.N. system, so that it can fulfill its charter mandate "to employ international machinery for the promotion of the economic and social advancement of all peoples." We welcome the thoughtful report by the Secretary-General's group of twenty-five experts on structural reform in the U.N. system. We will seriously consider its recommendations. In our view, an improved U.N. organizaiton must include:

· rationalization of the U.N.'s fragmented assistance programs;

· strengthened leadership within the central Secretariat and the entire U.N. system for development and economic cooperation:

· streamlining of the Economic and Social Council;

· better consultative procedures to insure effective agreement among members with a particular interest in a subject under consideration; and

· a mechanism for independent evaluation of the implementation of programs.

The United States proposes that 1976 be dedicated as a year of review and reform of the entire U.N. development system. An intergovernmental committee should be formed at this session, to begin work immediately on recommendations that can be implemented by the General Assembly in its 1976 session. We consider this a priority in any strategy for development.

Mr. President [Abdelaziz Bouteflika, Foreign Minister of Algeria], Mr. Secretary-General, colleagues, ladies and gentlemen: I began today with the statement that we have, this week, an opportunity to improve the condition of mankind. This fact alone represents an extraordinary change in the human condition. Throughout history, man's imagination has been limited by his circumstances—which have now fundamentally changed. We are no longer confined to what Marx called "the realm of necessity." And it has always been the case that the wisest realists were those who understood man's power to shape his own reality.

The steps we take now are not limited by our technical possibilities, but only by our political will. If the advanced nations fail to respond to the winds of change, and if the developing countries choose rhetoric over reality, the great goal of economic development will be submerged in our common failure. The speeches made here this week will be placed alongside many other lofty pronouncements made over decades past in this organization on this subject, buried in the archives of oblivion.

But we would not all be here if we did not believe that progress is possible and that it is imperative.

The United States has proposed a program of action. We are prepared to contribute, if we are met in a spirit of common endeavor.

· We have proposed steps to improve basic economic security

—to safeguard the world economy, and particularly the developing countries, against the cruel cycles that undermine their export earnings.

· We have proposed measures to improve developing countries' access to capital, new technology, and management skills to lift themselves from stagnation onto the path of accelerating growth.

· We have proposed structural improvements in the world trading system, to be addressed in the ongoing multilateral trade negotiations, to enhance developing countries' opportunities to earn their own way through trade.

· We have proposed a new approach to improving market conditions in food and other basic commodities, on which the economies and indeed the lives of hundreds of millions of people depend.

· We have proposed specific ways of giving special help to the development needs of the poorest countries.

My government does not offer these proposals as an act of charity, nor should they be received as if due. We know that the world economy nourishes us all; we know that we live on a shrinking planet. Materially as well as morally, our destinies are intertwined.

There remain enormous things for us to do. We can say once more to the new nations: We have heard your voices. We embrace your hopes. We will join your efforts. We commit ourselves to our common success.

ELEVEN

GLOBAL PEACE,
THE MIDDLE EAST,
AND THE UNITED STATES

*Address to the Cincinnati Chamber of
Commerce, September 16, 1975*

As AMERICA enters its two hundredth year as a free nation our role has grown central to the peace and progress of the world. We have become the engine of the global economy, the rock of security for those who share our values, the creative force in building international institutions, and the pioneer in science and technology.

Americans have carried the burdens of world leadership for a generation. They have done so with dedication and good will, but understandably they ask when and if their labors can cease. They want to know what our purposes are in international affairs. They sense that the world needs us, but they ask: Do we need the world?

The past three decades have taught us that our commitment to global leadership is not an act of choice but a recognition of reality. Awesome weapons can span continents in minutes. The international economic system thrives or declines as one. Conflict in faraway regions has vast political, security, and economic repercussions here at home. Communications make us instantly aware of developments in every corner of the globe —of the travel of diplomats, the movement of troops, or the hunger of little childen. World peace and American security, global well-being and American prosperity have become virtually inseparable.

The past three decades have also taught us that our contribution is indispensable. We cannot solve every problem, but few solutions are possible without us. Other countries must do more, but we cannot ignore the responsibility that rests on us. If we do not help resist aggression, if we do not work for a dynamic world economy, if we do not promote liberty and justice, no other nation can—at least no other nation that shares our values.

Americans have a right to be proud of how they have met this challenge. Through five administrations of both political parties we led in assisting Europe and Japan recover from the devastation of the Second World War. We helped create a trading and monetary system that has spread prosperity in our own land and around the world. We forged alliances with the major democracies that have kept the global peace for a generation. We have mediated and helped resolve conflicts. We have fed the hungry, educated men and women from other lands, and welcomed those who flee oppression to our shores. With all humility we can say that no other nation in history has made comparable efforts on such a scale.

But history has rewarded our exertions with new challenges. The world has been transformed over the thirty years since World War II partly because of the success of this nation's policies.

The Design of Global Peace. In the early years of the postwar period we were militarily and economically the world's predominant power. Our allies were recovering; new nations were just coming into being; potential adversaries were restrained by our nuclear supremacy.

Today's world is radically different. The industrialized nations are strong and self-confident; our alliances are cooperative endeavors between equals. We have preserved the world balance of power; but in the process both superpowers have acquired the capacity to destroy civilized life in a matter of hours. The growth of the world's economic system has spread economic power more widely among the new nations; they seek a greater role in international affairs and a larger share of the world economy.

The United States remains the largest single factor in international affairs. But we must learn what most other nations in history have known: that one country can neither escape from the world nor dominate it. We can no longer overwhelm problems with our resources. We no longer have the luxury of simple choices.

Thus, beyond the issues that make daily headlines, we have sought to conduct a foreign policy that takes account of the fundamental changes in the international order. We cannot afford oscillation between extremes of crusading and isolation. We must maintain a steady course which offers hope for long-term international stability and progress—a course which Americans can support, which gives courage to our allies and pause to our adversaries.

Our first priority is the vigor of our alliances with the great democracies of the Atlantic community and Japan. We formed these ties a generation ago to protect weaker friends against military danger. Today we work together as equals on issues going far beyond security. We have coordinated our efforts to ease tensions with the East; we have built new institutions of energy cooperation; we have developed common approaches to the developing countries; and we have begun to harmonize our economic policies to move together toward noninflationary economic recovery. The vitality of Western democracy and the solidarity of our alliances are an essential factor of global stability.

On the basis of allied cohesion and strength, we have also sought to place our relations with the Communist countries on a more stable and long-term basis. For thirty years, mankind's hopes for peace and its fear of war have turned on the relationship between the United States and the Soviet Union.

Today strategic nuclear parity has transformed international politics. Your government—in any administration—must manage a basic conflict of values and interests with the Soviet Union in the shadow of nuclear holocaust. Never before in history have the weapons of war been so devastating and so ill-suited to the pursuit of specific policy objectives. Therefore the United States has engaged the Soviet Union in negotiations on the limitation of strategic armaments. We have solved political disputes, such as Berlin, and restrained great-power conflict in the Middle East to give both sides a continuing stake in positive political relations. We have begun more normal contacts in trade and scientific, technical, and cultural exchanges. And we have regularized our consultations at the highest level.

The necessity of coexistence in the shadow of nuclear peril does not mean a coincidence of moral purpose. This country knows the moral difference between freedom and tyranny. But we shall also never lose sight of the fact that in the age of nuclear weapons, peace, too, is a moral imperative. We shall insist on reciprocity but we believe that incentives for cooperation and penalties for intransigence are more effective than rhetorical posturing. We shall keep up our military strength second to none; but we will not succumb to the illusion that military power offers the final answer to international problems. On the basis of firmness and flexibility, strength and willingness to negotiate, we shall strive to moderate conflicts and to bring a more secure world to future generations.

As we have maintained alliance cohesion and begun to ease tensions with the Communist powers, a new dimension has been added to the spectrum of international issues before us: the future of the relationship between developed and developing countries. The vast and growing problems of energy, food, raw materials, and economic development now face us in all their complexity as the fundamental issues of the last quarter of the twentieth century.

These problems are not technical or, at bottom, even economic. They go to the heart of the question of international order: whether the world can accommodate the needs of all nations; whether countries will regulate their affairs by cooperation or by confrontation; whether international relations will reflect the search for mutual benefit and common progress or turn into tests of strength. The United States is in a better position than any other nation to go it alone or to face such a test of strength; but we know that ultimately the whole world will suffer.

The United States has made its position clear. At the U.N. Special Session called to discuss these issues two weeks ago, I pledged our country to a cooperative, understanding approach. I said that we are prepared to work with other nations to put the technological and economic genius of the modern age in the service of all mankind. The United States is convinced that the developed and the developing nations working together can achieve through cooperation what neither can extort through economic warfare or ideological pressure—economic advance for all our peoples.

In this spirit the United States presented a comprehensive and detailed program for economic and social cooperation to the Special Session. These proposals and this attitude will guide us in future discussions with the less developed nations. The results at the Special Session, which just concluded today, were constructive. Discussions took place in a conciliatory spirit, and the final document produced considerable convergence between between the developed and the developing countries and the outlines of a consumer program of action.

Cooperation must remain a two-way street. If nations wield their special strengths as weapons, the promise of global progress will give way to the perils of global confrontation.

The most critical immediate issue, of course, is the question of the price of oil. We and our partners in the International Energy Agency have already taken major steps to conserve oil and to establish financial structures that will help us cope with the impact of rising oil prices. Much still remains to be done. But the United States, in cooperation with other industrial nations, will make a determined effort to reverse the conditions that have enabled oil prices to be set unilaterally. The United States cannot, and will not, entrust its political and economic destiny to decisions made elsewhere.

At the same time we are ready to seek a new relationship with the oil-producing nations. We ought to be partners, not adversaries. Consumers must have reliable access to oil supplies at reasonable prices. To invest their new oil wealth, the producers must become major importers of our products. We are ready to cooperate with the oil producers in linking our economies on equitable terms.

Next month the oil producers, developing countries, and industrial countries will meet to launch a dialogue on energy, raw materials, development, and finance first proposed by President Giscard d'Estaing of France. We have worked hard to make these meetings possible. We will work hard to make them a success. They provide us the opportunity to shape new constructive relationships in the world economy.

But another oil price rise would severely jeopardize these hopes. It could set off a relentless sequence of action and reaction to the detriment of all countries, developed and developing. This vicious cycle must be avoided. The possibilities of a cooperative world order depend upon it.

Peace in the Middle East. There is no more vivid example of the stake that we have in the world around us, and the decisive contribution that this nation can make, than the conflict in the Middle East.

The Congress is now deliberating on the recent Egyptian-Israeli agreement. As it does so, it is important for the American people to understand why the United States is involved, what strategy we have pursued, the significance of the agreement, and where we will go from here.

The Middle East lies at the crossroads of three continents. Because of the area's strategic importance, and because it provides the energy on which much of the world depends, outside powers have continued to involve themselves in its conflicts, often competitively.

For the United States a diplomatic role in the Middle East is not a preference but a matter of vital interest:

· Because of our historical and moral commitment to the survival and security of Israel;

· Because of our important concerns in the Arab world, an area of more than 150 million people and the site of the world's largest oil reserves;

· Because perpetual crisis in the Middle East would severely strain our relations with our most important allies in Europe and Japan;

· Because upheaval in the Middle East jeopardizes the

world's hopes for economic recovery, threatening the well-being of the industrial nations and the hopes of the developing world; and

· Because tension in the Middle East increases the prospect of direct U.S.-Soviet confrontation with its attendant nuclear risk.

Each successive Middle East crisis has presented us with painful choices between our many commitments and interests. And each successive crisis accelerates the trends of radicalism in the area, putting greater pressures on Ameria's friends in the moderate Arab world and heightening all the tensions and dangers.

The stake of every American in peace in the Middle East was dramatically and concretely illustrated by the Middle East war of 1973:

· The oil embargo, coupled with the OPEC [Organization of Petroleum Exporting Countries] price increases, cost Americans half a million jobs and over $10 billion in national output. It added at least 5 percentage points to the price index, contributing to the worst inflation since World War II. It set the stage for a serious worldwide recession, from which we are only now recovering two years later.

· Partly because of their greater dependence on Middle East oil, our principal allies in Western Europe and Japan separated from us over Middle East policy in the most serious strain in our alliances since they were founded.

· The 1973 crisis tested the course of U.S.-Soviet relations, leading us briefly to the verge of confrontation in the October 24 alert.

The October war also set in train momentum that is now irreversible. Events can be channeled toward diplomatic progress, or they can pull us headlong toward another war. This is why the United States, since October 1973, has been actively engaged in promoting a peaceful solution. We have no illusions about the difficulties. The Middle East has seen more than its share of dashed hopes and disappointment. But progress depends crucially, even decisively, on the United States. Time and again the parties have turned to us for mediation. Time and again we have acceded to these requests because we are convinced that stagnation invites disaster. The next Middle East war will pose greater risks, complexities, and dangers and cause more dislocations than any previous conflict.

What, then, has been our approach? For nearly three decades it was axiomatic that *all* issues pertaining to *all* the countries involved had to be addressed comprehensively: the final frontiers of Israel and the reciprocal guarantees of peace of the Arab states; the future of the Palestinians; the status of Jerusalem; and the question of international guarantees should all be considered together. But for thirty years it proved nearly impossible even to begin the process of negotiation. Every attempt to discuss a comprehensive solution failed —from the partition plan, to the Lausanne conference, to the Rogers plan and the Four Powers talks of 1969 and 1970, to the U.N. Security Council deliberations. To discuss simultaneously issues of such complexity, between countries whose deep mutual mistrust rejected even the concept of compromise, was futile until a minimum of confidence had been established. In the long history of the Arab-Israeli conflict, it is a new and relatively recent development that opinion in the Arab world has begun to think in terms of recognizing a sovereign Israel and that Israel has begun to see peace as a tangible goal rather than a distant dream.

The United States therefore concluded that instead of seeking to deal with all problems at once we should proceed step by step with the parties prepared to negotiate and on the issues where some room for maneuver seemed possible. We believed that once the parties began a negotiating process, they would develop a stake in success. Solutions to problems more easily negotiable would build mutual confidence. On each side a sense would grow that negotiations could produce benefits and that agreements would be kept—agreements that could become building blocks for a final peace. Ultimately we expected that the step-by-step process would bring about, for the first time, the basic political conditions needed for the overall settlement called for by Security Council Resolution 338. This remains our goal.

Progress since the October war has been without precedent since the beginning of the Arab-Israeli conflict. Security Council Resolution 338 launched a negotiating process and the first Geneva conference. Agreements to separate the opposing forces and establish U.N. buffer zones to strengthen the cease-fire were successfully negotiated between Egypt and Israel in January 1974 and between Syria and Israel in May 1974.

The role of the United States was crucial in helping the parties reach these agreements. It reflected the fact that only we had developed strong relationships of trust with all parties. Major Arab countries that broke diplomatic relations with the United States in 1967 moved in 1973 and 1974 to restore their ties with us, creating a new climate of confidence and thereby the conditions for progress. And our traditional friendship with Israel has been reinforced in the crucible of crisis and the long months of close association in negotiations.

The momentum of progress was interrupted in the summer and fall of 1974: first by our Presidential succession; then by the decision of the Arab summit at Rabat which made negotiations over the West Bank impossible. When negotiations were resumed in March of this year, they first ended in deadlock. We therefore reexamined our approach asking whether we should continue the step-by-step strategy or move directly to the Geneva conference and a comprehensive approach. The imminent crisis we feared as a result of the March deadlock did not materialize—almost solely because everyone expected that the United States, in one way or another, would resume its effort.

The President consulted widely with Congressional and civic leaders, with our Ambassadors from the area, and with the Middle East parties. He met with King Hussein [of Jordan], President Sadat [of Egypt], Prime Minister Rabin [of Israel], and Syrian Foreign Minister Khaddam. We benefited from the views of the new Saudi leadership which is continuing the policy of the highly respected late King Faisal.

The President concluded that the time was still not ripe for a comprehensive approach. In the wake of an apparent failure, the intractability of the issues would only be compounded by their being combined. Bringing all the parties, including the most irreconcilable, together in one dramatic public negotiation was an invitation to a deepened stalemate. This could discredit the whole process of negotiation and create a slide toward war. It was widely understood that the momentum of diplomatic progress had to be restored before Geneva was convened to consider the broader issues. Therefore, at the request of both sides, the United States resumed its step-by-step effort. The result was the new agreement between Egypt and Israel which was signed in Geneva on September 4.

The agreement is fair and balanced.

· Territorially, it provides for withdrawal of Israeli forces from the eastern coast of the Gulf of Suez and fom the strategic Sinai passes. Egypt recovers a significant portion of its territory, including the economically important oil fields.

· Militarily, the agreement reaffirms the cease-fire. It widens the buffer zone and extends the limitations of forces that were negotiated in the disengagement agreement of January 1974. These balanced provisions markedly reduce the danger of surprise attack that figured centrally in the wars of 1967 and 1973.

· Politically, the agreement—which remains in force until it is superseded by another one—commits both sides to a peaceful solution to the Middle East conflict, and to refrain from use or threat of force or of military blockade. It permits nonmilitary Israeli cargoes to go through the newly reopened Suez Canal.

Both Prime Minister Rabin and President Sadat have hailed the agreement as a possible turning point. It represents the most far-reaching practical test of peace—political, military, and psychological—in the history of the Arab-Israeli conflict. For the first time Israel and an Arab state have taken a step, not just to halt fighting or to disentangle the forces but to reduce the danger of future war and to commit themselves to peaceful settlement of the conflict. The effort that went into it and the inhibitions that both sides had to overcome reflect a serious determination to end a generation of violence. And both sides have affirmed that the agreement is a significant step in a process that must be continued toward a just and durable peace.

The achievement owes much to the courage of leaders on both sides. President Sadat and his government moved Egypt on the path of moderation and development. They have understood that a political process offered the only realistic hope for the achievement of all Arab interests. Credit is due equally to the courage of Prime Minister Rabin and the Government of Israel. Israel's dilemma is that to obtain peace it must give up tangible assets, such as territory, for intangible concessions, such as assurances and recognition. Israel's leaders realized that only negotiation offered a hope to achieve what Israel has sought for twenty-seven years: new political conditions that would mean acceptance by its neighbors in return for withdrawal from territory. They had the wisdom to recognize that the time had come to start this difficult, even painful, process.

The presence of 200 civilian Americans to assist with the early-warning system in the small area of the passes is a limited, but crucial, American responsibility. It was not a role we sought. We accepted it at the request of both sides only when it became totally clear that there would be no agreement without it and only on carefully limited terms. We agreed because failure would have posed grave risks for the United States.

In the aftermath of Indochina the concerns of some Americans about this presence are understandable. But the two cases are totally different. The American presence in the Sinai is not a step into conflict; it is a move which gives added insurance against conflict. It is limited to two hundred volunteer civilians by agreement with both sides. They will be stationed in a small, but important, sector of the U.N. neutral zone. They are not combat personnel or advisers engaged on one side of an ongoing war. They serve both sides at their request and complement the U.N. presence from such countries as Canada, Sweden, Austria, and Finland.

Our presence in the area is not new. Indeed thirty-six Americans are at this moment serving with the U.N. Truce Supervision Organization in the Middle East. Americans have been serving in this capacity for over twenty-five years.

The agreement provides the President the right to withdraw the American personnel if they are in jeopardy. We are prepared, as well, to accept a congressional proposal making the withdrawal mandatory in case of hostilities. In short, what we have proposed to the Congress and the American people is not an engagement in war, but an investment in peace.

There will also be deliberation in the Congress over military and economic assistance to the parties. We will submit our recommendations within a month. This assistance is not part of the agreement, itself. Indeed most of the assistance we shall request would have been sought even if there were no agreement. But in the present context our aid takes on new significance; it is central to our policy and vital to the chances for a lasting peace in the Middle East.

Economic and military support for Israel's security has been American policy during five administrations. Last May seventy-six Senators wrote to President Ford urging that the United States *"be responsive to Israel's urgent economic and military needs."* The Administration's request for new assistance to Israel is responsive to this call. It will reflect long-standing criteria of assistance. Only a small part grows out of new requirements arising from the agreement.

The case for aid to Egypt is equally strong. Egypt has taken important steps toward peace and closer relations with the West. Egypt deserves our encouragement. American technology and capital, public and private, can strengthen all the constructive tendencies in the Middle East. The symbolic and substantive significance of American support to Egypt is immeasurable.

Thus the additional burden of U.S. assistance is modest—infinitely smaller than the demonstrated costs of another war, which in 1973 required direct appropriations to Israel of $2.2 billion in addition to the indirect costs. But its role is crucial: It reduces the incentives for war; it, too, is an investment in peace.

Where do we go from here?

The Egyptian-Israeli agreement is a step in a continuing process. The agreement states explicitly that the parties shall continue the negotiating efforts to reach an overall, final peace settlement in accordance with resolution 338.

The path ahead will be difficult. In the immediate future,

we must begin the implementation of the Egyptian-Israeli agreement. This must await the deliberation and decision of the Congress. When this is settled and if the agreement goes into effect, we will start our consultations with all concerned to assure that there is consensus on the next step. We will not move precipitously, because we want confidence to build. We will not move without careful preparation, because we want the process to continue to succeed.

But the effort to achieve a lasting peace must resume. The Egyptian-Israeli agreement has created new opportunities for the future—but these opportunities must be seized, or they will disappear. The United States did not help negotiate this agreement in order to put an end to the process of peace but to give it new impetus. There can be no stagnation, for the area remains tense and volatile.

For our part, we stand ready to assist as the parties desire. We will seriously encourage a negotiation between Syria and Israel. We are prepared to consult all countries concerned, including the Soviet Union, about the timing and substance of a reconvened Geneva Conference. And we are fully aware that there will be no permanent peace unless it includes arrangements that take into account the legitimate interests of the Palestinian people.

The United States seeks no special advantage in the Middle East. It has always been our policy that the nations of the region should be free to determine their own relationships with any outside power. Therefore the United States would not understand and would be obliged to oppose efforts by any outside power to thwart the Egyptian-Israeli agreement.

In the search for a final peace the United States is prepared to work with the Soviet Union. We are cosponsors of the Security Council resolutions that launched this hopeful course of negotiation; we are cochairmen of the Geneva peace conference which met at an early crucial phase. While we have had important differences with the Soviet Union over the substance of a settlement, our two countries have held parallel views that the Middle East situation poses grave dangers and that partial steps must be part of, and contribute to, progress toward a comprehensive solution.

In the Middle East there is a yearning for peace surpassing any known for a generation. Let us seize this historic opportunity. The suffering and bravery of the peoples of the Middle East demand it; the highest interests of the United States require it.

This is why the American people, their Congress, and the President, are, to an extraordinary degree, united on the course of our Middle East policy. And this is why we will not cease our effort.

Conclusion. We Americans have spent the better part of a decade apologizing to ourselves and the world for what we thought we had become. We have spent most of the last three years enmeshed in a national tragedy that caused many to lose sight of what our country has meant, and continues to mean, to the billions abroad who look to the United States as a beacon of freedom and hope.

Today the issues that threatened our unity and confidence are in the process of being put behind us. A world of turmoil, danger, and opportunity cries out for our purposeful leadership. There is no doubt of our physical capacity and technical skill. But we must put them in the service of a common purpose.

After a decade of challenge and crises, we must strive to insure that our government will be united, that our people will have confidence, that our country will be strong, and that our freedoms will flourish. As we enter the year of a political campaign at home and an era of unprecedented challenge abroad, a spirit of unity and bipartisanship becomes our international, as well as national, duty. We cannot afford a year and a half of partisan warfare. Our foreign policy must be a common enterprise of all Americans, for what we do—or fail to do—will inevitably affect events for many years to come.

If the past two years of effort in the Middle East have lessened the dangers of war and set that part of the world on the road to peace—as I pray they have—it is the United States that has made the difference. It is the United States alone, among the world's nations, that Israel and its Arab neighbors were prepared to trust. It has been deeply moving for me to observe, after all the travails and self-doubts of the last decade, the confidence that others have in us. The nations of the Middle East have thus done us a service in reminding us of how in serving our international responsibility we also serve our own highest goals.

In the final analysis it is our own principles and hopes that define our obligation. America has always stood for something beyond our own material success: We have always believed—correctly—that we meant something to others. Our Founding Fathers spoke of the rights and hopes of all men. Our belief in the inalienable rights of man is no less compelling today—no less worthy of sacrifice—than it was two hundred years ago when a few dreamers came together in Philadelphia to proclaim history's only truly permanent revolution.

TWELVE

THE PERMANENT CHALLENGE OF PEACE: U.S. POLICY TOWARD THE SOVIET UNION

Address to the Commonwealth Club and the World Affairs Council of Northern California, San Francisco, February 3, 1976

AMERICA enters its third century and its forty-eighth Presidential election with unmatched physical strength, a sound foreign policy design, yet scarred by self-doubt. In the past decade and a half we have seen one President assassinated, another driven from office, and a third resign. We have lived through the agony of Vietnam and Watergate. We are still struggling to overcome the bitterness and division that have followed in their wake. We face no more urgent task than to restore our national unity and our national resolve.

For we, the strongest free nation, cannot afford the luxury of withdrawing into ourselves to heal our wounds. Too much depends upon us—peace or war, prosperity or depression, freedom or tyranny. Too much is at stake for America to paralyze itself tearing up the past, seeking sensational headlines in the present, or offering panaceas for the future. For our own well-being—American lives and American jobs—will be affected if we permit our domestic disunity and turmoil to cause us to falter in meeting our international responsibilities.

And so it is imperative that the national debate in this election year—the greatest demonstration of how free people govern themselves—strengthen, not undermine, our confidence and our capacity to carry out an effective national policy. It is essential that we quickly rebuild our national unity—the sense that we are all part of a shared enterprise.

It is in this spirit that I intend today to discuss America's relations with the world's other superpower—the Soviet Union. In recent months that relationship has become—as it should be —an important part of our national debate. I want to explain the Administration's view of the conditions that gave rise to the policy known as "détente," the goals we seek, and the relationship of our Soviet policy to the overall design of American diplomacy.

The United States is today confronted by one challenge unprecedented in its own history and another challenge without precedent in the history of the world. America finds itself, for the first time, permanently and irrevocably involved in international affairs. At the same time the catastrophic nature of nuclear war imposes upon us a necessity that transcends traditional concepts of diplomacy and balance of power—to shape a world order that finds stability in self-restraint and, ultimately, cooperation.

For the first century and a half of our history our peace and security were provided for us by two oceans, the shield of the British navy, and equilibrium among the European powers. The success of our democracy at home, and the absence of direct threat from abroad, nourished our sense of uniqueness and fostered the illusion that it was up to America to choose whether and when we would participate in the world.

Since de Tocqueville it has been a cliché that Americans, as a people, are slow to arouse, but that once aroused we are a tremendous and implacable force. Thus, even when we ventured forth in foreign affairs, we identified our exertion as a temporary disruption of our tranquility.

Our history, except for the Civil War, was without the tragedies and the sense of practical external limits that so colored the experience of almost every other people.

Our successes seemed to teach us that any problem could be solved—once and for all—by determined effort. We considered peace natural, stability normal, and foreign involvement appropriate only so long as needed to remove some temporary threat or disorder. We entered World War I as "the war to end wars," and to make the world "safe for democracy." We fought World War II until "unconditional surrender."

Even in the first twenty-five years after World War II—an era of great creativity and unprecedented American engagement in foreign affairs—we acted as if the world's security and economic development could be conclusively insured by the commitment of American resources, know-how, and effort. We were encouraged—even impelled—to act as we did by our unprecedented predominance in a world shattered by war and the collapse of the great colonial empires. We considered our deployment of troops in Europe and elsewhere to be temporary. We thought that the policy of containment would transform the Soviet Union and that a changed Soviet society would then evolve inexorably into a compatible member of a harmonious international community.

At the same time the central character of moral values in American life always made us acutely sensitive to the purity of means—and when we disposed of overwhelming power we had a great luxury of choice. Our moral certainty made compromise difficult; our preponderance often made it seem unnecessary.

Today, while we still have massive strength, we no longer enjoy meaningful nuclear supremacy. We remain the world's most productive and innovative economy, but we must now share leadership with Western Europe, Canada, and Japan;

we must deal with the newly wealthy and developing nations; and we must make new choices regarding our economic relations with the Communist countries. Our democratic principles are still far more valued by the world's millions than we realize, but we must also compete with new ideologies which assert progressive goals but pursue them by opposite methods.

Today, for the first time in our history, we face the stark reality that the challenge is unending; that there is no easy and surely no final answer; that there are no automatic solutions. We must learn to conduct foreign policy as other nations have had to conduct it for so many centuries—without escape and without respite, knowing that what is attainable falls short of the ideal, mindful of the necessities of self-preservation, conscious that the reach of our national purpose has its limits. This is a new experience for Americans. It prompts nostalgia for a simpler past. As before in our history it generates the search for scapegoats, holding specific policies responsible for objective conditions.

It is precisely because we no longer predominate but must pursue a long-term course that there is a premium today on our constancy and purposefulness. We cannot afford to swing recklessly between confrontation and abdication. We must not equate tough rhetoric with strong action, nor can we wish away tough realities with nostalgic hopes. We can no longer act as if we engage ourselves in foreign affairs only when we choose—or only to overcome specific problems—so that we can then shift our priorities back to our natural concern with ourselves. The reality is that there can be no security without our vigilance and no progress without our dedication.

It is in this context that U.S.-Soviet relations must be seen.

Contemporary Challenge of U.S.-Soviet Relations. The issue of how to deal with the Soviet Union has been a central feature of American policy for three decades. What is new today is the culmination of thirty years of postwar growth of Soviet industrial, technological, and military power. No American policy caused this; no American policy could have prevented it. But American policy can keep this power from being used to expand Soviet influence to our detriment; we have the capacity to enable allies and friends to live with a sense of security; we possess the assets to advance the process of building an international order of cooperation and progress.

We must do so, however, in unprecedented conditions. In previous periods rivalry between major powers has almost invariably led to war. In our time, when thermonuclear weapons threaten casualties in the hundreds of millions, such an outcome is unthinkable. We must manage a fundamental clash of ideologies and harness the rivalry of the nuclear superpowers, first into coexistence and then mold coexistence into a more positive and cooperative future.

In the period after World War II our nightmare was that the Soviet Union, after consolidating its occupation of Eastern Europe, might seek to spread its control to other contiguous areas in Europe and Asia. Our policies, therefore, sought to build alliances and positions of military strength from which we could contain and isolate the Soviet Union. In this manner the Soviet Union might be forced to settle for peace; transformations might occur within Soviet society that would curb expansionist tendencies and make the U.S.S.R., over time, into a more cooperative participant in the international system.

These policies served us and our allies well. Soviet expansion was checked. Behind our shield of security and with our assistance, our friends and allies in Western Europe restored their economies and rebuilt their democratic institutions.

Yet the hope that these policies would produce permanent stability, positive evolution of the Soviet system, and greater normality was only partially realized. In the immediate post-war period the aggressiveness of Soviet ideology in the Stalinist era obscured some of the real weaknesses of the Soviet state. Indeed as late as 1962 during the Cuban missile crisis, the United States enjoyed a five-to-one superiority in strategic missiles, a three-to-one superiority in strategic bombers, total naval superiority everywhere, and rough equality on the ground in Europe.

Gradually with the acquisition of nuclear technology and the transformation of the international system through de-colonization, the Soviet Union began to emerge as a first-class military power.

In strategic military terms the U.S.S.R. has achieved a broad equality with the United States, as was inevitable for a large nation whose rulers were prepared to impose great sacrifices on their people and to give military strength the absolute top priority in resources. With only half of our gross national product, Soviet military expenditures exceed those of the United States.

For the first time in history the Soviet Union can threaten distant places beyond the Eurasian land-mass—including the United States. With no part of the world outside the range of its military forces, the U.S.S.R. has begun to define its interests and objectives in global terms. Soviet diplomacy has thrust into the Middle East, Africa, and Asia. This evolution is now rooted in real power, rather than a rhetorical manifestation of a universalist doctrine, which in fact has very little validity or appeal.

Coping with the implications of this emerging superpower has been our central security problem for the last several years. This condition will not go away. And it will perhaps never be conclusively "solved." It will have to be faced by every Administration for the forseeable future.

Our policy must deal with the consequences. The emergence of ambitious new powers into an existing international structure is a recurrent phenomenon. Historically, the adjustment of an existing order to the arrival of one or more new actors almost invariably was accompanied by war—to impede the upstart, to remove or diminish some of the previously established actors, to test the balance of forces in a revised system. But in the nuclear era, when casualties in a general nuclear war will involve hundreds of millions in a matter of days, the use of force threatens utter catastrophe. It is our responsibility to contain Soviet power without global war, to avoid both abdication as well as unnecessary confrontation.

This can be done, but it requires a delicate and complex policy. We must strive for an equilibrium of power, but we must move beyond it to promote the habits of mutual restraint, coexistence, and, ultimately, cooperation. We must stabilize a new international order in a vastly dangerous environment, but our ultimate goal must be to transform ideological conflict into constructive participation in building a better world.

This is what is meant by the process called "détente"—not the hunger for relaxation of tension, not the striving for agreements at any price, not the mindless search for friendly atmosphere which some critics use as naive and dangerous caricatures.

The policies pursued by this Administration have been designed to prevent Soviet expansion but also to build a pattern of relations in which the Soviet Union will always confront penalties for aggression and also acquire growing incentives for restraint. These goals are well within our capacities. Soviet power is evolving with considerable unevenness. Soviet society is no longer totally cut off from contact with or the influences of the world around it nor is it without its own needs for outside relationships. It is the great industrial democraries, not the Soviet Union, that are the engine of the world economy and the most promising partners for the poorer nations.

The industrial democracies, if they face their challenges with confidence—if they do not mesmerize themselves with the illusion of simple solutions—possess vast strengths to contain Soviet power and to channel that power in constructive directions.

Our essential task is to recognize the need for a dual policy that simultaneously and with equal vigor resists expansionist drives and seeks to shape a more constructive relationship. We must prevent the Soviet Union from translating its growing strength into global or regional preponderance. But we must do so without escalating every cisis into a massive confrontation. In recent years the United States has firmly resisted attempts by the Soviet Union to establish a naval base in Cuba, to impede the access routes to Berlin, to exploit the explosive situation in the Middle East. Recently we have sought to halt blatant intervention in Angola—until prevented from doing so by congressional action.

At the same time we have an historic obligation to mankind to engage the Soviet Union in settlements of concrete problems and to push back the shadow of nuclear catastrophe. At the very least we owe it to our people to demonstrate that its Government has missed no opportunity to achieve constructive solutions and that crises which occur were unavoidable. For whatever the rhetoric, Americans will not support confrontations they consider contrived. This is why the United States has set forth principles of responsible relations in the nuclear age: respect for the interests of all, restraint in the uses of power, and abstention from efforts to exploit instability or local conflicts for unilateral advantage. The United States has sought to give life to these principles in major negotiations on arms control, the prevention of accidental war, and in the settlement of political issues such as Berlin. And we have begun to construct a network of cooperative agreements in a variety of functional areas—economic, scientific, medical, environmental, and others—which promise concrete benefits if political conditions permit their full implementation and further development. It has been our belief that, with patience, a pattern of restraints and a network of vested interests can develop which will give coexistence a more hopeful dimension and make both sides conscious of what they would stand to lose by reverting to the politics of pressure, confrontation, and crisis.

This policy reflects the deepest aspirations of the American people.

In the early 1970s, when current U.S.-Soviet relations were shaped, our Nation had already passed through traumatic events and was engaged in an anguishing war. There were riots in the streets and on the campuses demanding rapid progress toward peace. Every new defense program was challenged—including the ABM [antiballistic missile] which was approved by only one vote, the development of multiple warheads, the Trident submarine, and the B-1 bomber. Successive Congresses passed resolutions urging the Administration to reorder our national priorities away from defense. We were continually attacked for not making concessions in the strategic arms limitation talks [SALT]. The Congress and many interest groups pressed continually for the opening up of East-West trade and agitated against the Administration's approach of linking progress in economic relations with prior progress in political relations. Throughout the course of 1970 and 1971 we were involved in a series of crises with the Soviet Union and were often accused of provocation or bellicosity in the process.

Thus, only a few short years ago, the pressures in this country and from our allies were overwhelmingly to move rapidly toward better relations with Moscow. We resisted these pressures then, just as we now refuse to let ourselves be stampeded in the opposite direction. In the Administration's view the country needs a balanced policy, combining firmness and conciliation, strong defense and arms control, political principles and economic incentives. And it must be a policy for the long term, that the American people can sustain, offering promise of a constructive future.

It is, therefore, ironic that our national debate seems now in many respects to have come full circle. The conditions in which détente originated are largely forgotten. Those who pressed for concessions and unilateral restraint toward Moscow now accuse the Government of being too conciliatory. Those who complain about our failure to respond with sufficient vigor to Soviet moves are often the very ones who incessantly seek to remove this country's leverage for influence or action—through restrictions on trade and credit, through weakening our intelligence capabilities, through preventing aid to friends who seek to resist Soviet aggression.

The restrictions on trade and credit are a case in point. The human rights issue is a matter of deep and legitimate concern to all Americans. But the congressional attempt to link it openly with economic relations, without subtlety or understanding of Soviet politics, both deprived us of economic levers and sharply reduced Soviet emigration. Other industrial countries have stepped in to provide credits and technology, with less concern for the objective of inducing political restraint which we had envisaged.

So let us understand the scope and limits of a realistic policy:

· We cannot prevent the growth of Soviet power, but we can prevent its use for unilateral advantage and political expansion.

· We cannot prevent a build-up of Soviet forces, but we

have the capacity—together with our allies—to maintain an equilibrium. We cannot neglect this task and then blame the Soviet Union if the military balance shifts against us.

· We have the diplomatic, economic, and military capacity to resist expansionism, but we cannot engage in a rhetoric of confrontation while depriving ourselves of the means to confront.

· We must accept that sovereign states, especially of roughly equal power, cannot impose unacceptable conditions on each other and must proceed by compromise.

· We must live with the reality of the nuclear threat, but we have it in our power to build a new relationship that transcends the nuclear peril.

So let us end the defeatist rhetoric that implies that Soviet policy is masterful, purposeful, and overwhelming while American policy is bumbling, uncertain, and weak. Let us stop pretending that somehow tough rhetoric and contrived confrontations show confidence in America. The opposite is true. Those who are prepared to base their policy on reality, those who assert that the American people will support a complex policy of firmness and conciliation and that this policy will succeed, show a real faith in our capacities and our future. We have a design and the material assets to deal with the Soviet Union. We will succeed if we move forward as a united people.

Against this background let me discuss two current issues that illustrate the two strands of policy that we are concurrently pursuing:

· the strategic arms limitation talks in which we are seeking to shape a more positive future, and

· the Angolan situation, where we are attempting to curb Soviet expansionism.

Strategic Arms Limitation. There is one central fact that

distinguishes our era from all previous periods—the existence of enormously destructive weapons that can span unlimited distances almost instantaneously. No part of the globe is beyond reach. No part of the globe would be spared the effects of a general nuclear exchange.

For centuries it was axiomatic that increases in military power could be translated into almost immediate political advantage. It is now clear that new increments of strategic weaponry do not automatically lead to either political or military gains. Yet in the nature of things, if one side expands its strategic arsenal, the other side will inevitably match it. The race is maintained partly because a perceived inequality is considered by each side as politically unacceptable even though it has become difficult to define precisely what purely military purpose is served.

We thus face a paradox: At current and foreseeable levels of nuclear arms, it becomes increasingly dangerous to invoke them. In no crisis since 1962 have the strategic weapons of the two sides determined the outcome. Today these arsenals increasingly find their purpose primarily in matching and deterring the forces of the opponent. For under virtually no foreseeable circumstance could the United States—or the Soviet Union—avoid 100 million dead in a nuclear exchange. Yet the race goes on because of the difficulty of finding a way to get off the treadmill.

To be sure, there exist scenarios in planning papers which seek to demonstrate how one side could use its strategic forces and how in some presumed circumstance it would prevail. But these confuse what a technician can calculate with what a responsible statesman can decide. They are invariably based on assumptions such as that one side would permit its missile silos to be destroyed without launching its missiles before they are actually hit—on which no aggressor would rely where forces such as those possessed by either the United States or the U.S.S.R. now and in the years ahead are involved.

This condition imposes a unique and heavy responsibility on the leaders of the two nuclear superpowers. Sustaining the nuclear competition requires endless invocations of theoretical scenarios of imminent or eventual nuclear attack. The attempt to hedge against all conceivable contingencies—no matter how fanciful—fuels political tensions and could well lead to a self-fulfilling prophecy. The fixation on potential strategic arms imbalances that is inherent in an unrestrained arms race diverts resources in strategically unproductive areas—particularly away from forces for local defense, where shortfalls and imbalances could indeed be turned rapidly to our disadvantage. If no restraint is developed the competition in strategic arms can have profound consequences for the future of international relations, and indeed of civilization.

The United States, therefore, has sought and achieved, since 1963, a series of arms control agreements which build some restraint into nuclear rivalry. There was a significant breakthrough to limit strategic weapons in 1972. If the 1974 Vladivostok accord leads to a new agreement, an even more important advance will have been made.

Yet at this critical juncture, the American people are subjected to an avalanche of charges that SALT is a surrender of American interests. There are assertions that the United States is falling behind in the strategic competition and that SALT has contributed to it. There are unsupportable charges that the Soviets have systematically violated the SALT agreements.

None of this is accurate.

Where are the facts?

First of all, American policy decisions in the 1960s set the level of our strategic forces for the 1970s. We then had the choice between continuing the deployment of large, heavy throwweight missiles like the Titan or Atlas, or undertaking development and deployment of large numbers of smaller, more flexible ICBM's [intercontinental ballistic missiles], or combinations of both types. The Administration then in office chose to rely on an arsenal of 1,000 small, sophisticated, and highly accurate ICBM's and 656 submarine-launched missiles on 41 boats, along with heavy bombers; we deployed them rapidly and then stopped our buildup of launchers unilaterally in the 1960s when the programs were complete. Only 54 of the heavy Titans were retained and still remain in the force.

The Soviets made the opposite decision; they chose larger, heavier missiles; they continued to build up their forces through the 1906s and 1970s; they passed our numerical levels by 1969–70 and continued to add an average of 200 missiles a year until stopped by the first SALT agreement.

Thus, as a consequence of decisions made a decade ago by both sides, Soviet missiles are superior in throwweight while ours are superior in reliability, accuracy, diversity, and sophistication, and we possess larger numbers of warheads. In 1972 when the SALT agreement was signed, the Soviet Union was still building at the rate of 90 land-based and 120 sea-based launchers a year, while we were building none, as a result of our own repeatedly reaffirmed unilateral decisions of a decade previously. Since new American programs to redress the balance had only recently been ordered, there was no way to reduce the numerical gap before the late 1970s, when more modern sea-based missiles and bombers were scheduled to become operational.

The interim SALT agreement of 1972 froze overall numbers of launchers on both sides for five years—thereby limiting the momentum of Soviet programs without affecting any of ours. It stopped the Soviet build-up of heavy missile launchers. It forced the Soviets to agree to dismantle 210 older land-based missiles to reach permitted ceilings on missile-carrying sub-marines. The agreed-upon silo limitations permitted us to increase the throwweight of our own missiles, if we decided on this avenue of improving our strategic forces. We have so far chosen not to do so, although, through research and development, we retain the option. By any measure the SALT agreements prevented the then-evolving gap in numbers from widening, while enabling us to retain our advantage in other categories and easing the problem of redressing the balance when new programs became operational. What no negotiation could do is reverse by diplomacy the results of our own long-standing decisions with respect to weapons design and deployment.

Moreover the SALT agreements ended for an indefinite period the prospect of a dangerous and uncertain competition in antiballistic missile defense—a competition that promised no strategic advantage but potentially serious instabilities and the expenditure of vast sums of money.

The first SALT agreements were, therefore, without question in the American national interest. In the five-year respite gained by the 1972 interim agreement, it was our intention to negotiate a long-term pact on offensive weapons that would firmly fix both sides at an equal level once our new programs became operational. This is precisely what President Ford achieved at Vladivostok in November 1974.

In this accord in principle, both sides agreed on a ceiling of 2,400 strategic weapons covering strategic systems and heavy bombers—but not counting any of our forward-based aircraft in Europe or our allies' strategic weapons, many of which can reach Soviet soil. The ceiling of 2,400 is lower than the level the Soviet Union already has reached; it would require the dismantling of many Soviet weapons while the planned levels and composition of our forces would not need to be reduced or changed. An equal ceiling of 1,320 was placed on numbers of strategic weapons with multiple warheads. Soviet heavy missile launchers will remain frozen. These limits would cap the strategic competition in numbers for a ten-year period, yet preserve all the programs we need to assure deterrence and strategic sufficiency.

Obviously no single agreement can solve every problem. This is not a question of loopholes but of evolving technology, with respect to which we intend to remain vigilant. We will negotiate carefully to make certain that the national interest and national security are protected. But if we succeed in turning the Vladivostok accord into a ten-year agreement, we will have crossed the threshold between total, unrestrained competition and the difficult but promising beginning of long-term strategic equilibrium at lower levels of forces. The United States and the Soviet Union have already agreed to turn to reductions in strategic forces in the next phase of the negotiations starting in 1977.

One would have thought that these accomplishments would speak for themselves. Instead they have triggered a flood of charges which mislead the American people and our friends, give a wrong impression of irresoluteness to our adversaries, and complicate the prospects for a new agreement that is in the overriding national interest.

No charge is more irresponsible and potentially more dangerous than the allegation that the United States has knowingly tolerated violations of the first SALT agreements.

What are the facts?

A Standing Consultative Commission was created by the agreements of 1972 precisely to consider disputes or ambiguities in implementation. Such incidents were almost certain to arise in a first, quite limited agreement between longstanding adversaries possessing weapons systems of great complexity whose growth is verified not by some neutral policing mechanism but by each side's own intelligence systems. Every questionable activity that has arisen has been systematically analyzed by this Government and considered by the President and his advisers. Whenever any question remained, it was then promptly raised with the Soviets. All instructions to the American representative on the Consultative Commission reflected the unanimous views of all U.S. agencies concerned and the data and assessment produced jointly by them. No one had a bias in favor of absolving the Soviets—an inherently malicious charge. No one prevented all questionable or suspicious activities from being raised with the Soviets. And not all the questioned activities were on the Soviet side.

All of these issues have been, and will continue to be, seriously handled and dealt with through a process that has proved effective. Yet irresponsible charges continue to lump together incidents that have been explained or are still being considered with wild allegations that have no foundation. They sometimes put forward inaccurate figures and data which often can be refuted only by divulging sensitive intelligence information. Yet with all the recent flurry of allegations, no recommendations are made of what countermeasures we should take or how to assess the significance of any given alleged violation.

In what way do the alleged violations affect the strategic equation? In what manner, if any, have we been foreclosed from protecting ourselves? Would those who inaccurately allege violations simply throw over all the agreements regardless of the benefits they provide the United States? Would they halt the negotiation of further agreements? What purpose is served by leading our public and the Soviet Union to believe —totally incorrectly—that the United States is blind to violations or that its Government deliberately deceives its people? Can anyone seriously believe that this Administration which has strenuously resisted Communist advances in every part of the world—and is often strongly criticized for it—would ignore Soviet violations of a formal agreement?

I can assure you that this Administration will not tolerate violations. It will continue to monitor Soviet compliance meticulously. It will pursue energetically all ambiguities or signs of noncompliance. But it will not be driven by demagoguery to make false or hasty judgments. No department or agency charged with responsibility for this problem holds the view that any violations have occurred.

As we assess SALT we must face squarely one question: What is the alternative to the agreements we have and seek? If the SALT process falters, we must consider what new or additional strategic programs we would undertake, their likely cost, and above all, their strategic purpose. An accelerated strategic build-up over the next five years could cost as much as an additional $20 billion. Failing a satisfactory agreement, this will surely be the path we must travel. It would be a tragically missed opportunity. For, in the process of such a build-up, and the atmosphere it would engender, it would be difficult to return to serious negotiations for some time. Tensions are likely to increase; a new, higher baseline will emerge from which future negotiations would eventually have to begin. And in the end neither side will have gained a strategic advantage. At the least they will have wasted resources. At worst they will have increased the risks of nuclear war.

Of course the Soviet Union must ponder these alternatives as well. Their sense of responsibility must equal ours if there is to be an equitable and durable agreement based on strict reciprocity. We consider a SALT agreement important, but we will take no chances with our national security.

Let me sum up:

· We will never stand for the violation of a solemn treaty or agreement, and we will remain alert.

· We will never tolerate a shift in the strategic balance against us—by violations of agreements, by unsatisfactory agreements, or by neglect of our own programs; we will spend what is necessary to maintain strategic sufficiency.

· The President is determined to pursue the effort to negotiate a saner strategic balance on equitable terms—because it is in our interest, and because we have an obligation to our own people and to world peace.

The Soviet Union and Angola. As the United States strives to shape a more hopeful world, it can never forget that global stability and security rest upon an equilibrium between the great powers. If the Soviet Union is permitted to exploit opportunities arising out of local conflicts by military means, the hopes we have for progress toward a more peaceful international order will ultimately be undermined.

This is why the Soviet Union's massive and unprecedented intervention in the internal affairs of Africa with nearly $200 million of military equipment, its advisers, and its transport of the large expeditionary force of eleven thousand Cuban combat troops must be a matter of urgent concern.

Angola represents the first time that the Soviets have moved militarily at long distance to impose a regime of their choice. It is the first time that the United States has failed to respond to Soviet military moves outside the immediate Soviet orbit. And it is the first time that Congress has halted national action in the middle of a crisis.

When one great power tips the balance of forces decisively in a local conflict through its military intervention—and meets no resistance—an ominous precedent is set, of grave consequence even if the intervention occurs in a seemingly remote area. Such a precedent cannot be tolerated if a lasting easing of tensions is to be achieved. And if the pattern is not broken now, we will face harder choices and higher costs in the future.

The United States seeks no unilateral goals in Angola: We have proposed a cease-fire; withdrawal of all outside forces—Soviet, Cuban, and South African; cessation of foreign military involvement, including the supply of equipment; and negotiations among all three Angolan factions. This approach has the support of half the nations of Africa.

Last summer and fall, to halt a dangerously escalating situation, the United States provided financial support through African friends to those in Angola—the large majority—who sought to resist Soviet and Cuban domination. Using this as leverage we undertook an active diplomacy to promote an African solution to an African problem. We acted quietly to avoid provoking a major crisis and raising issues of prestige.

At first it was feared that the Soviet-backed faction, because of massive Soviet aid and Cuban mercenaries, would dominate totally by Independence Day, November 11. Our assistance prevented that. African determination to oppose Soviet and Cuban intervention became more and more evident. On December 9 the President warned Moscow of the consequences of continued meddling and offered to cooperate in encouraging a peaceful outcome that removed foreign influence. The Soviet Union appeared to have second thoughts. It halted its airlift from December 9 until December 24.

At that point the impact of our domestic debate overwhelmed the possibilities of diplomacy. It was demanded that we explain publicly why our effort was important—and then our effort was cut off. After the Senate vote to block further aid to Angola, Cuba more than doubled its forces and Soviet military aid was resumed on a large scale. The cooperativeness of Soviet diplomacy declined. Since then the situation has continued to deteriorate.

As our public discussion continues, certain facts must be understood. The analogy with Vietnam is totally false; this Nation must have the maturity to make elementary distinctions. The President has pledged that no American troops or advisers would be sent to Angola, and we were prepared to accept legislative restrictions to that effect, in addition to the War Powers Act which already exists. What was involved was modest assistance to stabilize the local balance of forces and make possible a rapid political settlement in cooperation with African countries.

It is charged that the Administration acted covertly, without public acknowledgement. That is correct, for our purpose was to avoid an escalated confrontation that would make it more difficult for the Soviets to back down, as well as to give the greatest possible scope for an African solution. Angola was a case where diplomacy without leverage was likely to be impotent, yet direct military confrontation would involve needless risks. This is precisely one of those grey areas where unpublicized methods would enable us to influence events short of direct conflict.

And we complied totally with Congress' new standard of executive-legislative consultation on secret activities. Beginning in July, and through December, we discussed the Angolan situation and what we were doing about it with more than two dozen Senators, 150 Congressmen, and over 100 staff members of both Houses. Eight congressional committees were briefed on twenty-four separate occasions. We sought in these briefings to determine the wishes of Congress, and there was little sign of active opposition to our carefully limited operations.

It is said that the Russians will inevitably be eased out by the Africans themselves over a period of time. That may or may not prove true. But such an argument, when carried to its logical conclusion, implies that we can abandon the world to interventionist forces and hope for the best. And reliance on history is of little solace to those under attack, whose future is being decided now. The degree of Soviet and Cuban intervention is unprecedented; they will have effectively determined the outcome. There is no evidence to support the claim that they will be quickly removed or that other nations may not draw damaging conclusions dangerous to our long-term interests.

It is maintained that we should meet the Soviet threat in Angola through escalated methods of pressure such as altering our position on SALT or grain sales. But these arrangements benefit us as well as the Soviet Union and are part of the long-term strategy for dealing with the Soviet Union. History has proved time and again that expansion can be checked only when there is a local balance of forces; indirect means can succeed only if rapid local victories are foreclosed. As the President has pointed out, the Soviet Union has survived for nearly sixty years without American grain; it could do so now. Cutting off grain would still lose Angola. We would duplicate the experience of the Trade Act, which interrupted the trade relationship with the U.S.S.R. to insure emigration—and ended up with neither.

Let us not bemuse ourselves with facile slogans about not becoming the world's policeman. We have no desire to play such a role. But it can never be in our interest to let the Soviet Union act as the world's policeman. There are many crises in the world where the United States cannot and should not intervene. But here we face a blatant Soviet and Cuban challenge, which could have been overcome if we had been allowed to act prudently with limited means at the early stage. By forcing this out onto center stage, our divisions simultaneously escalated the significance of the crisis and guaranteed our impotence.

To claim that Angola is not an important country, or that the United States has no important interests there, begs the principal question. If the United States is seen to waver in the face of massive Soviet and Cuban intervention, what will be the perception of leaders around the world as they make decisions concerning their future security? And what conclusions will an unopposed superpower draw when the next opportunity for intervention beckons?

Where are we now?

The Government has a duty to make clear in the Soviet Union and Cuba that Angola sets no precedent, that this type of action will not be tolerated again. It must reassure adjacent countries they will not be left exposed to attack or pressure from the new Soviet-Cuban foothold. Congress and the executive must come together on this proposition—in the national interest and in the interest of world peace.

The Administration will continue to make its case however unpopular it may be temporarily. Let no nation believe that Americans will long remain indifferent to the dispatch of expeditionary forces and vast supplies of arms to impose minority governments—especially when that expeditionary force comes from a nation in the Western Hemisphere.

National Strength and the Debate at Home. We live in a world without simple answers. We hold our values too dear to relinquish defending them; we hold human life too dear to cease the quest for a secure peace. The first requirement of stability is to maintain our defenses and the balance of power. But the highest aim of policy in the nuclear age must be to create out of the sterile equilibrium of force a more positive relationship of peace.

America has the material assets to do the job. Our military might is unmatched. Our economic and technological strength dwarfs any other. Our democratic heritage is envied by hundreds of millions around the world.

Our problems, therefore, are of our own making—self-doubt, division, irresolution. We must once again become a confident, united, and determined people.

Foreign countries must be able to deal with America as an entity, not as a complex of divided institutions. If our divisions paralyze our international efforts, it is America as a whole that will suffer. We have no more urgent task than restoring the partnership between the American people, the Congress, and the Executive. A new partnership can enable the President of the United States, in his constitutionally-determined role, to address the world with the central authority of the spokesman of a united and purposeful America.

Debate is the essence of democracy. But restraint is the cement of national cohesion. It is time to end the self-torment and obsession with our guilt which have threatened to paralyze us for too many years. It is time to stop dismantling our national institutions and undermining our national confidence.

Let us learn—even in an election year—the self-discipline to shape our domestic debates into a positive, not a destructive, process.

One of the forgotten truths of our history is that our Founding Fathers were men of great sophistication in foreign affairs. They understood the balance of power; they made use of the divisions of Europe for the advantage of our own Revolution. They understood the need for a strong executive to conduct the Nation's diplomacy. They grasped that America required economic, political, and moral links with other nations. They saw that our ideals were universal and they understood and welcomed the impact of the American experiment on the destines of all mankind.

In our age whose challenges are without precedent, we need once again the wisdom of our Founding Fathers. Our ideals must give us strength—rather than serve as an excuse for abdication. The American people want an effective foreign policy. They want America to continue to help shape the international order of the coming generation according to our ideals. We have done great things as a united people. We have it in our power to make our third century a time of vibrancy and hope and greatness.

THIRTEEN

THE AMERICAS IN A
CHANGING WORLD

Address to the U.S.-Venezuelan Symposium II,
Macuto (Caracas), Venezuela,
February 17, 1976

THE Western Hemisphere has for centuries symbolized man's readiness to grasp his own destiny. When I placed a wreath at the tomb of Simon Bolivar yesterday, I recalled the depth of his faith and wonder at the future of the Americas. Today, more than a century later, the promise of our hemisphere is more alive than ever—and more important to each of our countries and to the world.

Today I want to discuss with you the challenges that history has posed to our hemispheric friendship, the efforts we have made in the recent period to address these challenges, and the compelling responsibility we face today and tomorrow.

Our Special Relationship. I have come to this continent because the United States believes that Latin America has a special place in our foreign policy.

This belief is the product of history. We won our national independence together in the same era. We confronted the similar challenges of pioneer peoples developing the resources of bountiful unexplored continents. We shaped democratic institutions and spurred economic growth, conscious that we benefited greatly from our relationship with each other. We have long shared a common interest in shielding our hemisphere from the intrusion of others. We led the world in building international organizations to serve our cooperative endeavors for both collective security and economic progress.

The United States has always felt with Latin America a special intimacy, a special bond of collaboration, even in the periods of our isolation from world affairs. Even now, when our countries are major participants in world affairs, when our perceptions of contemporary issues are not always identical, there remains a particular warmth in the personal relationships among our leaders and a special readiness to consider the views of our neighbors. On many issues of United States policy—economic, political, or security—the American people and Congress give special consideration to our hemispheric ties.

The problem we face today is that history—and indeed the very growth and success we have all achieved—have complicated our relationship. What used to be a simple perception of hemispheric uniqueness, and a self-contained exclusive relationship, has become enmeshed in the wider concerns we all now have in the rest of the world.

· The United States is conscious of a global responsibility to maintain the world balance of power, to help resolve the age-old political conflicts that undermine peace, and to help shape a new international order encompassing the interests and aspirations of the 150 nations that now comprise our planet. And so our vision now reaches beyond the Western Hemisphere. We have major alliances with the Atlantic community and Japan, as well as this hemisphere; we have growing ties of friendship with many nations. In a nuclear age we have an inescapable responsibility to manage and stabilize our relations with the major Communist powers and to try to build a safe and more constructive future. The problem of peace in this generation means for us, the United States, a

permanent involvement in world affairs in all their dimensions
—maintaining security, promoting a healthy trade and monetary system and economic development, and creating a stable
and just and universal system of political relations.

· At the same time Latin American nations have grown in
power and influence and become major forces in their own
right on the world scene. This is one of the most striking
events of this era. Your economies are among the most advanced of the developing world. But your role is not a product of economic strength alone; its roots are deeper—your
traditions of personal and national dignity, concern for legal
principle, and your history of peace. Your sense of regional
identity has become more important—to you—and to the
world. We accept and respect these developments, and the new
organizations like SELTA [Latin American Economic System],
which now speak to your own collective interests. We trust
that they will not be used for confrontation; for that could
complicate our relations and hinder solutions to problems. We
are confident that the increased sense of Latin American
identity, and the institutions which serve it, can be a constructive and vital force for cooperation on a wider basis. This
will be our attitude toward these institutions.

—The countries of Latin America have done more than
grow internally and strengthen their regional associations.
They have established new ties outside the hemisphere—trade
relations with the European Community and Japan and a
growing sense of solidarity with developing nations in Africa
and Asia. Such global involvement is inevitable; inevitably
also, it creates new and conflicting pressures on more traditional friendships.

· The challenge of economic development has become a
worldwide concern and is being addressed on a global, and
not simply hemispheric, basis. Venezuela is now cochairman

of the Conference on International Economic Cooperation and has discharged this responsibility with great wisdom. Similarly the energies of the United States are increasingly focused on international organizations and issues of global scope. We have made major and comprehensive proposals to the U.N. General Assembly Special Session, the World Food Conference, and the Conference on International Economic Cooperation. Recent events have taught us all that global prosperity is indivisible; no nation can prosper alone.

· Finally the United States continues in this era to feel a special concern for its hemispheric relations. Our profound conviction is that if we cannot help to solve the burning issues of peace and progress with those with whom we have such longstanding ties of sentiment and experience of collaboration, we have little hope of helping to solve them elsewhere.

To put it positively we feel strongly that our cooperation as equals in this hemisphere can be a model for cooperation in the world arena. The challenge we face is that we must reconcile these distinct but intersecting dimensions of concern. We must define anew the nature and purposes of our hemispheric condition. We must understand its meaning and its promise. We must adapt it to our new global condition. We must summon it, develop it, and use it for our common objectives.

The United States values its bilateral ties with your countries, without any intention of pursuing them in order to break up your regional solidarity. We want to preserve our hemispheric ties and adapt them to the moral imperatives of this era, without hegemony, free of complexes, aimed at a better future.

All the nations of the hemisphere are mature countries. The variety of intersecting relationships and concerns reflects the vitality of our nations and the increasingly important roles we play in the world. We in the Americas are granted by history a unique opportunity to help fashion what your Foreign Minister has called a "new equilibrium" among all nations.

Dialogue and Progress. The experience of our recent past has much to teach us. During the early 1960s the Alliance for Progress stimulated great expectations of rapid development. The enthusiasm with which our countries embraced the Alliance Charter clearly exceeded our collective perserverance and understated the magnitude of the challenge. But great human and financial resources were mobilized; now institutions were created that remain basic instruments for cooperation. And ultimately the Alliance left an even greater moral imprint. By the end of the 1960s internal development and social change had become an imperative for all governments in Latin America, regardless of political coloration. The United States is proud of its contribution.

In this decade this hemisphere has been swept up in the tides of the global economy that now have an increasing significance to our national plans and expectations.

At Viña del Mar [Chile] in 1969, the nations of Latin America staked out a new agenda of issues reflecting what we have since come to call interdependence—the conditions of world trade, multinational corporations, and technology transfer—as well as more traditional issues such as economic assistance. In the spirit of inter-American cooperation, the United States attempted to respond. My Government endorsed, and worked for, measures to improve Latin America's access to our markets and those of other industrial countries, to improve the flow of private capital, to reform the inter-American system, and to insure consideration for Latin American concerns in international forums.

Less than a month after becoming Secretary of State in 1973 [October 5], I called for a new dialogue between Latin

America and the United States to reinvigorate our relations by addressing together the new challenges of an interdependent world. I believed that in the past the United States had too often sought to decide unilaterally what should be done about inter-American relations. I felt that Latin America must have a stake in our policies if those policies were to be successful. I said that we were ready to listen to all Latin American concerns in any forum.

Latin America chose to conduct the dialogue on a strictly multilateral basis, presenting common positions to the United States. First in Bogotá, then in Mexico City, the agenda of issues that had been set out in Viña del Mar was updated to account for changed circumstances and new concerns.

At Tlatelolco [Mexico], and again in Washington, I joined my fellow Foreign Ministers in informal meetings, supplementing our regular encounters in the OAS [Organization of American States] and United Nations. A thorough and heartening dialogue took place. For the next twelve months, United States and Latin American representatives met in a continuous series of political and technical discussions. These meetings were interrupted almost precisely a year ago, in reaction to certain provisions of the United States Trade Act of 1974— the very act that implemented the system of generalized preferences first proposed in Viña del Mar.

All of us have something to learn from this experience. First, we can now see that the new dialogue, as it was conducted, only partially met the psychological requirements of our modern relationship.

The United States was prepared to work with the other nations of the hemisphere to improve and perfect the undeniable community that has existed under the name of the inter-American system for almost a century. Yet the explicitness of our approach to the concept of community led many in Latin

America to think that the United States wanted to maintain or create a relationship of hegemony. This misunderstanding obscured the reality that the hemisphere was in transition, between dependence and interdependence, between consolidation and political growth, and that the old community based on exclusivity was being transformed into a more open community based on mutual interests and problem solving.

The United States, perhaps underestimating the psychological weight of history, had conceived a dialogue as a means of adjusting its policies through compromises arising from a common search for solutions with Latin America.

The Latin American nations still seemed to think that the United States, with its great strengths and responsibilities, could act unilaterally to resolve all issues, that any compromise was surrender, that Latin America should propose and the United States should respond. The United States, on the other hand, looked upon dialogue as a prolonged process of give-and-take, in which progress would come incrementally, as our representatives analyzed the problems and negotiated solutions.

Latin America demanded quick results—each meeting became a deadline by which time the United States had to show "results" or be judged lacking. But as economic difficulties beset us all in a period of world recession, it became obvious that if Latin American aspirations were expressed to the people of the United States in terms of categorical and propagandistic demands, they could not elicit a sufficiently positive response.

Both sides oversimplified the nature of the problem: The Latin American nations did not always perceive that the issues were among the most difficult that the international community has faced, because they go to the heart of the structure and interaction of entire societies. The United States did not sufficiently take into account that Latin America had experienced years of frustration in which lofty promises by the United States had been undone by the gradualism of the American political system, which responds less to abstract commitments than to concrete problems. Hence the charge of neglect on one side and the occasional feeling on the other side of being beseiged with demands.

But if the new dialogue has not yet yielded results, it nevertheless expresses a constructive mode of dealing with our problems and realizing the aspirations of the hemisphere. The United States is prepared to make a major effort to invigorate our hemispheric ties. My trip here underlines that purpose.

We have learned something basic about the hemisphere itself. In the past both the United States and Latin America have acted as if the problems of the hemisphere could be solved exclusively within the hemisphere. Today the Americas—North and South—recognize that they require a global as well as a regional vision if they are to resolve their problems. For the United States a homogeneous policy toward an entity called "Latin America" presents new problems, in terms both of global concerns and of the real diversity of Latin America. Nor can the burden of adjustment to a new hemispheric equilibrium be borne wholly by the United States. We are prepared to make a major contribution, and we are willing to cooperate fully with Latin American regional institutions that come into being to this end.

But both sides need a new approach. The United States is prepared to give more systematic consideration to Latin America's quest for regional identity. On the other hand Latin America must overcome its own apprehensions about our policies. In the past, whenever we emphasized the regional aspects of our relationships, we have been accused of forcing problems into an inter-American system which we dominated;

when we emphasized the bilateral mode, we were accused of a policy of divide and rule. Each side must understand the problems and purposes of the other.

We thus all know our challenge. We must now turn it into our opportunity. As far as the United States is concerned, we are prepared to make a major effort to build upon our historic ties a cooperative effort to construct a better future.

Interdependence and Our Common Future. Where do we go from here? What is the answer? Wherein lies the purpose of our relationship in the modern era?

Our starting point must be to recognize that an era of interdependence makes collaborative endeavor more, not less, important to any country that wishes to preserve control over its own national destiny.

We in this hemisphere won our glory in fighting for national independence and defending it in the face of foreign threats; we have built societies embodying the tradition of democracy; we have dedicated our human energies to the development of our natural resources, with impressive results.

Yet even as we celebrate our birth as nations and our centuries of achievement, we encounter a new challenge to our independence. It comes not from foreign armies but from gaps and strains revealed within the very international economic system that each of our nations, in its own way, has done much to create.

Since the Enlightenment, which produced the faith in reason and progress that inspired our revolutions, we have all believed that the growth of a global economy would nurture a world community bringing universal advancement. Yet now we find that the international system of production—which still has the potential to provide material progress for all— has become subject to uncertainties and inefficiencies and international conflicts.

Nowhere is this challenge more vivid than in Latin America. With the higher stage of development that your economies have reached has come the awareness of greater vulnerability to fluctuations in export earnings, to increases in the costs of imports, and to the ebb and flow of private capital. Yet your more complex and more open economies can also respond more vigorously to, and profit more readily from, positive trends in the world economic system.

Interdependence for the Americas is, therefore, a positive force and an opportunity. We must manage it, harness it, and develop it for our common benefit.

Our economic dilemmas give rise, in our times, to political imperatives. Rapidly changing external events affect all our peoples profoundly—their livelihoods, their material standards, their hopes for the future, and—most fundamentally—their confidence that our systems of government can successfully encounter the challenges before us. And the requirement for action is political will.

Our societies derive their strength from the consent and dedication of our peoples. Can our democratic system cope with the strains of social change and the frustrations of what is inevitably a long historical process? Can nations find the wisest path in an era when our problems are too vast to be solved by any nation acting alone? Will we succumb to the temptation of unilateral actions, advantageous in their appearance but not their reality? Can we reconcile our diversity and the imperative of our collaboration?

I believe we have every cause for optimism. The requirements of interdependence make patent the genius of our special hemispheric traditions, values, and our institutions. Pluralism and respect for the rights of others are indispensable to the harmony of the international order. For to seek to impose radical changes without the consent of all those who would be affected is to ignore political reality. Equally, to deny a voice to any who are members of the international community is to insure that even positive achievement will ultimately be rejected.

Therefore the traditions of this hemisphere—democracy, justice, human and national dignity, and free cooperation—are precisely the qualities needed in the era of global interdependence. National unity without freedom is sterile; technological progress without social justice is corrupt; nationalism without a consciousness of the human community is a negative force.

Therefore our permanent quest for progress in this hemisphere must take into account global as well as regional realities. It must reflect the differing interests of each country. And our global efforts respectively must draw on the vitality of our own relationships as a source of dynamism, strength, and inspiration.

The United States has attempted to make a constructive contribution in this context.

Last September in New York, addressing the Latin American Foreign Ministers attending the U.N. General Assembly, I pointed out that several of our initiatives before the Seventh Special Session has been designed to be particularly relevant to Latin American concerns. And I pledged that in the necessary negotiations in other forums, and in all aspects of our relations, we would remember that each Latin American country was different, and we would be responsive to the distinctive national interests of our friends in the hemisphere.

My New York comments raised contradictory speculations. The explicit introduction of global considerations into our Latin American policy was variously interpreted as implying either that the United States denied the existence of a special relationship with Latin America or that it sought to build on that relationship to constitute a new bloc in world affairs. The recognition of the uniqueness of each country—and particularly my statement that "no single formula" could encompass our desire for warm and productive relations with each nation in the hemisphere—were interpreted by some to imply that the United States was about to embark on a new crusade to maintain its power through a policy of special bilateral deals designed to divide the countries of Latin America against each other and preclude their ties with countries outside the hemisphere.

These speculations reflect the suspicions and uncertainties of a fluid global environment. They reflect problems we must jointly overcome. They do not reflect United States policy.

The fundamental interests of the United States require an active and constructive role of leadership in the task of building peace and promoting economic advance. In this hemisphere the legacy of our history is a tradition of civilized cooperation, a habit of interdependence, that is a sturdy foundation on which to seek to build a more just international order. And it is absurd to attempt to create a broader world community by tearing down close cooperative relations that have already existed in our part of the globe.

Therefore the United States remains committed to our *common* pledge at Tlatelolco [February 1974] to seek "a new, vigorous spirit of inter-American solidarity." This must mean today not an artificial unanimity or unrealistic pleas for unilateral action. As we agreed at Tlatelolco, interdependence has become a physical and moral imperative: It is a reality of mutual dependence and a necessity of cooperation on common problems. To face real problems we must now deal effectively among ourselves, we must identify our real needs and priorities; given the hemisphere's diversity, that can often be achieved bilaterally and subregionally better than regionally.

In this spirit of working solidarity, the United States pledges:

· *To take special cognizance of the distinctive requirements of the more industrialized economies of Latin America—and of the region as a whole*—in our efforts to build a more equitable international order. We believe the major Latin American countries need concessional foreign assistance less than they need support for their drive to participate in the international economy on a more equal footing with the industrialized nations. To help overcome fluctuations in export earnings and continued import and debt-servicing needs, we have secured a development security facility in the IMF [International Monetary Fund] and a substantial increase in access to IMF resources. To facilitate access to long-term development capital on commercial terms, we have proposed a new international investment trust and have begun a program of technical assistance to countries entering established capital markets.

In a similar vein we support expanded capitalization of international financial institutions such as the International Finance Corporation and the Inter-American Development Bank. A U.S. contribution of $2.25 billion to a new multiyear replenishment of the Inter-American Development Bank is now before the U.S. Congress. President Ford has given his full support.

To promote the growth and market stability of commodities of importance to Latin America, we favor producer-consumer cooperation in specific commodities and a reduction in the barriers to increased processing of raw materials in exporting countries.

We are prepared to undertake other practical steps.

The nations of Latin America have shown considerable interest in the transfer of modern technology. We support this, in principle and in practice. The challenge here, as elsewhere, is to develop mechanisms to achieve practical results.

It may be that SELA [Latin American Economic System] can turn to this question and suggest the means by which we could cooperate. We are prepared to respond positively.

In addition we must recognize that the private sector, private initiative, and private capital can play important roles in the development and application of new scientific and technological advances to local needs and conditions. The degree to which private capital is prepared to devote its considerable resources of talent and knowledge to this task will depend on the climate for its participation. It is for this reason that we state again our willingness to discuss codes of conduct, which can provide guidelines for the behavior of transnational enterprises. No subject is more sensitive—or more vital—for the private sector has played the critical role in bringing about growth; its resources exceed by far those now available for governmental aid. Yet for it to be effective the proper environment must be created. This is a major test for our cooperative efforts.

To increase trading opportunities we now permit many industrial products of developing countries to enter the United States without duty. And we favor special and differentiated treatment in the multilateral trade negotiations through concentration on products of interest to Latin America. This is already apparent in the talks we have had on tropical products. On all such multilateral issues we are prepared to have prior consultation with the nations of Latin America.

· *To maintain direct assistance to the neediest nations in this hemisphere* still oppressed by poverty and natural disaster, the great bulk of our bilateral concessional assistance to Latin America—nearly $300 million annually—is now allocated to the region's poorest nations to meet basic needs in health, education, and agriculture. At this moment the United States has joined other countries in a massive response to the devastating earthquake in Guatemala. In addition we continue to support expansion of multilateral concessional assistance through the fund for special operations of the Inter-American Development Bank and the soft-loan windows of other international financial institutions active in Latin America. These activities, supplemented by new programs in agricultural development and to assist balance-of-payments shortfalls, make an important contribution to our common responsibility toward the neediest.

· *To support Latin American regional and subregional efforts to organize for cooperation and integration.* The United States has provided technical and financial assistance to the movement of regional and subregional integration, including the development banks of the Andean Pact, the Central American Common Market, and the Caribbean Common Market. We are eager to assist these integration movements and others that may arise in the future. In addition we see in SELA a new possibility for cooperation among the nations of Latin America on common regional problems and projects. We welcome SELA and will support its efforts at mutual cooperation as its members may deem appropriate.

· *To negotiate on the basis of parity and dignity our specific differences with each and every state—both bilaterally and, where appropriate, multilaterally.* We intend to solve problems before they become conflicts. We stand ready to consult with other Governments over investment disputes when those disputes threaten relations between our Governments. As you all know, the United States and Panama are continuing to move forward in the historic negotiations on a Panama Canal treaty to establish a reliable long-term relationship between our two nations. In the interim between now and the final Law of the Sea Conference, we will continue to attempt to find solutions to issues relating to fisheries and the seas which have complicated our relations in the past. It is the earnest hope of my country that within a year a treaty of Caracas will be signed on the law of the sea.

· *To enforce our commitment to mutual security* and the Bolivarian ideal of regional integrity against those who would seek to undermine solidarity, threaten independence, or export violence. Last July at San José, the nations of the Americas agreed upon revisions to the Inter-American Treaty of Reciprocal Assistance—the Rio Treaty. In so doing they reaffirmed their commitment to take collective action against aggression—whether it comes from without or within the hemisphere. The United States regards this treaty as a solemn international obligation. We are resolved to carry out the commitment it places upon us.

· *To work to modernize the inter-American system* to respond to the needs of our times, to give direction to our common actions. The member states have already taken a major step forward in revising and reaffirming the Rio Treaty. In the months ahead the OAS will be considering the report of its Special Committee on Reform. More is at stake than the text of the charter; the member states are also beginning to focus on the structure and processes of the organization itself. The United States believes that the OAS has an important future of service to the hemisphere. We stand ready to work with others to modernize and strengthen it, to make it a more effective instrument for regional cooperation.

The application of these principles is a matter of common concern. We have had a special relationship for 150 years and more; the very intimacy of our ties imposes upon us the duty of rigorous and responsible self-assessment. We should set ourselves concrete deadlines—to complete the process before the end of this year.

We should use the months ahead constructively and productively. It is time that all of us in the hemisphere put aside slogans and turn from rhetoric to resolve. Let us go beyond the debate whether the United States is patronizing or neglecting or seeking to dominate its neighbors. Let us not dispute whether the Latin American nations are being unreasonable or peremptory or seeking to line up against their northern partner.

Instead let us focus on our goals and the need for common effort and get down to serious business. Many forums and forms are available. I propose that we identify the most fruitful areas for our common effort and set ourselves the goal of major accomplishment this year. At the OAS meeting in June we can review where we stand and discuss what further needs to be done. At the last General Assembly we adopted the informal style of the new dialogue, successfully, to facilitate open and frank discussions of major issues. I propose that we do so again and that we concentrate, at this next ministerial meeting, on the nature of our fundamental relationship.

Our common problems are real enough; a common response will give living reality to the heritage and promise of the hemisphere and the enduring truth that the nations of this hemisphere do indeed have—and will continue to have—a special relationship.

FOURTEEN

FOREIGN POLICY AND
NATIONAL SECURITY

*Address to the World Affairs Council and
Southern Methodist University, Dallas,
March 22, 1976*

I HAVE come here today to talk to you about the vital and intimate relationship between America's foreign policy and our national security.

As Secretary of State I am not, of course, directly involved in the preparation of our defense budget or in decisions regarding particular weapons programs. But as the President's principal advisor on foreign policy, no one knows better than I that a strong defense is crucial for our role in the world. For a great and responsible power, diplomacy without strength would be empty. If we were weak we could not negotiate; we could only hope or accommodate. It is the confidence of strength that permits us to act with conciliation and responsibility to help shape a more peaceful world.

Other nations must not be led to doubt either our strength or our resolution. For how others see us determines the risks they are prepared to run and the degree to which they are willing to place confidence in our policies. If adversaries consider us weak or irresolute, testing and crises are inevitable. If allies doubt our constancy, retreat and political shifts are certain.

And so, as Secretary of State, I am inevitably a partisan of a strong America and a strong defense as the underpinning of a strong foreign policy. I have a responsibility to make clear to the American people and to other nations that our power is indeed adequate to our current challenges, that we are improving our forces to meet changing conditions, that America understands its interests and values and will defend them, and that the American people will never permit those hostile to us to shape the world in which we live.

I do not accept the propositions that other nations have gained military ascendancy over us, that the Administration has neglected our defenses, or that negotiations to reduce the threat of nuclear war are unwise. These charges sound remarkably like the "missile gap" claims which aroused anxieties in 1960 only to dissolve suddenly a few weeks after the election.

We do face serious challenges to our security. They derive from the unprecedented conditions of the thermonuclear age, the ambiguities of contemporary power, and the perpetual revolution in technology. Our task is to understand the real and permanent requirements of our security, rather than to be seduced by the outmoded vocabulary of a simpler time.

What are the national security issues we face? What is the true condition of our national defense?

· First, the inevitable growth of Soviet economic and military power has produced essential strategic equality. We cannot halt this growth, but we must counterbalance it and prevent its use for political expansion.

· Second, America remains the most powerful nation in the world. It will remain so, if the Congress approves the President's proposed defense budget. But evolving technology and the military programs of others impose upon us the need for constant vigilance and continuing major effort.

· Third, technology has revolutionized the instruments

of war and introduced an unparalleled complexity into the perceptions of power and the choices that we must make to maintain it. The defense establishment we have today is the product of decisions taken ten to fifteen years ago. Equally, the decisions we make today will determine our defense posture in the 1980s and beyond. And the kind of forces we have will determine the kind of diplomacy we are able to conduct.

· Fourth, as nuclear arsenals grow, the horrors of nuclear war become ever more apparent while at the same time the threat of all-out nuclear war to deter or resist less than all-out aggression becomes ever less plausible. Under the umbrella of strategic equivalence, testing and probing at the local and regional levels become more likely. Hence over the next decade we must increase and modernize the forces—air, land, and sea—for local defense.

· Fifth, while a weak defense posture produces a weak foreign policy, a strong defense does not necessarily produce a strong foreign policy. Our role in the world depends as well on how realistically we perceive our national interests, on our unity as a people, and on our willingness to persevere in pursuit of our national goals.

· Finally, for Americans, physical strength can never be an end in itself. So long as we are true to ourselves, every Administration has the obligation to seek to control the spiral of nuclear weapons and to give mankind hope for a more secure and just future.

Let me discuss each of these challenges.

The Long-Range Challenge of Defense. To cope with the implications of Soviet power has become a permanent responsibility of American defense and foreign policy. Sixty years of Soviet industrial and economic growth, and a political system that gives top priority to military buildup, have—inevitably—

brought the Soviet Union to a position of rough equilibrium with the United States. No policy or decision on our part brought this about. Nothing we could have done would have prevented it. Nothing we can do now will make it disappear.

But while we cannot prevent the growth of Soviet military strength, we can and must maintain the strength to balance it and insure that it will not be used for political expansion. There is no alternative to a substantial defense budget over the long term. We have a permanent responsibility and need a steady course that does not change with the fads of the moment. We cannot afford the oscillation between assaults on defense spending and cries of panic, between cuts of $40 billion in Administration defense budget requests over seven years and charges of neglect of our defenses.

This claim on our perseverance is a new experience for Americans. Throughout most of our history we have been able to mobilize urgently in time of war and then to disarm unilaterally when victory was achieved. After World War II we rapidly demobilized our armies, relying largely on our nuclear monopoly to preserve the peace. Thus when the Korean war broke out we were little better prepared than we had been ten summers previously. Only recently have we begun to understand—and then reluctantly—that foreign policy and military strategy are inextricably linked, that we must maintain defense preparedness over the long term, and that we will live for as far ahead as we can see in a twilight between tranquility and open confrontation. We need a defense posture that is relevant to our dangers, comprehensible to our friends, credible to our adversaries, and that we are prepared to sustain over the long term.

The Imperatives of Technology. Technology has transformed the conditions and calculations of military strength in unprecedented fashion.

The paradox of contemporary military strength is that a momentous increase in the element of power has eroded the traditional relationship of power to policy. Until the end of World War II, it would never have occurred to a leader that there might be an upper limit to useful military power. Since the technological choices were limited, strength was largely defined in quantitative terms. Today the problem is to insure that our strength is relevant to our foreign policy objectives. Under current conditions, no matter how we or our adversaries improve the size or quality of our strategic arsenals, one over-riding fact remains: An all-out strategic nuclear exchange would kill hundreds of millions on both sides in a matter of hours and utterly devastate the nations involved.

Thus the current strategic problem is virtually the diametric opposite of the historic one. Planners used to pursue increased overall power. Today we have a total strength unimaginable a generation ago, but we must design, diversify, and refine our forces so that they are relevant to—and able to support—rational foreign policy objectives. Historically military planners could treat the technology of their time as stable; today technology revolutionizes military capabilities in both strategic and tactical forces every decade and thus presents policy-makers with an ever-increasing spectrum of choice.

And yet the choices we make now will not, in most cases, really affect the structure of our forces for from five to ten years—the time it takes to design new weapons, build them, and deploy them. Thus the policies Administrations are able to carry out are largely shaped by decisions in which they took no part. Decisions made in the 1960s largely determined our strategic posture for the 1970s. We can do little to change the impact of those earlier decisions; the Administration in power in the 1980s will be able to do little to change the impact of the decisions we make today. This is a sobering challenge, and it turns national security policy into a nonpartisan responsibility.

In choosing among the options that technology gives us, we—and every Administration—must keep certain principles in mind.

· First, we must not simply duplicate Soviet choices. The Soviet Union has a different geopolitical problem, a different force structure, and perhaps a different strategic doctrine.

· Second, because of the costs of modern forces, we face complex choices. In many areas we face a trade-off between quantity and quality, between numbers and sophistication.

· Third, because of our higher wage scales—particularly for our volunteer forces—any increase in our forces will weigh much more heavily on our economy than on that of adversaries whose pay scales are only a fraction of ours. For this reason, and the value we place on human life, we have always had an incentive, indeed an imperative, to put a premium on technology—where we are superior—rather than sheer numbers.

· Fourth, we must see beyond the numbers game. Quality confers advantages as much as quantity and can sometimes substitute for it. Yet even we cannot afford every weapon that technology makes possible.

· Fifth, at some point numbers count. Technology cannot substitute indefinitely for numerical strength. The belief that there is an unlimited amount of fat to be cut in the defense budget is an illusion. Reductions almost inevitably translate into a reduction of effectiveness.

America possesses the economic and technological foundation to remain militarily preeminent; we can afford whatever military forces our security requires. The challenge we face is not to our physical strength—which is unequalled—but to our will to maintain it in all relevant categories and to use it when necessary to defend our interests and values.

Strategic Forces and Strategic Arms Limitation. Our nation's security requires, first and foremost, strategic forces that can deter attack and that insure swift and flexible retaliation if aggression occurs.

We have such forces today. Our technology has always been ahead of the U.S.S.R. by at least five years; with appropriate effort we can insure that this will continue to be the case.

We are determined to maintain the strategic balance at whatever level is required. We will never allow the balance to be tipped against us either by unilateral decision or a buildup of the other side, by a one-sided agreement or by a violation of an agreement.

But we must be clear what maintaining the balance means. We must not mesmerize ourselves with fictitious "gaps." Our forces were designed according to different criteria than those of the Soviet Union; their adequacy must be judged by our strategic needs, not theirs.

In the middle 1960s we could have continued the deployment of heavy throwweight missiles, following the Titan or the Atlas. But the Administration then in office decided instead to rely—in addition to our large bomber force—on an arsenal of 1,000 new, relatively light, sophisticated, and extremely accurate intercontinental ballistic missiles [ICBMs] and 656 submarine-launched missiles on 41 boats. We deployed these systems rapidly, halting our buildup of launchers in the 1960s when it was judged that technological improvements were more important than an increase in numbers.

The Soviet Union chose a different course. Because of its more limited technological capabilities, it emphasized missiles whose greater throwweight compensated for their substantially poorer accuracy. But—contrary to the expectations of American officials in the 1960s—the Soviets also chose to expand their numbers of launchers beyond what we had. Thus the

Soviets passed our numerical levels by 1970 and continued to add an average of two hundred missiles a year—until we succeeded in halting this buildup in the SALT [Strategic Arms Limitation Talks] agreement of 1972.

Therefore—as a consequence of unilateral decisions made a decade ago by both sides—Soviet missile forces today are somewhat larger in number and considerably heavier in throwweight, while ours are superior in reliability, accuracy, diversity, and sophistication. We possess far larger numbers of warheads—eighty-five hundred to their twenty-five hundred —and we have several hundred more strategic bombers.

Whether we move in the direction of greater throwweight will largely depend on recommendations made by the Department of Defense and the Joint Chiefs of Staff; it is not essentially a foreign policy decision. But in making it we will be governed by our need, not by a compulsion to duplicate the Soviet force structure. The destructiveness of missiles depends on a combination of explosive power and accuracy. For most purposes, as accuracy improves, explosive power becomes less important—and heavy land-based missiles become, in fact, more vulnerable. Since we have stressed accuracy, we may decide that we do not need to approach the level of throwweight of Soviet weapons, although nothing—certainly no SALT agreement—prevents us from substantially increasing our throwweight if we choose.

Whatever our decision regarding technical issues, no responsible leader should encourage the illusion that America can ever again recapture the strategic superiority of the early postwar period. In the 1940s we had a nuclear monopoly. In the 1950s and early 1960s we had overwhelming preponderance. As late as the Cuban missile crisis of 1962, the Soviet Union possessed less than 100 strategic systems while we had thousands.

But today, when each side has thousands of launchers and

many more warheads, a decisive or politically significant margin of superiority is out of reach. If one side expands or improves its forces, sooner or later the other side will balance the effort. The Soviet Union first developed an ICBM; we matched it. We then added a lead in numbers of strategic missiles to the lead we already had in bombers; they caught up and surpassed us in missile numbers although we still remain far ahead in numbers of bombers. When our Trident submarines are in production by the end of this decade, we will begin to redress that numerical imbalance as well as improve the flexibility and survivability of our forces.

We were the first to put modern ballistic missiles on submarines and we were the first to put multiple warheads on missiles. Although we remain ahead in both categories, the Soviets found ways to narrow the gap. And the same will be true in the future, whether in missile accuracy or submarine, aircraft, or cruise missile technology.

The pattern is clear. No net advantage can long be preserved by *either* side. A perceived inequality could shake the confidence of other countries, even when its precise military significance is difficult to define. Therefore, we certainly will not permit a perceived or actual imbalance to arise against us and the Soviet Union is likely to follow similar principles. The probable outcome of each succeeding round of the strategic arms race will be the restoration of equilibrium, at a higher and costlier level of forces and probably with less political stability. Such temporary advantages as can be achieved are not strategically decisive. The long leadtimes for the deployment of modern weapons should always permit countermeasures to be taken. If both sides remain vigilant, neither side will be able to reduce the effects of a counterblow against it to acceptable levels.

Those who paint dark vistas of a looming U.S. inferiority

in strategic weapons ignore these facts and the real choices facing modern leaders.

No nuclear weapon has ever been used in modern wartime conditions or against an opponent possessing means of retaliation. Indeed, neither side has even tested the launching of more than a few missiles at a time; neither side has ever fired them in a North-South direction as they would have to do in wartime. Yet initiation of an all-out surprise attack would depend on substantial confidence that thousands of reentry vehicles launched in carefully coordinated attacks—from land, sea, and air—would knock out all their targets thousands of miles away, with a timing and reliability exactly as predicted, before the other side launches any forces to preempt or retaliate and with such effectiveness that retaliation would not produce unacceptable damage. Any miscalculation or technical failure would mean national catastrophe. Assertions that one side is "ahead" by the margins now under discussion pale in significance when an attack would depend on decisions based on such massive uncertainties and risks.

For these reasons, the strategic arsenals of the two sides find their principal purpose in matching and deterring the forces of the opponent and in making certain that third countries perceive no inequality. In no recent crisis has an American President come close to considering the use of strategic nuclear weapons. In no crisis since 1962—and perhaps not even then—has the strategic balance been the decisive factor. Even in Korea, when we possessed an overwhelming superiority, it was not relevant to the outcome.

It is against this background that we have vigorously negotiated mutual limitations in strategic arms. There are compelling reasons for pursuing such talks.

· Since successive rounds of competitive programs will almost certainly yield only equilibrium, we have sought to regulate the competition and to maintain the equivalence that will exist in any case at lower levels.

· Stabilizing the strategic balance frees resources to strengthen our forces in areas where they are most needed; it will ease the problem of enhancing our capabilities for regional defense and in sea power—the areas where an imbalance could have serious geopolitical consequences.

· Agreed limitations and a more calculable strategic relationship will facilitate efforts to reduce political confrontations and crises.

·And, finally, the American people expect their leaders to pursue every responsible approach to peace and stability in the thermonuclear era. Only then can we expect them to support the sacrifices necessary to maintain our defensive strength.

We have made progress toward these goals. In the 1972 SALT agreements we froze antiballistic missile systems in their infancy and thus avoided potentially massive expenditures and instabilities. We halted the momentum of the Soviet missile buildup for five years—a period in which, because of the long leadtimes involved, we had no capacity for deployment of our own. We intended to use that five-year interval to negotiate a longer-term and more comprehensive agreement based on numerical equality and, failing that, to close the numerical gap by our own efforts as our modernization programs developed.

This is precisely what President Ford achieved at Vladivostok a year and a half ago and what we are trying to enshrine in a binding treaty that would run through 1985. Both sides would have equal ceilings on missiles, heavy bombers, and on multiwarhead missiles; this would require the Soviets to dismantle many weapons, while our planned forces would not be affected. And neither the weapons of our allies nor our forward-based nuclear systems—such as carriers and tactical aircraft—would be included; these had been Soviet demands since 1969.

These are major accomplishments which are overwhelmingly in our interest, particularly when we compare them to the situation which could have prevailed had we failed to achieve restraints on Soviet programs. Nevertheless very important issues remain to be resolved. We will make every effort to conclude a satisfactory agreement, but we will be driven solely by the national interest and not by arbitrary or artificial deadlines.

The SALT agreements are the opposite of the one-sided concessions to the U.S.S.R. so often portrayed. Soviet offensive programs were slowed; none of ours were affected. Nor has the Administration countenanced Soviet violations of the first SALT agreement, as has been irresponsibly charged. In fact, we have carefully watched every aspect of Soviet performance. It is the unanimous view of all agencies of our Government—only recently reconfirmed—that no Soviet violation has occurred and that none of the ambiguous actions that we have noted and raised has affected our security. But we will remain vigilant. All ambiguous information will be carefully analyzed. No violations will be tolerated. We will insist on full explanations where questionable activity has occurred.

We will maintain the strategic balance at whatever level is required—preferably within the limits of successful SALT negotiations, but if necessary without those limits. We will not heed those who maintain that all that is required are limited, minimum deterrence forces—to threaten the Soviet civilian population. To follow their advice would deprive us of all options save capitulation and the massive destruction of civilian life; it would create a large numerical imbalance against us which could have significant political consequences, possibly tempting our adversaries and upsetting our friends.

But neither will we be deflected by contrived and incredible scenarios, by inflated versions of Soviet strength, or by irresponsible attacks on SALT, into diverting defense resources away from vital areas—the forces for regional and local defense and our Navy. For these are the areas where shortfalls and imbalances can rapidly turn into geopolitical shifts that jeopardize our fundamental interests and those of our allies.

Military Strength for Regional Defense. Under conditions of nuclear parity, world peace is more likely to be threatened by shifts in local or regional balances—in Europe, the Middle East, Asia, Latin America, or Africa—than by strategic nuclear attack. Thus our forces that can be used for local defense deserve our particular attention and increased resources.

The issue is not the simplistic one of the size of the Soviet Army. There is nothing new about the size of the Soviet Army. During the entire postwar period, the Soviet standing army has always been larger than ours; at times it has been three times the size. The Soviet Union has a much greater landmass to defend and perceives major defense problems both in Eastern Europe and on its Asian front where nearly half of the Soviet Army is now stationed. We, by contrast, enjoy the shields of friendly neighbors and wide oceans. And we are linked with close allies with substantial forces of their own.

The new and long-foreseen problem is that under conditions of nuclear balance our adversaries may be increasingly tempted to probe at the regional level. This temptation must be discouraged. If leaders around the world come to assume that the United States lacks either the forces or the will to resist while others intervene to impose solutions, they will accomodate themselves to what they will regard as the dominant trend. And an unopposed superpower may draw dangerous conclusions when the next opportunity for intervention beckons. Over time, the global balance of power and influence will inevitably shift to the advantage of those who care nothing about America's values or well-being.

Thus our strong capability for local and regional defense is essential for us and, together with our allies, we must build up these forces. In a crisis the President must have other choices than capitulation or resort to strategic nuclear weapons.

We are not the world's policeman—but we cannot permit the Soviet Union or its surrogates to become the world's policeman either, if we care anything about our security and the fate of freedom in the world. It does no good to preach strategic superiority while practicing regional retreat.

This was the issue in Angola. The United States had no significant stake in a purely Angolan civil war. The issue was —and remains—the unacceptable precedent of massive Soviet and Cuban military intervention in a conflict thousands of miles from their shores—with its broad implications for the rest of Africa and, indeed, many other regions of the world. The danger was, and is, that our inaction—our legislatively imposed failure even to send financial help to Africans who sought to resist—will lead to further Soviet and Cuban pressures on the mistaken assumption that America has lost the will to counter adventurism or even to help others do so.

It is time, therefore, to be clear that as far as we are concerned, Angola has set no precedent. It is time that the world be reminded that America remains capable of forthright and decisive action. The American people know that the United

States cannot remain aloof if basic principles of responsible international conduct are flouted and the geopolitical balance is threatened by a pattern of outside interventions in local conflicts.

The United States has made clear its strong support for majority rule and minority rights in southern Africa. We have no stake in and we will give no encouragement to illegal regimes there. The President and I have made clear that rapid change is required and that the opportunity for negotiated solutions must be seized. We will make major efforts to promote these objectives and to help all parties to return to the negotiating table. The proposals made today by [British] Foreign Secretary [James] Callaghan in the House of Commons seem to us a most constructive approach. We welcome them.

But let no one believe that American support can be extorted by the threat of Cuban troops or Soviet arms. Our cooperation is not available to those who rely on Cuban troops. The United States cannot acquiesce indefinitely in the presence of Cuban expeditionary forces in distant lands for the purpose of pressure and to determine the political evolution by force of arms.

We have issued these warnings before. I repeat them today. The United States will not accept further Cuban military interventions abroad.

We are certain that the American people understand and support these two equal principles of our policy—our support for majority rule in Africa and our firm opposition to military intervention.

Angola reminds us that military capabilities by themselves cannot solve our foreign policy problems. No matter how massive our arsenals or how flexible our forces, they will carry little weight if we become so confused in our decision-making and so constrained in defining our interests that no one believes we will ever act when challenged.

The issue is not an open-ended commitment or a policy of indiscriminate American intervention. Decisions on whether and how to take action must always result from careful analysis and open discussion. It cannot be rammed down the throats of an unwilling Congress or public.

But neither can we avoid decisions when their time has clearly come. Global stability simply cannot survive the presumption that our natural choice will always be passivity; such a course would insure that the world will witness dangerous challenges and major changes highly inimical to our interests and our ideals.

The Strength and Will of America. If America's defense is to match the Nation's, needs it must meet three basic requirements.

· Our strategic forces must be sufficient to deter attack and credibly maintain the nuclear balance.

· Our forces for regional defense, together with those of our allies, must be clearly capable of resisting threat and pressure.

· And at home we must once again unite behind the proposition that aggression unresisted is aggression encouraged. We must be prepared to recognize genuine threats to the global balance, whether they emerge as direct challenges to us or as regional encroachment at a greater distance. And we must be prepared to do something about them.

These are the real issues our leaders now face and will surely face in the future. They require answers to some hard questions, such as the following: Where can our defense dollars be most productively spent? What programs are needed that are not already underway? What would be the costs of these programs and over what period of time? What, if anything, would we have to give up? What are the premises of our defense policy—against what threats and with what diplomacy?

Administration and critics alike must answer these questions if we are to have an effective national policy. And in this spirit, I have spoken today about the relationship between defense and foreign policy.

Military strength is crucial to America's security and well-being. But we must take care not to become so obsessed with power alone that we become a "Fortress America" and neglect our ultimate political and moral responsibilities.

Our Nation is the beacon of hope to all who love freedom not simply because it is strong, but because it represents mankind's age-old dream of dignity and self-respect. Others before us have wielded overwhelming military power and abdicated moral responsibility or engendered fear and hatred. Our resources—military, industrial, technological, economic, and cultural—are beyond challenge; with dedication and effort they shall remain so. But a world of tenuous balance, of a nuclear equilibrium constantly contested, is too barren and perilous and uninspiring. America has always stood for something deeper than throwing its weight around; we shall see to it that we shall never relinquish our moral leadership in the search for a just and lasting peace.

We have gone through a difficult decade not because we were weak, but because we were divided. None of our setbacks have been caused by lack of American power or even lack of relevant power. The fundamental challenge to America, therefore, is to generate the wisdom, the creativity, and the will to dedicate ourselves to the peace and progress of humanity.

America's ultimate strength has always been the conviction and basic unity of its people. And despite a decade and more

of testing—despite assassination, war, and institutional crisis
—we still remain a vital and optimistic and confident people.

It is time once again for Americans to hold their heads
high. It is important to recall once again some fundamental
truths:

· that we are still the strongest Nation on the face of the
earth;

· that we are the most generous Nation in history—we have
fed the starving, opened our arms and our hearts to refugees
from other lands, and given more of our substance to the poor
and downtrodden around the world than any other nation;

· that we are needed to maintain the world's security;

· that we are essential to any hopes for stability and human
progress;

· that we remain the bulwark of democracy and the land of
promise to millions who yearn for freedom and a better life for
themselves and their children;

· that we, therefore, have a responsibility to hold high the
banner of freedom and human dignity for all mankind.

Our record of achievements should be but prologue to what
this generation of Americans has it within its power to accomplish. For the first time in history we can work with others
to create an era of peace and prosperity for all mankind. We
shall not fail.

With faith in the goodness and the promise of America we
shall master our future. And those who celebrate America's
tricentennial will look back and say that this generation of
Americans was worthy of the ideals and the greatness of our
history.

FIFTEEN

SOUTHERN AFRICA AND THE UNITED STATES: AN AGENDA FOR COOPERATION

Address delivered at a luncheon in Secretary Kissinger's honor hosted by President Kenneth Kaunda, Lusaka, Zambia, April 27, 1976

PRESIDENT FORD has sent me here with a message of commitment and cooperation.

I have come to Africa because in so many ways, the challenges of Africa are the challenges of the modern era. Morally and politically, the drama of national independence in Africa over the last generation has transformed international affairs. More than any other region of the world, Africa symbolizes that the previous era of world affairs—the colonial era—is a thing of the past. The great tasks you face—in nationbuilding, in keeping the peace and integrity of this continent, in economic development, in gaining an equitable role in world councils, in achieving racial justice—these reflect the challenges of building a humane and progressive world order.

I have come to Africa with an open mind and an open heart to demonstrate my country's desire to work with you on these great tasks. My journey is intended to give fresh impetus to our cooperation and to usher in a new era in American policy.

The United States was one of the prime movers of the process of decolonization. The American people welcomed the new nations into the world community and for two decades

367

have given aid and encouragement to economic and social progress in Africa. And America's responsibilities as a global power give us a strong interest today in the independence, peace, and well-being of this vast continent comprising a fifth of the world's land surface. For without peace, racial justice, and growing prosperity in Africa we cannot speak of a just international order.

There is nothing to be gained in a debate about whether in the past America has neglected Africa or been insufficiently committed to African goals. The United States has many responsibilities in the world. Given the burden it has carried in the postwar period, it could not do everything simultaneously. African nations too have their own priorities and concerns, which have not always accorded with our own. No good can come of mutual recrimination. Our differing perspectives converge in a common purpose to build a secure and just future for Africa. In active collaboration there is much we can do; in contention or apart we will miss great opportunities. President Ford, the American Government and people are prepared to work with you with energy and goodwill if met in the same spirit.

So it is time to put aside slogans and to seek practical solutions. It is time to find our common ground and act boldly for common ends.

Africa is a continent of hope—a modern frontier. The United States, from the beginning, has been a country of the frontier, built by men and women of hope. The American people know from their history the meaning of the struggle for independence, for racial equality, for economic progress, for human dignity.

I am not here to give American prescriptions for Africa's problems. Your program must be African. The basic decisions and goals must be African. But we are prepared to help.

Nor am I here to set African against African, either among your Governments or among factions of liberation movements. African problems cannot be solved and your destiny cannot be fulfilled except by a united Africa. America supports African unity. We urge all other countries to do the same.

Here in Africa the range of mankind's challenges and potential can be seen in all its complexity and enormous promise. The massive power and grandeur of nature is before us in all its aspects—as the harsh master and as a bountiful servant of mankind. Here we can feel the rich and living cultures which have changed and invigorated art, music, and thought around the world. And here, on this continent, we are tested—all of us—to see whether our future will be determined for us or by us, whether humanity will be the victim or the architect of its destiny.

The Problem of Southern Africa. Of all the challenges before us, of all the purposes we have in common, racial justice is one of the most basic. This is a dominant issue of our age, within nations and among nations. We know from our own experience that the goal of racial justice is both compelling and achievable. Our support for this principle in southern Africa is not simply a matter of foreign policy but an imperative of our own moral heritage.

The people of Zambia do not need to be reminded of the importance of realizing this goal. By geography and economic necessity Zambia is affected directly and grievously by strife in southern Africa. Political stability in this region means more to Zambia than to many others. Yet Zambia has chosen to stand by its principles by closing its border with Rhodesia and enduring the economic consequences. This is a testimony to the determination of the people of this country and to the statesmanship of its great leader, President Kaunda.

And it was in this city seven years ago that leaders of east and central African states proclaimed their manifesto on southern Africa.

One is struck by the similarity of philosophy in the American Declaration of Independence and the Lusaka Manifesto. Two hundred years ago Thomas Jefferson wrote: "We hold these Truths to be self-evident, that all Men are created equal, that they are endowed by their Creator with certain unalienable Rights, that among these are Life, Liberty and the Pursuit of Happiness—That to secure these Rights, Governments are instituted among Men, deriving their just Powers from the Consent of the Governed . . ."

And seven years ago the leaders of east and central Africa declared here in Lusaka that "by this Manifesto we wish to make clear, beyond all shadow of doubt, our acceptance of the belief that all men are equal, and have equal rights to human dignity and respect, regardless of color, race, religion or sex. We believe that all men have the right and the duty to participate, as equal members of the society, in their own Government."

There can be no doubt that the United States remains committed to the principles of its own Declaration of Independence. It follows that we also adhere to the convictions of the Lusaka Manifesto.

Therefore, here in Lusaka, I reaffirm the unequivocal commitment of the United States to human rights, as expressed in the principles of the United Nations Charter and the Universal Declaration of Human Rights. We support self-determination, majority rule, equal rights, and human dignity for all the peoples of southern Africa—in the name of moral principle, international law, and world peace.

On this occasion I would like to set forth more fully American policy on some of the immediate issues we face—in Rhodesia, Namibia, and South Africa—and then to sketch our vision of southern Africa's hopeful future.

Rhodesia. The U.S. position on Rhodesia is clear and unmistakable. As President Ford has said, "The United States is totally dedicated to seeing to it that the majority becomes the ruling power in Rhodesia." We do not recognize the Rhodesian minority regime. The United States voted for, and is committed to, the U.N. Security Council resolutions of 1966 and 1968 that imposed mandatory economic sanctions against the illegal Rhodesian regime. Earlier this year we cosponsored a Security Council resolution, which was passed unanimously, expanding mandatory sanctions. And in March of this year we joined with others to commend Mozambique for its decision to enforce these sanctions even at great economic cost to itself.

It is the responsibility of all who seek a negotiated solution to make clear to the Rhodesian minority that the world community is united in its insistence on rapid change. It is the responsibility of those in Rhodesia who believe in peace to take the steps necessary to avert a great tragedy.

U.S. policy for a just and durable Rhodesian solution will therefore rest on ten elements:

· First, the United States declares its support in the strongest terms for the proposals made by British Prime Minister [James] Callaghan on March 22 of this year—that independence must be preceded by majority rule which, in turn, must be achieved no later than two years following the expeditious conclusion of negotiations. We consider these proposals a basis for a settlement fair to all the people of Rhodesia. We urge that they be accepted.

· Second, the Salisbury regime must understand that it cannot expect U.S. support either in diplomacy or in material help at any stage in its conflict with African states or African liberation movements. On the contrary, it will face our unrelenting opposition until a negotiated settlement is achieved.

· Third, the United States will take steps to fulfill completely its obligation under international law to mandatory economic sanctions against Rhodesia. We will urge the Congress this year to repeal the Byrd Amendment—which authorizes Rhodesian chrome imports to the United States—an act inconsistent with U.N. sanctions. In parallel with this effort we will approach other industrial nations to insure the strictest and broadest international compliance with sanctions.

· Fourth, to insure that there are no misperceptions on the part of the leaders of the minority in Rhodesia, the United States, on the conclusion of my consultations in black Africa, will communicate clearly and directly to the Salisbury regime our view of the urgency of a rapid negotiated settlement leading to majority rule.

· Fifth, the U.S. Government will carry out its responsibility to inform American citizens that we have no official representation in Rhodesia nor any means of providing them with assistance or protection. American travelers will be advised against entering Rhodesia; Americans resident there will be urged to leave.

· Sixth, as in the case of Zambia a few years ago, steps should be taken—in accordance with the recent U.N. Security Council resolution—to assist Mozambique, whose closing of its borders with Rhodesia to enforce sanctions has imposed upon it a great additional economic hardship. In accordance with this U.N. resolution, the United States is willing to provide $12.5 million of assistance.

· Seventh, the United States—together with other members of the United Nations—is ready to help alleviate economic hardship for any countries neighboring Rhodesia which decide to enforce sanctions by closing their frontiers.

· Eighth, humanitarian provision must be made for the thousands of refugees who have fled in distress from Rhodesia into neighboring countries. The United States will consider sympathetically requests for assistance for these refugees by the U.N. High Commissioner for Refugees or other appropriate international organizations.

· Ninth, the world community should give its support to the people of Rhodesia as they make the peaceful transition to majority rule and independence and should aid a newly independent Zimbabwe. To this end we are ready to join with other interested nations in a program of economic, technical, and educational assistance to enable an independent Zimbabwe to achieve the progress and the place in the community of nations to which its resources and the talents of all its people entitle it.

· Finally, we state our conviction that whites as well as blacks should have a secure future and civil rights in a Zimbabwe that has achieved racial justice. A constitutional structure should protect minority rights together with establishing majority rule. We are prepared to devote some of our assistance programs to this objective.

In carrying out this program we shall consult closely with the Presidents of Botswana, Mozambique, Tanzania, and Zambia.

We believe these are important measures. We are open-minded with respect to additional actions that can help speed a resolution. The United States will consult closely with African leaders, especially the four Presidents, and with other friends on the Rhodesian problem. For the central fact that I have come here to stress is this: The United States is wholly committed to help bring about a rapid, just, and African solution to the issue of Rhodesia.

Namibia. Rhodesia is the most urgent but by no means the only critical problem in southern Africa. The status of Namibia has been a source of contention between the world community and South Africa for over three decades.

The territory of South-West Africa turned into a source of serious international discord following World War II. When the United Nations refused to accede to South Africa's proposal for annexation of the territory, South Africa declined to enter into a trusteeship agreement and since then has refused to recognize the United Nations as the legal sovereign. In 1966 the General Assembly terminated South Africa's mandate over the territory. In 1971 the International Court of Justice concluded that South Africa's occupation of Namibia was illegal and that it should withdraw.

The United States voted for the 1966 General Assembly resolution. We were the only major power to argue before the International Court that South African occupation was illegal. And in January 1976 the United States voted in favor of the U.N. resolution condemning the occupation of Namibia and calling for South Africa to take specific steps toward Namibia's self-determination and independence.

We are encouraged by the South African Government's evident decision to move Namibia toward independence. We are convinced that a solution can be found which will embody equal rights for the entire population and at the same time protect the interests of all who live and work there. But we are concerned that South Africa has failed to announce a definite timetable for the achievement of self-determination, that all the people and all political groupings of Namibia have not been allowed to take part in determining the form of government they shall one day have, and that South Africa continues to deny the United Nations its proper role in establishing a free and independent Namibia.

Therefore the United States position is as follows:

· We reiterate our call upon the South African Government to permit all the people and groups of Namibia to express their views freely, under U.N. supervision, on the political future and constitutional structure of their country.

· We urge the South African Government to announce a definite timetable acceptable to the world community for the achievement of self-determination.

· The United States is prepared to work with the international community, and especially with African leaders, to determine what further steps would improve prospects for a rapid and acceptable transition to Namibian independence. We are convinced that the need for progress is urgent.

· Once concrete movement toward self-determination is underway, the United States will ease its restrictions on trade and investment in Namibia. We stand ready to provide economic and technical assistance to help Namibia take its rightful place among the independent nations of the world.

South Africa. Apartheid in South Africa remains an issue of great concern to those committed to racial justice and human dignity.

No country, no people can claim perfection in the realm of human rights. We in America are aware of our own imperfections. But because we are a free society, our problems and our shortcomings are fully aired and made known to the world. And we have reason to take pride in our progress in the quest for justice for all in our country. The world community's concern with South Africa is not merely that racial discrimination exists there. What is unique is the extent to which racial discrimination has been institutionalized, enshrined in law, and made all-pervasive.

No one—including the leaders of black Africa—challenges the right of white South Africans to live in their country. They are not colonialists; historically, they are an African people. But white South Africans must recognize as well that the world will continue to insist that the institutionalized separation of the races must end. The United States appeals to South Africa to heed the warning signals of the past two years. There is still time to bring about a reconciliation of South Africa's peoples for the benefit of all. But there is a limit to that time —a limit of far shorter duration than was generally perceived even a few years ago.

A peaceful end to institutionalized inequality is in the interest of all South Africans. The United States will continue to encourage and work for peaceful change. Our policy toward South Africa is based upon the premise that within a reasonable time we shall see a clear evolution toward equality of opportunity and basic human rights for all South Africans. The United States will exercise all its efforts in that direction. We urge the Government of South Africa to make that premise a reality.

In the immediate future, the Republic of South Africa can show its dedication to Africa—and its potential contribution to Africa—by using its influence in Salisbury to promote a rapid negotiated settlement for majority rule in Rhodesia. This, we are sure, would be viewed positively by the community of nations, as well as by the rest of Africa.

A Vision of the Future. Southern Africa has all the prerequisites for an exciting future. Richly endowed with minerals, agricultural and hydroelectric potential, a favorable climate, and, most important, great human resources, it needs only to overcome the human failure of racial strife to achieve bright prospects for all its peoples.

Let us all strive to speed the day when this vision becomes a reality.

The United States stands ready to work with the nations of southern Africa to help them achieve the economic progress which will give meaning to their political independence and dignity to their struggle for equality.

As you know, Deputy Secretary [of State Charles W.] Robinson, an expert in economic development, is accompanying me on this visit. This is the first time that an American Secretary of State and Deputy Secretary together have come on such a mission, reflecting the importance we attach to the economic development of southern Africa. Mr. Robinson and I are discussing development needs with African officials in the various capitals and we shall continue these consultations at the UNCTAD [U.N. Conference on Trade and Development] meeting in Nairobi next week. After my return to Washington, based on what we have learned, we will urgently study a new aid program for this continent.

Africa and its friends face a dual challenge—immediate and long-term growth. In the short term, economic emergencies can arise from natural disasters or sharp swings in global economic conditions over which developing nations have little control. These economic shocks must be dealt with if the nations of the region are to maintain their hard-won progress toward development. For example, the sharp drop in world copper prices has had a devastating impact on the economies of Zambia and Zaire. The United States will deal with this problem in its bilateral assistance programs for these countries and in our programs for multilateral action—to be proposed at UNCTAD next week—for resource developmet, buffer stocks, and earnings stabilization.

But our basic concern must go beyond responding to emergencies. We need to develop urgently programs to lay the foundations for sustained growth to enable the developing nations of southern Africa to deal effectively with global economic shocks and trends.

Let me mention four that are especially relevant to southern Africa: trained local manpower, rural development, advanced technology, and modern transportation.

· For Namibia and Zimbabwe training programs should be intensified now so that needed manpower will be ready when majority rule is attained. Existing programs to train Namibian and Zimbabwean refugees as administrators and technicians should be expanded as rapidly as possible. We have requested additional funds from Congress for this purpose. We urge other donors and international organizations to do more.

· Development for all of southern Africa involves a process of transforming rural life. We are prepared to assist in agricultural development, in health programs, in manpower training, in improving rural transportation—through both bilateral and multilateral programs.

· A revolution in development planning could be achieved by the use of satellites to collect vital information on crops, weather, water resources, land use, and mineral exploration. The United States has already shared with developing nations information from our earliest Earth resources survey satellites. We are now prepared to undertake much larger programs to apply this technology to Africa—including training programs and the development of training facilities and satellite receiving stations in Africa itself.

· Perhaps the most critical long-term economic need of southern Africa is a modern system of regional transportation. The magnitude of the effort extends beyond the capacity of any one nation or group of nations. For this reason the United States proposes that the World Bank undertake as a priority matter the organization of a multilateral consultative group of donors to develop a modern regional transportation system for southern Africa. For our part we promise our full cooperation in working out a long-term program and in financing appropriate portions of it.

· And finally, I can announce today that we expect to triple our support for development programs in southern and central Africa over the next three years.

In addition the United States has offered leadership in many international forums to promote development through multilateral cooperation. The industrial nations, the newly wealthy oil producers, and the developing countries themselves must collaborate for the goal of development. Africa is a principal beneficiary of the many U.S. initiatives in multilateral institutions and programs—to enhance economic security through supporting export earnings in the face of sharp economic swings, to promote growth through better access to capital markets and technology transfers, to accelerate agricultural production, to improve the conditions of trade and investment in key commodities, and to address the special needs of the poorest nations.

Many of the proposals we have made are already being implemented. Next week in Nairobi I will put forward new proposals to further advance progress in relations between developed and developing nations.

Conclusion. Today I have outlined the principles of American policy on the compelling challenges of southern Africa.

Our proposals are not a program made in America to be passively accepted by Africans. They are an expression of common aspirations and an agenda of cooperation. Underlying it is our fundamental conviction that Africa's destiny must remain in African hands.

No one who wishes this continent well can want to see

Africans divided either between nations or between liberation movements. Africans cannot want outsiders seeking to impose solutions or choosing among countries or movements. The United States, for its part, does not seek any pro-American African bloc confronting a bloc supporting any other power. Nor do we wish to support one faction of a liberation movement against another. But neither should any other country pursue hegemonial aspirations or bloc policies. An attempt by one will inevitably be countered by the other. The United States, therefore, supports African unity and integrity categorically as basic principles of our policy.

There is no better guarantee against outside pressure from any quarter than the determination of African nations in defense of their own independence and unity. You did not build African institutions to see outside forces fragment them into competing blocs. The United States supports Africa's genuine nonalignment and unity. We are ready for collaboration on the basis of mutual respect. We do so guided by our convictions and our values. Your cause is too compatible with our principles for you to need to pursue it by tactics of confrontation with the United States; our self-respect is too strong to let ourselves be pressured either directly or by outside powers.

What Africa needs now from the United States is not exuberant promises or emotional expressions of good will. What it needs is a concrete program which I have sought to offer today. So let us get down to business. Let us direct our eyes toward our great goals—national independence, economic development, racial justice—goals that can be achieved by common action.

Africa in this decade is a testing ground of the world's conscience and vision. That blacks and whites live together in harmony and equality is a moral imperative of our time. Let us prove that these goals can be realized by human choice, that justice can command by the force of its rightness instead of by force of arms.

These are ideals that bind all the races of mankind. They are the mandate of decency and progress and peace.

This drama will be played out in our own lifetime. Our children will inherit either our success or our failure. The world watches with hope, and we approach it with confidence.

So let it be said that black people and white people working together achieved on this continent—which has suffered so much and seen so much injustice—a new era of peace, well-being, and human dignity.

SIXTEEN

THE INDUSTRIAL
DEMOCRACIES:
THE IMPERATIVE OF
COOPERATION

*Address to the International Institute for
Strategic Studies, inaugurating the Alastair
Buchan memorial lecture series, London,
June 25, 1976*

LADIES and gentlemen, friends: On my arrival in Washington seven years ago, one of my first acts was to gather a group of senior scholars of European affairs to have them give their advice to a new President on relations with our allies. The chairman of that group was Alastair Buchan.

He should not be held responsible for the results. But it was only natural to seek his counsel. For Alastair was more than a distinguished expert; he was a consummate man of the West. A Scot by birth, he considered himself, and referred to himself, as a European. He lived many years in the United States and visited us often, applying his incisive mind to the study of America and its role in the world. He was a champion of the importance, indeed the inevitability, of the transatlantic tie between North America and Europe.

Beneath the skeptical air was a passionate commitment to the values and traditions we cherish as Western civilization. Sir Peter Ramsbotham [U.K. Ambassador to the United States] said in his eulogy of Alastair in Washington that no other countryman of his had contributed more to the understanding of international affairs and the strategic implications of nuclear power in the latter half of the twentieth century. But Alastair's focus was not simply the structure of global politics and the roots of war; it was the central role of the West in preserving peace and giving it moral purpose.

This institute is a monument to his quest.

Alastair had that combination of intellect and compassion known as wisdom. It motivated the great contribution he made to scholarship and to a generation's understanding of the transformation of international relationships. He has left his mark on every person in this hall. During the last seven years, he never hesitated to scold me in all friendship when he thought that American policy did not do justice to the great cause of European-American cooperation. I would like to think that, had he lived, he would feel that, after many starts, we have made great strides in strengthening the unity of the West. And if that were his conviction, I for one would be very proud.

"Structural changes," Alastair wrote, "are occurring in the relative power and influence of the major states; there has been a quantitative change of colossal proportions in the interdependence of Western societies and in the demands we make on natural resources; and there are qualitative changes in the preoccupations of our societies." He then posed the question: "Can the highly industrialized states sustain or recover a quality in their national life which not only satisfies the new generation, but can act as an example or attractive force to other societies?"

All of us who wish to honor Alastair's memory must do so in the way he would want most of all—by proving that the answer to his question is yes. A world that cries out for economic advance, for social justice, for political liberty, and for a stable peace needs our collective commitment and contribution. I firmly believe that the industrial democracies working together have the means, if they have the will, to shape creatively a new era of international affairs. Indeed we are doing so on many fronts today, thanks no little to the clarity Alastair brought to our purposes and directions.

A generation ago, Western statesmen fashioned new institutions of collaboration to stave off a common threat. Our progress after thirty years has been striking. Global war has been deterred, and all of the industrial democracies live with an enhanced sense of security. Our economies are the most prosperous on earth; our technology and productive genius have proven indispensable for all countries seeking to better the welfare of their peoples, be they Socialist or developing. Our societies represent, more than ever, a beacon of hope to those who yearn for liberty and justice and progress. In no part of the world and under no other system do men live so well and in so much freedom. If performance is any criterion, the contest between freedom and communism, of which so much was made three decades ago, has been won by the industrial democracies.

And yet at this precise moment, we hear in our countries premonitions of decline, anxieties about the travail of the West and the advance of authoritarianism. Can it be that our deeper problems are not of resources but of will, not of power but of conception?

We who overcame great dangers 30 years ago must not now paralyze ourselves with illusions of impotence. We have already initiated the construction of a new system of international relations—this time on a global scale. We must summon the determination to work toward it in unity and mutual confidence.

For America, cooperation among the free nations is a moral, and not merely a practical, necessity. Americans have never been comfortable with calculations of interest and power

alone. America, to be itself, needs a sense of identity and collaboration with other nations who share its values.

Our association with Western Europe, Canada, and Japan
thus goes to the heart of our national purpose. Common endeavors with our sister democracies raise the goals of our foreign policy beyond physical survival, toward a peace of human
progress and dignity. The ties of intellectual civilization,
democratic tradition, historical association, and more than a
generation of common endeavor bind us together more firmly
than could any pragmatic conception of national interest
alone. The unity of the industrial democracies has been the
cornerstone of American foreign policy for 30 years, and it
will remain so for as far ahead as we can see.

So I would like to pay tribute to Alastair this evening by
addressing the issues he raised: Can America, Europe, and
the industrial democracies meet the challenge of the world's
future? What is the state of our relationship?

The U.S. and a United Europe. In 1973, with Vietnam at
last behind us and fresh from new initiatives with China and
the Soviet Union, the United States proposed that the collaboration of the industrial democracies be given new impetus.
Military security, while still crucial, was no longer sufficient to
give content or political cohesion to our broader relationship
or to retain support for it from a new generation. We faced
important East-West negotiations on European security and
force reductions; a fresh agenda of international economic
problems; the challenge of shaping anew our relationship with
the developing world; and the need to redefine relations between America and a strengthened and enlarged European
Community.

It is academic to debate now whether the United States
acted too theoretically in proposing to approach these challenges through the elaboration of a new Atlantic declaration,

or whether our European friends acted wisely in treating this proposal as a test case of European identity. The doctrinal arguments of 1973 over the procedure for Atlantic consultations, or whether Europe was exercising its proper global role, or whether economic and security issues should be linked, have in fact been settled by the practice of consultations and cooperation unprecedented in intensity and scope. The reality and success of our common endeavors have provided the best definition and revitalization of our relationship. There is no longer any question that Europe and the United States must cooperate closely, under whatever label, and that the unity of Europe is essential to that process.

In its early days, the European Community was the focus of much American idealism, and perhaps of some paternalism, as we urged models of federal unity and transatlantic burden-sharing on our European friends. By now, leaders on both sides of the Atlantic have come to understand that European unity cannot be built by Americans or to an American prescription; it must result from European initiatives.

The evolution of European initiatives—both its successes and its setbacks—inevitably gives rise to new questions about whether the United States still welcomes European unification. Let me take this occasion to emphasize our conviction that European unity is crucial for Europe, for the West, and for the world. We strongly support and encourage it.

We have perhaps become a little more sophisticated about our contribution to the process. We no longer expect that it will grow from the desire to ease American burdens. If Europe is to carry a part of the West's responsibilities in the world, it must do so according to its own conceptions and in its own interest. Alastair Buchan wrote: "It is impossible to inspire Western Europe to political unity or to encourage Japanese self-reliance unless they have the freedom and confidence to define their interests in every sphere, interests which must be reconciled with those of the United States but not subordinated to them."

The United States endorses this principle wholeheartedly. It is not healthy for the United States to be the only center of initiative and leadership in the democratic world. It is not healthy for Europe to be only a passive participant, however close the friendship and however intimate the consultation.

We therefore welcome the fact that Europe's role in global affairs is gaining in vigor and effectiveness. A vital and cohesive Western Europe is an irreplaceable weight on the scales of global diplomacy; American policy can only gain by having a strong partner of parallel moral purposes.

Of course we do not want Europe to find its identity in opposition to the United States. But neither does any sensible European. Of course there will be disagreements between us of tactics, and sometimes of perspectives, if not of ends. But I do not believe that Americans have so lost confidence in ourselves that we must inhibit the role of others, with whom we may have occasional differences, but who share our highest values. The wisest statesmen on the two sides of the ocean have always known that European unity and Atlantic partnership are both essential and mutually reinforcing.

So let us finally put behind us the debates over whether Europe's unity has American support. We consider the issue settled. Let us rather address ourselves to the urgent challenges of mutual concern which a uniting Europe, the United States, and all industrial democracies must face together—common defense, East-West relations, and the international economy.

Security and the Democracies. Security is the bedrock of all that we do. A quarter-century ago, the American defense commitment to Europe provided the shield behind which Western Europe recovered its economic health and political vitality. Today our collective alliance defense—and the U.S.-Japanese relationship—continue to be essential for global stability. But the nature of security and strategy has fundamentally changed since the time when our alliances were founded:

· The Soviet Union has recovered from the devastation of World War II and pressed vigorously ahead on the path of industrial growth. Possessing resources on a continental scale, and imposing on its people enormous sacrifices in the name of its ideology, the U.S.S.R. has developed its economic strength and technology to a point where it can match the West in many sectors of industrial and military power. It shows no signs of changing its priorities.

· For centuries it was axiomatic that increases in military power could be translated into almost immediate political advantage. It is now clear that in strategic weaponry new increments of weapons or destructiveness do not automatically lead to either military or political gains. The destructiveness of strategic weapons has contributed to the emergence of nuclear stalemate. Neither side, if it acts with minimum prudence, will let the balance tip against it, either in an arms race or in an agreement to limit arms.

· Beneath the nuclear umbrella, the temptation to probe with regional forces or proxy wars increases. The steady growth of Soviet conventional military and naval power and its expanding global reach cannot be ignored. Conventional forces and military assistance to allies assume pivotal importance. We must insure that the strength and flexibility of all forces capable of local defense are enhanced. And we must conduct a prudent and forceful foreign policy that is prepared to use our strength to block expansionism.

These new realities demand from us steadiness, above all. Democratic societies have always fluctuated in their attitude toward defense—between complacency and alarmist concern. The long leadtimes of modern weapons and their complexity make both these aberrations dangerous. We cannot afford alternation between neglect and bursts of frenzy if we are to have a coherent defense program and public support for the necessary exertions. We need an allied defense posture that is relevant to our dangers, credible to both friends and adversaries, and justifiable to our peoples. And we must be prepared to sustain it over the long term.

It is imperative that we maintain the programs that insure that the balance is preserved. But we owe it to ourselves to see the military balance in proper perspective. Complacency may produce weakness, but exaggeration of danger can lead to a loss of will. To be sure, there has been a steady buildup of Soviet military power. But we have also seen to the steady growth and improvement of our own forces over the same period.

· We have always had to face Soviet ground forces larger than our own—partly because of the Soviet Union's definition of its needs as a power in the heart of the Eurasian landmass, with perceived threats on both flanks. Its naval power, while a growing and serious problem, is far weaker than combined allied naval strength in terms of tonnage, firepower, range, access to the sea, experience, and seamanship.

· The United States, for its part, is expanding its army from thirteen to sixteen divisions through new measures of streamlining forces; we are increasing our combat forces in Europe; we plan to station a new army brigade on the critical sector of the north German plain; we are augmenting our naval forces. Our European allies have completed major programs to build common infrastructure. We have undertaken new joint efforts of standardization and interoperability of allied forces.

· U.S. strategic forces are superior in accuracy, diversity, reliability, survivability, and numbers of separately targetable nuclear warheads. We have a commanding lead in strategic bombers. In addition there are American deployments overseas and the nuclear forces of two Atlantic allies.

· Even with our different priorities, the economic and technological base which underlies Western military strength remains overwhelmingly superior in size and capacity for innovation. The Soviet Union suffers endemic weakness in its industry and agriculture: Recent studies indicate that this chronic inefficiency extends even into their military sector to a much greater extent than realized before.

These strengths of ours demonstrate that our present security posture is adequate and that it is well within our capacities to continue to balance the various elements of Soviet power. To maintain the necessary defense is a question of leadership more than of power. Our security responsibility is both manageable and unending. We must undertake significant additional efforts for the indefinite future. For as far ahead as we can see, we will live in a twilight area between tranquility and open confrontation.

This is a task for both sides of the Atlantic. Our defense effort within the alliance will be importantly affected by the degree to which the American public is convinced that our allies share similar perceptions of the military challenge and a comparable determination to meet it. The greatest threat to the alliance would occur if, for whatever reason—through misreading the threat, or inattention to conventional forces, or reductions of the defense efforts of allies, or domestic developments within NATO members—U.S. public support for NATO were weakened.

The challenge of building sufficient hardware is easier than those of geopolitical understanding, political coordination and, above all, resolve. In the nuclear age, once a change in the geopolitical balance has become unambiguous, it is too late to do anything about it. However great our strength, it will prove empty if we do not resist seemingly marginal changes whose cumulative impact can undermine our security. Power serves little purpose without the doctrines and concepts which define where our interests require its application.

Therefore, let us not paralyze ourselves by a rhetoric of weakness. Let us concentrate on building the understanding of our strategic interests which must underlie any policy. The face is that nowhere has the West been defeated for lack of strength. Our setbacks have been self-inflicted, either because leaders chose objectives that were beyond our psychological capabilities or because our legislatures refused to support what the executive branch believed was essential. This—and not the various "gaps" that appear in the American debate in years divisible by four—is the deepest security problem we face.

East-West Relations. As long ago as the Harmel Report of December 1967, the Atlantic alliance has treated as its "two main functions" the assurance of military security and realistic measures to reduce tensions between East and West. We never considered confrontation, even when imposed on us by the other side, or containment an end in itself. Nor did we believe that disagreements with the Soviet Union would automatically disappear. On the contrary, the very concept of "détente" has always been applicable only to an adversary relationship. It was designed to prevent competition from sliding into military hostilities and to create the conditions for the relationship to be gradually and prudently improved.

Thus alliance policy toward the East has had two necessary

dimensions. We seek to prevent the Soviet Union from transforming its military power into political expansion. At the same time we seek to resolve conflicts and disputes through negotiation and to strengthen the incentives for moderation by expanding the area of constructive relations.

These two dimensions are mutually reinforcing. A strong defense and resistance to adventurism are prerequisites for efforts of conciliation. By the same token, only a demonstrated commitment to peace can sustain domestic support for an adequate defense and a vigilant foreign policy. Our public and Congress will not back policies which appear to invite crises; nor will they support firmness in a crisis unless they are convinced that peaceful and honorable alternatives have been exhausted. Above all, we owe it to ourselves and to future generations to seek a world based on something more stable and hopeful than a balance of terror constantly contested.

However we label such a policy, it is imposed by the unprecedented conditions of the nuclear age. No statesman can lightly risk the lives of tens of millions. Every American president, after entering office and seeing the facts, has come to President Eisenhower's view that "there is no . . . alternative to peace."

Our generation has been traumatized by World War II, because we remember that war broke out as a result of an imbalance of power. This is a lesson we must not forget. But neither must we forget the lesson of World War I, when war broke out despite an equilibrium of power. An international structure held together only by a balance of forces will sooner or later collapse in catastrophe. In our time this could spell the end of civilized life. We must therefore conduct a diplomacy that deters challenges if possible and that contains them at tolerable levels if they prove unavoidable; a diplomacy that resolves issues, nurtures restraint, and builds cooperation based on mutual interest.

This policy has critics in all our countries. Some take for granted the relative absence of serious crises in recent years, which the policy has helped to bring about, and then fault it for not producing the millenium, which it never claimed. Some caricature its objectives, portraying its goals in more exalted terms than any of its advocates, and then express dismay at the failure of reality to conform to this impossible standard. They describe détente as if it meant the end of all rivalry; when rivalry persists, they conclude that détente has failed and charge its advocates with deception or naivete. They measure the success of policy toward adversaries by criteria that should be reserved for traditional friendships. They use the reality of competition to attack the goal of coexistence, rather than to illustrate its necessity.

In fact, this policy has never been based on such hope or gullibility. It has always been designed to create conditions in which a cool calculus of interests would dictate restraint rather than opportunism, settlement of conflicts rather than their exacerbation. Western policies can at best manage and shape, not assume away, East-West competition.

A pivot of the East-West relationship is the U.S.-Soviet negotiation on limitation of strategic arms. Increasingly, strategic forces find their function only in deterring and matching each other. A continuing buildup of strategic arms, therefore, only leads to fresh balances, but at higher levels of expenditures and uncertainties. In an era of expanding technological possibilities, it is impossible to make rational choices of force planning without some elements of predictability in the strategic environment. Moreover, a continuing race diverts resources from other needed areas such as forces for regional

defense, where imbalances can have serious geopolitical consequences. All these factors have made arms limitation a practical
interest of both sides, as well as a factor for stability in the
world.

We have made considerable progress toward curbing the
strategic arms race in recent years. We will continue vigorously
to pursue this objective in ways which protect Western interests and reflect the counsel of our allies.

In defining and pursuing policies of relaxing tensions with
the East, the unity of the industrial democracies is essential.
Our consultations have been intensive and frequent, and the
record of Western cohesion in recent years has been encouraging—in the negotiations leading to the Four Power
Agreement on Berlin; in the mutual and balanced force reduction talks; in the SALT negotiations [Strategic Arms Limitation Talks]; and in the preparation for the European Security
Conference.

Allied cooperation, and the habits of consultation and coordination which we have formed, will be even more important in the future. For as the policy of relaxing tensions
proceeds, it will involve issues at the heart of all our interests.

No one should doubt the depth of our commitment to this
process. But we also need to be clear about its limits and about
our conception of reciprocity:

· We should require consistent patterns of behavior in different parts of the world. The West must make it clear that coexistence requires mutual restraint, not only in Europe and in
the central strategic relationship but also in the Middle East,
in Africa, in Asia—in fact, globally. The NATO foreign ministers, at their Oslo meeting last month, stressed the close link
between stability and security in Europe and in the world as
a whole. We must endorse this not only by our rhetoric, but
above all by our actions.

· We should make clear the tolerable definition of global ideological rivalry. We do not shrink from ideological competition. We have every reason for confidence in the indestructible power of man's yearning for freedom. But we cannot agree that ideology alone is involved when Soviet power is extended into areas such as southern Africa in the name of national liberation, or when regional or local instabilities are generated or exploited in the name of proletarian internationalism.

· We should not allow the Soviet Union to apply détente selectively within the alliance. Competition among us in our diplomatic or economic policies toward the East risks dissipating Western advantages and opening up Soviet opportunities. We must resist division and maintain the closest coordination.

The process of improving East-West relations in Europe must not be confined to relations with the Soviet Union. The benefits of relaxation of tensions must extend to Eastern, as well as Western, Europe.

There should be no room for misconceptions about United States policy:

· We are determined to deal with Eastern Europe on the basis of the sovereignty and independence of each of its countries. We recognize no spheres of influence and no pretensions to hegemony. Two American presidents and several cabinet officials have visited Romania and Poland as well as nonaligned Yugoslavia, to demonstrate our stake in the flourishing and independence of those nations.

· For the same reason, we will persist in our efforts to improve our contacts and develop our concrete bilateral relations in economic and other fields with the countries of Eastern Europe.

· The United States supports the efforts of West European

nations to strengthen their bilateral and regional ties with the countries of Eastern Europe. We hope that this process will help heal the divisions of Europe which have persisted since World War II.

· We will continue to pursue measures to improve the lives of the people in Eastern Europe in basic human terms—such as freer emigration, the unification of families, greater flow of information, increased economic interchange, and more opportunities for travel.

The United States, in parallel with its allies, will continue to expand relationships with Eastern Europe as far and as fast as is possible. This is a long-term process; it is absurd to imagine that one conference by itself can transform the internal structure of Communist governments. Rhetoric is no substitute for patient and realistic actions. We will raise no expectations that we cannot fulfill. But we will never cease to assert our traditional principles of human liberty and national self-determination.

The course of East-West relations will inevitably have its obstacles and setbacks. We will guard against erosion of the gains that we have made in a series of difficult negotiations; we will insure that agreements already negotiated are properly implemented. We must avoid both sentimentality that would substitute good will for strength, and mock toughness that would substitute posturing for a clear conception of our purposes.

We in the West have the means to pursue this policy successfully. Indeed we have no realistic alternative. We have nothing to fear from competition. If there is a military competition, we have the strength to defend our interests. If there is an economic competition, we won it long ago. If there is an ideological competition, the power of our ideas depends only on our will to uphold them.

We need only to stay together and stay the course. If we do so, the process of East-West relations can, over time, strengthen the fabric of peace and genuinely improve the lives of all the peoples around the world.

Our Economic Strength. One of the greatest strengths of the industrial democracies is their unquestioned economic preeminence. Partly because we are committed to the free market system which has given us this preeminence, we have not yet fully realized the possibilities—indeed the necessity—of applying our economic strength constructively to shaping a better international environment.

The industrial democracies together account for 65 percent of the world's production and 70 percent of its commerce. Our economic performance drives international trade and finance. Our investment, technology, managerial expertise, and agricultural productivity are the spur to development and well-being around the world. Our enormous capacities are multiplied if we coordinate our policies and efforts.

The core of our strength is the vitality and growth of our own economies. At the Rambouillet economic summit last November, at the Puerto Rico summit next week, in the OECD [Organization for Economic Cooperation and Development], and in many other forums, the major democratic nations have shown their ability to work together. But an extensive agenda still summons us. We will require further efforts to continue our recovery and promote noninflationary growth. We will need to facilitate adequate investment and supplies of raw materials. We must continue to avoid protectionist measures, and we must use the opportunity of the multilateral trade negotiations to strengthen and expand the international trading system. We need to reduce our vulnerability and dependence on imported oil through conservation, new sources of energy, and collective preparations for possible emergencies. And we must build on the progress made at Rambouillet and at Jamaica last January to improve the international monetary system.

Our central challenge is to pool our strengths, to increase our coordination, and to tailor our policies to the long term. On the basis of solid cooperation among ourselves, we must deal more effectively with the challenges of the global economy —such as our economic relations with the centrally planned Communist economies and with the scores of new nations concerned with development.

East-West economic interchange, while small in relative scale, is becoming an important economic and political factor. This growth reflects our fundamental strength. It carries risks and complications, both political and economic. But it also presents opportunities for stabilizing relations and involving the Communist countries in responsible international conduct. If the democracies pursue parallel policies—not allowing the Communist states to stimulate debilitating competition among us or to manipulate the process for their own unilateral advantage—East-West economic relations can be a factor for peace and well-being.

We must insure that benefits are reciprocal. We must avoid large trade imbalances which could open opportunities for political pressure. We should structure economic relations so that the Communist states will be drawn into the international economic system and accept its disciplines. When dealing with centrally controlled state economies, we have to realize that economic relations have a high degree of political content and cannot be conducted solely on the normal commercial basis. Obviously, profitability must be one standard. But we need a broader strategy, consistent with our free enterprise system, so that economic relations will contribute to political objectives. The industrial democracies should coordinate their policies to insure the orderly and beneficial evolution of East-West relations. To these ends the United States has proposed to the OECD that we intensify our analyses of the problems and opportunities inherent in East-West trade with a view to charting common objectives and approaches.

If the economic strength of the industrial democracies is important to the Socialist countries, it is vital for the developing world. These nations seek to overcome pervasive poverty and to lift the horizons of their peoples. They ask for an equitable share of global economic benefits and a greater role in international decisions that affect them.

The process of development is crucial not only for the poorer nations but for the industrial nations as well. Our own prosperity is closely linked to the raw materials, the markets, and the aspirations of the developing countries. An international order can be stable only if all nations perceive it as fundamentally just and are convinced that they have a stake in it. Over the long term, cooperative North-South relations are thus clearly in the interest of all, and the objectives of industrial and developing countries should be complementary.

However, the North-South dialogue has been far from smooth. Tactics of pressure and an emphasis on rhetorical victories at conferences have too often created an atmosphere of confrontation. Such attitudes obscure the fundamental reality that development is an arduous long-term enterprise. It will go forward only if both sides face facts without illusions, shunning both confrontation and sentimentality.

Far more is involved than the mechanical application of technology and capital to poverty. There must be within the developing country a sense of purpose and direction, determined leadership and, perhaps most important, an impulse for change among the people. Development requires national administration, a complex infrastructure, a revised system of education, and many other social reforms. It is a profoundly unsettling process that takes decades. For many new countries it is in fact even more difficult than similar efforts by the Western countries a century ago, for their social and geographic conditions reflect the arbitrary subdivisions of colonial rule. Some face obstacles which could not be surmounted even with the greatest exertions on their own. Their progress depends on how well the international community responds to the imperatives of economic interdependence.

It is senseless, therefore, to pretend that development can proceed by quick fixes or one-shot solutions. Artificial majorities at international conferences confuse the issue. Confrontational tactics will in time destroy the domestic support in the industrial countries for the forward-looking policy which the developing countries so desperately need.

The industrial democracies have special responsibilities as well. Development requires their sustained and collective cooperation. They represent the largest markets and most of the world's technology and capital. They have an obligation to show understanding for the plight of the poorest and the striving for progress of all developing nations. But they do the developing countries no favor if they contribute to escapism. If they compete to curry favor over essentially propagandistic issues, contributions will be diluted, resources will go unallocated, and unworkable projects will be encouraged.

The developing countries need from us not a sense of guilt but intelligent and realistic proposals that merge the interests of both sides in an expanding world economy:

First, we must develop further the mechanisms of our own

cooperation. To this end the United States has made a number of concrete proposals at the recently concluded OECD meeting.

Second, the industrial democracies should coordinate their national aid programs better so that we use our respective areas of experience and technical skill to best advantage. President Giscard's proposal for an integrated Western fund for Africa is an imaginative approach to regional development.

Third, we should regularly consult and work in close parallel in major international negotiations and conferences. The Conference on International Economic Cooperation, the multilateral trade negotiations, U.N. General Assembly special sessions, world conferences on food, population, environment or housing, and UNCTAD [U.N. Conference on Trade and Development] all can achieve much more if the industrial democracies approach them with a clear and coherent purpose.

Fourth, we should stop conducting all negotiations on an agenda not our own. We should not hesitate to put forward our own solutions to common problems.

Finally, we need a clear, longer-term strategy for development. The diverse elements of the process, including various forms of assistance, technology transfer, trade and financial policy, must be better integrated.

Cooperation among developed countries is not confrontation between North and South, as is often alleged. The fact is that a responsible development policy is possible only if the industrial democracies pursue realistic goals with conviction, compassion, and coordination. They must not delude themselves or their interlocutors by easy panaceas, or mistake slogans for progress. We make the greatest contribution to development if we insist that the North-South dialogue emphasize substance rather than ideology, and concentrate on practical programs instead of empty theological debates.

The Future of Democratic Societies. In every dimension of our activities, then, the industrial democracies enter the new era with substantial capacities and opportunities. At the same time, it would be idle to deny that in recent years the moral stamina of the West has been seriously challenged.

Since its beginnings, Western civilization has clearly defined the individual's relationship to society and the state. In southern Europe the humanism of the Renaissance made man the measure of all things. In northern Europe the Reformation, in proclaiming the priesthood of all believers and offering rewards for individual effort, put the emphasis on the individual. In England the sense of justice and human rights and responsibilities evolved in the elaboration of the common law. Two hundred years ago the authors of our Declaration of Independence drew upon this heritage; to them every human being had inalienable rights to life, liberty, and the pursuit of happiness. The state existed to protect the individual and permit full scope for the enjoyment of these rights.

Today in the West, thirty years after the Marshall Plan, our deepest challenge is that a new generation must explore again the issues of liberty and social responsibility in an era when societies have grown vastly in size, complexity, and dynamism. The modern industrial society, though founded in freedom and offering prosperity, risks losing the individual in the mass and fostering his alienation. The technical complexity of public issues challenges the functioning of democracy. Mass media and the weakening of party and group structures further the isolation of the individual; they transform democratic politics, adding new elements of volatility and unpredictability. The bureaucratic state poses a fundamental challenge to political leadership and responsiveness to public will.

Basic moral questions are raised:

· How do we inspire a questioning new generation in a relativist age and in a society of impersonal institutions?

· Will skepticism and cynicism sap the spiritual energies of our civilization at the moment of its greatest technical and material success?

· Having debunked authority, will our societies now seek refuge in false simplifications, demagogic certitudes, or extremist panaceas?

These questions are not a prediction but a test—a test of the creativity and moral fortitude of our peoples and leaders.

Western civilization has met such tests before. In the late fifteenth century Europe was in a period of gloomy introspection, preoccupied with a sense of despair and mortality. The cities which had sparked its revival following the Islamic conquests were in decline. Its territory was being diminished by the depredations of a powerful invader from the East. Its spiritual, economic, and cultural center—Italy—was a prey to anarchy and dismemberment.

And yet Europe at that very moment was already well launched on one of the world's periods of greatest political and intellectual advance. The Renaissance and Reformation, the great discoveries, the revival of humanistic values, the industrial and democratic revolutions—these were all to create the character and the dynamism of the Western civilization of which we, on both sides of the Atlantic, are the heirs.

Similarly today, the West has assets to meet its challenges and to draw from them the material for new acts of creation. It is our nations that have been the vanguard of the modern age. Intellectually and morally, it is our societies that have proven themselves the vast laboratory of the experiment of modernization. Above all, it is the Western democracies that originated—and keep alive today—the vision of political freedom, social justice, and economic well-being for all peoples. None of us lives up to this vision ideally, or all the time. But the rigorous standard by which we judge ourselves is what makes us different from totalitarian societies of the left or the right.

This, then, is our moral task:

First, as democratic governments we must redeem, over and over again, the trust of our peoples. As a nation which has accepted the burden of leadership, the United States has a special responsibility: We must overcome the traumas of the recent period, eradicate their causes, and preserve the qualities which world leadership demands. In Europe, wherever there has been a slackening in governmental responsiveness to the needs of citizens, there should be reform and revival.

Second, we must confront the complexities of a pluralistic world. This calls for more than specific technical solutions. It requires of leaders a willingness to explain the real alternatives, no matter how complicated or difficult. And it requires of electorates an understanding that we must make choices amidst uncertainty, where the outcome may be neither immediate nor reducible to simple slogans.

Third, we must clarify our attitudes toward political forces within Western societies which appeal to electorates on the ground that they may bring greater efficiency to government. But we cannot avoid the question of the commitment of these forces to democratic values, nor a concern about the trends that a decision based on temporary convenience would set in motion. At the same time, opposition to these forces is clearly not enough. There must be a response to legitimate social and economic aspirations and to the need for reforms of inadequacies from which these forces derive much of their appeal.

Finally, the solidarity of the democratic nations in the world is essential both as material support and as a moral symbol. There could be no greater inspiration of our peoples than the reaffirmation of their common purpose and the conviction that they can shape their fortune in freedom.

We cannot afford either a perilous complacency or immobilizing pessimism. Alastair Buchan posed his questions not to induce paralysis but as a spur to wiser action and fresh achievement.

We know what we must do. We also know what we can do. It only remains to do it.

SEVENTEEN

AMERICA AND ASIA

*Address to the Downtown Rotary Club and
the Chamber of Commerce, Seattle,
July 22, 1976*

A LITTLE more than two weeks ago this nation celebrated its two hundredth birthday. In the process of that celebration, Americans learned that despite the agony, the turmoil, and the constitutional crisis of the last decade, we are still proud to be Americans and still proud of what America means to the world. We felt once again that our country is free, and vibrant with life and change. We saw that tolerance and hope and dedication are far more a part of the American national character today than hatred, division, and despair.

To the generation that came to maturity in the late 1960s or early 1970s, these truths may have been apparent for the first time. For my generation it was, rather, a reminder of basic verities about America which had been in danger of being obscured by the turmoil of a decade. But for all of us, of whatever generation, it was an uplifting experience.

Certainly the events of one celebration, however inspiring, cannot by themselves solve the long-term problems that our nation will face in its third century. But they illuminate the road before us as we enter our electoral campaign. They tell us that it is time to move away from the counsels of timidity, fear, and resentment which have done so much to corrupt our public dialogue.

Ours is not a nation bent on domination, as we were told four years ago. Ours is not a nation in retreat, as we have been told too often this year. Ours is a nation which understands that America cannot be at peace if the world is at war; that America cannot be prosperous if the world is mired in poverty; that America cannot be true to its heritage unless it stands with those who strive for freedom and human dignity. In short we know that our lives, liberty, and pursuit of happiness depend on the world in which we live and that America's leadership is crucial to shaping what kind of world that will be.

We face today, as we have for several years, international conditions quite unlike those known by earlier generations of Americans. We have designed a foreign policy capable of mastering those new challenges; a foreign policy for the last quarter of the twentieth century based on four propositions:

· First, American strength is essential to the peace of the world and to the success of our diplomacy. We should not bemuse ourselves with false choices between defense or domestic needs, between security or social justice. Unless we pursue all these objectives we are likely to achieve none of them. Security cannot be the sole goal of our policy, but no other achievements can endure without it.

· Second, our alliances with the great democracies of North America, Western Europe, and Asia are the bedrock and the top priority of our foreign policy.

· Third, in an age of thermonuclear weapons and strategic balance, we have a moral, as well as a political, obligation to strive mightily toward the overriding goal of peace. We are ready to use our strength to resist blackmail or pressure; we must also be prepared to negotiate longstanding disputes, foster habits of moderation, and develop more constructive ties with potential adversaries. The American people and the people of the world ask for a peace more secure than a balance of terror constantly being contested.

· Fourth, security and peace are the foundation for addressing the positive aspirations of peoples. Prosperity, human rights, protecting the environment, economic development, scientific and technical advance, and cultural exchange have become major concerns of international diplomacy. In these spheres the destinies of nations are interdependent and a world of order and progress requires new forms of cooperation among all nations—rich and poor, industrialized and developing.

We want our children to live in a world of greater peace and justice. We want them to have the opportunity to apply their own genius, in their own time, to the betterment of mankind. To do so we, in our time, must help shape an international order that welcomes the participation of all nations and responds to the deepest concerns of all peoples.

We have come a long way already. We are at peace for the first time in more than fifteen years. Our collaboration with the great industrial democracies is steadily expanding into new fields, while its fundamental basis is stronger than it has been in years. We have made progress toward peace in the Middle East and, partly because of our unique role there, the elements for major new advances exist. In Asia, we have —as I will discuss in greater detail—solidified our ties with both our friends and our potential adversaries. Here in the Western Hemisphere we are building a new relationship based on equality and mutual respect. We have inaugurated a hopeful new policy in Africa. And with respect to the Soviet Union we have combined a determination to resist expansion with a readiness to build relations on a more stable and lasting basis; we are, and will be, conciliatory but vigilant.

The people of the Pacific Northwest hardly need to be told of the strength or role of America. Yours is a region but recently carved from a wilderness by men and women of courage and vision. Here the pioneer spirit that is so much a part of our history lives on, and from here America looks out across the Pacific toward the nations—new and old—of Asia. And it is America's relations with Asia that I would like to discuss with you today.

The Asian Dimension. No region in the world is more dynamic, more diverse, or more complex than Asia.

· In the past generation Americans have fought three major wars in Asia. We have learned the hard way that our own safety and well-being depend upon peace in the Pacific and that peace cannot be maintained unless we play an active part.

· Our prosperity is inextricably linked to the economy of the Pacific basin. Last year our trade with Asian nations exceeded our trade with Europe. Asian raw materials fuel our factories; Asian manufacturers serve our consumers; Asian markets offer outlets for our exports and investment opportunities for our business community.

· And our ties with Asia have a unique human dimension. For generations Americans have supplied an impulse for change in Asian societies; Asian culture and ideas in turn have touched our own intellectual, artistic, and social life deeply.

American foreign policy has known both great accomplishment and bitter disappointment in Asia. After World War II we sought above all to contain Communist expansion. We essentially succeeded. We forged a close alliance with democratic Japan. We and our allies assisted South Korea in defeating aggression. We provided for the orderly transition of the Philippines to full independence. We strengthened the ties with Australia and New Zealand that had been forged as allies in two wars. We spurred the development of the Pacific basin into a zone of remarkable economic vitality and growth.

By the late 1960s, however, old policies confronted new realities—American disenchantment with a war we would not win and could not end; acute rivalry between the major Communist powers; and, above all, Japan's burgeoning power and prosperity. It was becoming apparent that our commitments in Asia too often dictated our interests; that we sometimes acted as though our stake in our allies' security was greater than their own; that estrangement with China no longer served either nation's interests nor the cause of global stability; that our economic dealings not infrequently resembled patron-client relationships.

Throughout the first half of this decade, therefore, we have been fashioning a new policy for Asia. We have been bringing our commitments into balance with our interests. We have helped our allies and friends augment their own strength, while we have gradually reduced our own military presence in Asia by 130,000 men, in addition to the 550,000 troops we withdrew from Vietnam. We have strengthened our relations with Japan, begun a new relationship with the People's Republic of China, and searched for political solutions to Asian regional conflicts. We have encouraged Asian nations in their self-reliance and in their efforts at regional cooperation. We have welcomed Asian nations in new multilateral efforts to improve the global economic system.

While a great deal has been accomplished, Asia remains a region of potential turbulence. The collapse of Vietnam last year produced concern about a more general American retreat from Asia. Happily such fears have subsided, largely because American policy has buttressed the inherent strength and resilience of the nations of Asia. But there are no grounds for complacency. Soviet activity in Asia is growing. North and South Korea remain locked in bitter confrontation. Hanoi represents a new center of power, and its attitude toward its neighbors remains ambiguous and potentially threatening. Most developing nations remain afflicted by social and political tensions. And the scramble for oil and ocean resources raises the specter of possible future territorial disputes.

Much will depend on our actions and on the confidence of Asian nations in our steadiness. Indeed all the strands of our global policy meet in Asia:

· Peace in Asia is crucial for global peace.

· The need to resolve conflicts and to ease tensions is nowhere more acute than in Asia.

· And the effort to shape new patterns of international cooperation holds great promise in Asia where the developing nations are among the world's most dynamic and self-reliant.

Let me now discuss each of these challenges in turn.

Asian Security. First, the problem of security in Asia.

All the world's major powers—the United States, Japan, China, the Soviet Union, Western Europe—have significant interests in Asia. All would be directly affected by conflict there. Yet the security of none of these powers is determined exclusively—and in some cases not even primarily—by events in Asia. Therefore, no nation should believe that it can enhance its security by deflecting conflicts from one continent to another. If the European balance is upset, our security and the security of Asian countries will be affected. If the Asian balance is jeopardized, serious repercussions will be felt in Europe. Neither in Europe nor in Asia can we permit others to dictate our destiny or the destiny of those whose independence is of concern to us.

Security policy for Asia must, therefore, be formed in global terms. Yet its requirements are uniquely complex. In Europe two alliance systems face each other directly across a clear line drawn down the center of the continent. The principal danger is external attack by organized military forces. The strengths and weaknesses of both sides are relatively calculable.

In Asia the balance is more multiple and fluid. The focal point is not solely between East and West; it includes the contention between the two major Communist powers, and the threats are highly diverse.

In some areas, such as Korea, the principal danger lies in armed attack across an established frontier. In others, such as Southeast Asia, the more immediate threats involve insurgency. Governments confront the difficult challenge of nation-building. Most are burdened by complex social problems arising from religious, racial, and cultural differences. Virtually all must contend with armed dissidents who are frequently ready to accept ouside assistance.

As President Ford stated in Honolulu last December, the linchpin of our Asian security effort must be a strong and balanced U.S. military posture in the Pacific. Only if we are perceived to be clearly capable of supporting friends can we discourage aggression against them. Only by showing that we understand the necessities of the regional balance of power can we encourage free countries to see to their self-defense. To the extent that the nations of Asia achieve a margin of security, the political forces that stand for democracy and human liberty are encouraged. By the same token, unilateral withdrawals from Asia diminish our security as well as our influence even over the domestic evolution of friendly countries.

It goes without saying that an American commitment is vital only if it is perceived to be as much in the' interest of our allies as of ourselves. No nation should conduct its policy under the illusion that it is doing the United States a favor by permitting us to contribute to its defense. Those who seek to adjust their defense relationships with us will find us prepared to accommodate their desires in a spirit of reciprocity.

At the same time let there be no doubt about this Administration's firmness with regard to our treaty commitments. Allies needing our support will find us constant; adversaries testing our resolution will find us steadfast.

It is not possible to enumerate all our security interests in Asia in one speech. Let me therefore discuss three areas of special importance or complexity: Japan, Korea, and Southeast Asia.

No relationship is more important to the United States than our alliance with Japan. Mutual security remains fundamental to our collaboration, but in a new era we have extended our partnership to a broad range of common interests—easing tensions in Asia, solving regional and global problems, and combining our vast economic strengths to spur stable and noninflationary world economic growth.

In the early 1970s Japan and the United States passed through an inevitable period of adjustment from dependence and American predominance to equality and mutual responsibility. There were frictions over textiles and monetary policies and over the timing of our essentially parallel China policies. But these difficulties have been overcome; they proved to be the growing pains of a more mature and equal relationship. Today our relations with Japan are better than they have ever been. There are no significant bilateral disputes. We have developed a clearer common perception of our security requirements, which will be further enhanced by the recently formed Joint Committee on Defense Cooperation. We have injected greater balance and reciprocity into our economic relations. We have learned to identify and deal with potential difficulties before they become politically explosive. We have consulted with greater frequency and frankness and in greater depth than in any previous period. Both nations are displaying sensitivity to the intangibles of our relationship and have built a wide base of public support for closer cooperation.

Our relationship with Japan plays a central role in furthering stability and progress in Asia and the world. Our security relationship is crucial for the global balance of power. Japan is our largest overseas trading partner. Each of us seeks to improve relations with Moscow and Peking, to ease tensions in Korea, to encourage a stable political evolution in Southeast Asia. Each of us cooperates in the development of effective international efforts to promote stable economic growth, strengthen bonds among the industrial democracies, and shape more positive ties between the industrial and developing countries.

Japan and the United States share a common dedication to the principles of democracy. And so, close consultation on key regional and global issues is at the heart of our respective policies. The United States will make every effort to strengthen these bonds.

Americans fought and died to preserve South Korea's independence. Our experience and our sacrifice define our stake in the preservation of this hard-won stability; treaty obligations of mutual defense define our legal obligations. Our support and assistance will be available where they have been promised. In fulfilling our commitments we will look to South

Korea to assume the primary responsibility for its own defense, especially in manpower. And we will continue to remind the South Korean Government that responsiveness to the popular will and social justice are essential if subversion and external challenge are to be resisted. But we shall not forget that our alliance with South Korea is designed to meet an external threat which affects our own security, and that of Japan as well.

Difficult as the situation still remains in Korea, it is the friendly nations of Southeast Asia that, in the wake of Indochina, are facing the greatest adjustment to new conditions.

Nations which once looked to us for their security almost exclusively have been forced by events into greater self-reliance and broader cooperation among each other. The members of the Association of Southeast Asian Nations [ASEAN]—the Philippines, Indonesia, Thailand, Malaysia, and Singapore— are determined to preserve their independence by hastening the pace of regional consolidation. All face serious problems that are endemic to the process of development; all seek to sustain and expand their relations with us; all hope that we will retain an active interest in their destiny.

President Ford, in his speech in Honolulu last December and in his visits to the Philippines and Indonesia, affirmed our continuing interest in the well-being and safety of Southeast Asia. We shall encourage the efforts of the ASEAN countries to bolster their independence; we welcome Southeast Asian regional cooperation. Clearly our effort cannot substitute for, but only supplement, regional efforts. But we are prepared to continue to provide military assistance, though with greater emphasis on cash and credit sales. We will, as well, maintain our military presence in the Western Pacific, especially our mobile naval and air power. We are in the process of negotiating a new base agreement with the Philippines. We will promote new patterns of economic cooperation. And we will co-

operate with ASEAN countries, consistent with their own initiatives and concepts.

Easing Tensions to Strengthen Peace. Second, let me turn
to the problem of easing tensions.

In the thermonuclear age, we have no more important obligation than to push back the shadow of nuclear confrontation.
If crises occur they must not result from any lapse of vision
on our part. Accommodation without strength or principle
leads to appeasement; but in the thermonuclear age, reliance
on power—not coupled with a spirit of conciliation—can spell
catastrophe for all of mankind.

Thus the United States, in concert with its allies, seeks to
reach beyond security toward better relations—based on strict
reciprocity and principle—with former or potential adversaries.

No nation is more important to this process than the People's Republic of China. Together we have turned a dramatic
new page, following a generation of mutual suspicion and
hostility. There have long been deep sentimental attachments
between the American and the Chinese peoples which have
provided an important bond between our two nations even
in the most difficult times. But it was mutual necessity that
impelled us both to launch a fresh beginning in 1969. Our
shared concern that the world remain free from domination
by military force or blackmail—"hegemony" as we have described it in our various communiques—provided the strategic foundation for a new relationship. This mutual interest
continues and is the basis for durable and growing ties.

Both sides derive benefits from constructive relations—improved prospects for maintaining a global equilibrium, reduced dangers of conflict in Asia, mutually beneficial trade and
cultural exchanges, and expanded possibilities for cooperative
or parallel action on specific global issues. We have made
significant progress in improving relations with China over

the past several years. We have established liaison offices in each other's capitals. We have increased trade and promoted exchanges. Frequent and wide-ranging talks with Chinese leaders—including visits by two American Presidents and many Congressional delegations—have deepened our mutual understanding. On some international issues there is substantial compatibility in our perspective and, where our interests diverge, we are diminishing the risks of miscalculation.

It is important to recognize that China's perception of the United States as a strong and resolute force in international events is an important factor in shaping our relations. We will keep Chinese views in mind in framing our approach to important international questions. But, equally, if so subtle and complex a relationship is to prosper, the People's Republic of China must take our concerns and problems into account as well. We must deal with each other on the basis of equality and mutual benefit—and a continuing recognition that our evolving relationship is important for global stability and progress.

The new relationship between the United States and the People's Republic of China is now an enduring and important feature of the international scene. We are determined to work to improve it further. While difficult issues remain, we intend to continue to move toward the normalization of our relationship in keeping with the principles of the Shanghai Communique.

On the Korean Peninsula, too, we are prepared to make serious efforts to ease tensions.

In recent years North Korea and its friends have mounted a major diplomatic campaign—especially in the so-called nonaligned forums and the United Nations—to alter the institutional arrangements of the armistice agreement which ended hostilities in Korea twenty-three years ago and helps to keep the peace today. They insist upon unconditional dissolution of the U.N. Command, which, together with North Korea and China, is a signatory to the armistice agreement. They have gone so far as to claim that if the Command is dissolved, the armistice agreement itself would cease to exist. At the same time North Korea demands the unilateral withdrawal of American forces from Korea. They propose that the issues of peace and security on the peninsula be discussed in bilateral talks with the United States alone, excluding the Republic of Korea which represents two-thirds of the Korean population.

North Korea's proposals are designed not to promote peace but to isolate our ally, to precipitate unilateral American withdrawal, and to dissolve the existing legal arrangements into amorphous general negotiations.

The United States will never accept such proposals. No nation that truly believes in peace should support them; no country interested in genuine nonalignment should lend itself to so one-sided an approach.

We do not maintain that present arrangements in the Korean Peninsula must remain forever frozen. On the contrary, the United States favors new negotiations to promote security and to ease tensions there. We are prepared to discuss a new legal basis for the existing armistice. We are also ready to replace the armistice with more permanent arrangements.

But this Administration cannot, and will not, negotiate behind the back of our South Korean ally over issues which affect its very existence. Nor will the United States agree to terminate the U.N. Command without new arrangements which preserve the integrity of the armistice agreement—the only existing legal arrangement which commits the parties concerned to keep the peace—or which establish a new permanent legal basis. And the United States will not undermine stability and hopes for negotiation by withdrawing its forces unilaterally.

The United States position with respect to Korea is clear.

· First, we urge a resumption of serious discussions between North and South Korea.

· Second, if North Korea's allies are prepared to improve their relations with South Korea, then and only then will we be prepared to take similar steps toward North Korea.

· Third, we continue to support proposals that the United Nations open its doors to full membership for South and North Korea without prejudice to their eventual reunification.

· Finally, we are prepared to negotiate a new basis for the armistice or to replace it with more permanent arrangements in any form acceptable to all the parties.

In this spirit we proposed last September [22, 1975, at the U.N. General Assembly] a conference including North and South Korea, the United States, and the People's Republic of China—the parties most immediately concerned—to discuss ways of preserving the armistice agreement and of reducing tensions in Korea. We noted that in such a meeting we would be ready to explore possibilities for a larger conference to negotiate more fundamental and durable arrangements.

Today President Ford has asked me to call again for such a conference.

Specifically, the U.S. Government is prepared to meet with South Korea, North Korea, and the People's Republic of China during the coming session of the U.N. General Assembly. We propose New York, but we are ready to consider some other mutually agreeable place. We are willing to begin immediate discussions on issues of procedure and site. Such a conference could provide a new legal structure for the armistice if the parties agree. It could replace the armistice with more permanent arrangements. It could ease tensions throughout Asia.

We urge other parties to respond affirmatively. Any nation genuinely interested in peace on the peninsula should be prepared to sit down and talk with the other parties on ways to improve the existing situation.

Southeast Asia, as much as Northeast Asia, requires our careful attention. Indochina, an arena of war for generations, has yet to find a positive and peaceful role. Vietnam has been unified by force, producing a new and strong power in the region, and Communist regimes have taken over in Laos and Cambodia. The relations of the Indochinese states with one another are unsettled and unclear, as are Hanoi's longer-term ambitions. Our policy is designed to bolster the independence of our friends, encourage the restraint of former foes, and help chart a more constructive pattern of relations within the region.

We have said on many occasions that for us the Indochina war is over. We are prepared to look to the future; we are willing to discuss outstanding issues; we stand ready to reciprocate gestures of good will. We have conveyed our willingness to open discussions with the Vietnamese authorities, with both sides free to raise any issues they wish.

For us the Americans missing-in-action remain the principal concern. Let there be no mistake: There can be no progress toward improved relations with Hanoi without a wholly satisfactory accounting for these men. Nor will we yield to cynical efforts to use the anguish of American families to extort economic aid. If the Vietnamese meet our concerns for the missing-in-action and exhibit restraint toward their neighbors, they will find us ready to reciprocate and to join in the search for ways to turn a new page in our relations.

New Patterns of Cooperation. Beyond security, beyond the imperative of easing tensions, lies a new dimension of international relations—to help shape a global structure that responds to the aspirations of peoples and assures our children a world of prosperity, justice, and hope. We must meet this challenge because:

· There cannot be enduring tranquility in a world scarred by injustice, resentment, and deprivation;

· There cannot be assured prosperity in a world of economic warfare and failed development; and

· There cannot be an enduring international order in a world in which millions are estranged from decisions and practices which determine their national well-being.

As the world's strongest economy, the United States has accepted responsibility for leadership in this agenda of interdependence. In many international forums over several years, we have put forth comprehensive initiatives to produce concrete progress on the most compelling issues of our interdependent world—food, energy, commodities, trade, technology, the environment, and the uses of mankind's last frontiers, the oceans and outer space.

Nowhere are the possibilities and benefits of economic cooperation greater than in Asia. The record of developing countries in Asia is extraordinary. Most grew at annual rates of 6 to 7 percent a year for the entire decade prior to the 1973 oil embargo; Asian economies have flourished, even in the face of global recession.

The secret of their economic performance is no mystery. Rich in natural resources, fertile land, and industrious people, East Asia—with few exceptions—is not burdened with massive overpopulation. Most countries in the area possess talented entrepreneurs and skilled administrators; most governments have rejected the confining strait-jacket of statist economic practices; virtually all provide a hospitable climate for foreign investment.

If growth and vitality are a common feature, the developing

nations of Asia otherwise reflect a considerable diversity. Some, despite abundant resources, remain among the world's poorest in terms of per capita income. Others are rapidly approaching the ranks of the advanced nations. Some export principally raw materials and food-stuffs, while others have joined Japan as industrial workshops for the world.

Although the impulse for regional integration is apparent, the Asian-Pacific market economy is open and accessible to the world. The United States, Japan, and others supply capital, market, management skills, and technology. We in turn obtain from the developing countries of Asia reliable supplies of important raw materials, fair treatment of our investments, and expanding markets for our trade.

Economic development does not automatically insure tranquility between states or within them. But it can enhance the ability of governments to obtain public support, strengthen the legitimacy of institutions, and consolidate national independence. These factors are of particular importance for Asian nations beset—as they often are—by the problems of nation-building and domestic dissidence.

Cooperative relations between the industrialized nations and the developing nations of Asia are both inescapable and vital.

The United States and the developing nations of Asia share important interests.

· We should both value an international economic system which insures steady, noninflationary growth and expands the opportunities of our citizens.

· We must both recognize that if economic development is to strengthen stability, it must enhance national self-reliance. The developing nations of Asia need concessional foreign assistance far less than support for their efforts to participate in the international economy on a more equal footing.

· We must deal with each other on the basis of parity and dignity, seeking responsible progress on issues, to liberalize trade, to expand investment opportunities, and to transfer technology.

· We must cooperate to improve the effectiveness of established institutions such as the Asian Development Bank. We must be ready to create new instruments—for example, the proposed International Resources Bank—to address the new range of issues in the field of commodities.

The nations bordering the Pacific have an opportunity to usher in an era of cooperation which will enhance the prosperity of their peoples and give an impetus to the well-being of mankind.

America's Strength and Spirit. Three times in the past 35 years many thousands of American lives have been lost in wars on the Asian Continent. For us World War II began and ended there. A blatant Communist attempt to conquer Korea was defeated there. And the tragedy of Vietnam, with its fifty thousand [U.S.] dead and the wave of bitterness it created here at home, was played out there.

It must not happen again. It will not happen again if America's policy, profiting from the past, takes charge of its future, making aggression too costly to attempt and peace too tempting to reject.

Our greatest challenge abroad is to continue to act on the knowledge that neither peace nor prosperity—for ourselves or anyone else on our small planet—is possible without the wisdom and the continuing active involvement of the United States. Our size, our economy, our strength, and our principles leave us no alternative but to be concerned with events in the world around us.

Our greatest foreign policy need at home is steadiness, cohesion, and a realization that in shaping foreign policy we are engaged in an enterprise beyond party and not bounded by our electoral cycles. Today Americans—of whatever party or political conviction—can have confidence that their country, as always, has the substance and the strength to do its duty.

· We have the military and economic power, together with our allies, to maintain the balance of stability upon which global peace must rest.

· We have the wisdom to see that an enduring peace requires dedicated and realistic measures to reduce tension.

· And we have the vision to fashion new relationships among all nations in an interdependent world, to work toward a true and lasting world community.

The bond between America's spirit and America's achievement, between its courage and its responsibility, was expressed by a great poet here in Seattle. As Theodore Roethke said:

> I feel my fate in what I cannot fear.
> I learn by going where I have to go.

That is the American way. We are a people accustomed to, and capable of, forging our own destiny. We are ready, as Americans always have been ready, to face the future without fear. We shall go where we have to go. We shall do what we have to do.

INDEX